A

SUDAN SUNSET

Michael and Anne Tibbs

*Best wishes
Michael and Anne
December 2004*

A
SUDAN SUNSET

Michael and Anne Tibbs

Published in 1999 by Michael and Anne Tibbs
Welkin, Lynchmere, West Sussex..

Copyright. C Michael and Anne Tibbs 1999

ISBN – 0 – 9516727 – 1 –1

All rights reserved.

Printed by Hobbs the Printers Limited,
      Totton, Hampshire SO40 3WX.

We are both very grateful to all our friends and relations who have encouraged us to produce this book. We would especially like to record our thanks to everyone who has helped us. Our son Christopher and his wife Asha have allowed us to escape to their Isle of Wight retreat, so that we could concentrate. Christopher and his father-in-law Bula have been our main source of assistance when we have failed to get any response from our computer in spite of our constant references to the Idiots' Guide to Windows 95. Ray and Mel White have also come to the rescue on more than one occasion. Katharine Crompton, Anne's Godmother and cousin, has helped us with proof reading.

We hope we have not used any material without permission. Sadly many of the Sudan Political Service stalwarts are no longer with us, so if we have intruded on their preserves, we hope that they or their descendants will forgive us.

Anne has drawn all the pictures. The photographs, with one or two exceptions are ours. We are grateful to Christopher for the one on the cover. This was taken across the Nile at Shendi in 1983. He was staying there with Abdel Rahman's wife, Zeinab; the figure in the foreground is their son, Hashim.

Michael and Anne Tibbs.
August 1999

You will find photographs and drawings all through the book, but
the Colour sections are between pages 52/53, 100/101, 164/165 and 260/261.

Maps and Plans.
The Anglo Egyptian Sudan	vii
Kordofan	viii
Dar Messeria	50
Messeria migration zones	57
Our New Year Trek	116
Plan of Rigl el Fula	195

Please note
You can only order this book from us:-
Welkin, Lynchmere Ridge,
Haslemere, Surrey GU27 3PP

telephone	01428 643120
fax	01428 645304
e-mail	matibbs@welkin.fsnet.co.uk

CONTENTS

INTRODUCTION (ix)

1. **HOW IT ALL BEGAN.** 1
   Interview, arrival in Khartoum, settling in to El Obeid,
   Life in El Obeid.
2. **EL OBEID, THE FIRST YEAR.** 14
   Horses and polo, the races, St Peter's church,
   the new Governor, Duncan Cumming,
   Geoffrey and Mary Hawkesworth, visits to the Jebels.
3. **MARRIED LIFE BEGINS.** 27
   MECAS, first leave, visit to Northern Kordofan,
   Marriage, Dunnottar Castle, change of plan,
   The King's death, Anne's first visit to Nahud.
4. **OUR FIRST TREK TO THE MESSERIA.** 36
   with Donald Rae.
   Abu Zabad, Kasha, Tima, Lagawa, Keilak, Muglad,
   Tebeldia, Abyei, Muglad, Lagawa, Dilling.
5. **WESTERN KORDOFAN.** 51
   Law exam, Donald Rae, leave, arrival of John and
   Mary Hunter, Khartoum to El Obeid, the move
   to Nahud, Assistant DC's duties,
   Baggara. The Messeria, tribe and history.
   Return of the Hoggs.
6. **LIFE IN NAHUD.** 63
   Settling in, problems of distance, social life,
   arrival of Zeinab, Rachel's problems, Joanna Hogg.
7. **THE MUGLAD SHOW.** 74
   The 'proof', arrival of the Governor and notables,
   the show, nagara, the races, Rigl el Fula.
8. **SOME TRIALS OF LOCAL GOVERNMENT.** 80
   And the growth of Rigl el Fula.
   Anne's illness, horse trek with Babu, first Council meeting,
   financial problems, visit of Director of Local Government
   Council meetings.

9.	**HORSE TREK.**	**89**

El Odayia to Abu Zabad
Sheikh Mulah, visits to the feriks, Baggara wedding house.

10.	**SOME MATTERS DOMESTIC..**	**105**

Christmas, stores, health, the days' routine.
The TTO and a matter of sticks   **115**

11.	**NEW YEAR TREK.**	**117**

Saturday 3rd January - Thursday 3rd February 1953
El Odayia, Camel trek from Mumu, Rigl el Fula,
Muglad via Wadi el Ghulla, Babu's tea party, Mrs Babu,
Lagawa for Council meeting, Geoffrey McComas's announcement,
Keilak, Muglad, Abyei, Abiemnon, Bentiu with the Bowcocks,
giraffe, Abyad meeting, Anne gets her hair cut, Lagawa,
Nahud, 31 days out 1,100 miles.

12.	**THE NUBA .**	**143**

Kasha and Shifr, Wali meeting, Tima, Tulleshi, Kamdung
Abu Genouk, Tubuk, Nuba wrestling, Toraji.

13.	**THE DAGU.**	**159**

Dar el Kebir, election of a Sultan.

14.	**THE NGOK DINKA**	**162**

Abyei, the settlements and luaks, religion, Deng Majok, the
school, fishing, a cattle auction.

15.	**ABYEI AND ABIEMNON.**	**171**

The Province Judge's visit.
Trek, 3rd March 1953 Tebeldia, Muglad, Abyei,
RC church, Dinka dancing, The spear throwing case, Abiemnom
meeting, Muglad, Tibun, Rigl el Fula, Nahud.

16.	**ANNE'S 21st BIRTHDAY**	**179**

And the move to Rigl el Fula. Babu in Lynchmere.
Birthday picnic, the move and arrival on foot.

17.	**LIFE IN RIGL EL FULA,**	**185**

And the first Council Meeting.
The resthouse, visits from Governor, Geoffrey Hawkesworth and
Geoffrey McComas, John and Mary Hunter, the Council meeting,
Council tea party.

18.	**ANNE IN RIGL EL FULA AND OUR HOUSE.**	**196**

House approved, foundations dug, increase in our livestock, coffee
parties,.a slide show.

19.	**ELECTION FEVER.**	**205**

Anglo-Egyptian agreement signed, celebration tea party in Nahud, Electoral Commission, abortive visit to Lagawa, problems over the numbers of candidates, the 'token system', Abu Genouk, problems in Muglad.

20.	**A BUSY DECEMBER,**	**219**
	El Obeid to Abyei and back..	

Good bye to the Hawkesworths, slide party for the ladies, Abyei again, the White Fathers, Ma'an, Rigl el Fula. Christmas dairy in El Obeid.

21.	**THE GOVERNOR GENERAL'S VISIT.**	**227**

Trying out the new road, the death of Beshir, preparations. Finishing the house, arrival, tea on the road, dinner party, opening of the Council building and presentation of the new Warrant, the entertainments.

22.	**A VISIT TO IAN CUNNINSON.**	**238**

From Abyad to Abyei, visit to Ian Cuninson, our Anthropologist, at Omda Horgas's ferik.

23.	**NEARING THE END.**	**243**

Problems with the new order, visit from the Wherrals, Mohamed Ibrahim Abdel Hafiz leaves, opening of parliament cancelled, Nyama, Subu, Koiya and castor oil, Abyei, Grinti, 'portmanteau', Anne evacuated.

24.	**SAD FAREWELL.**	**250**

Water problems in Muglad, Dinka, Abyie again, Zacharia Bol Deng, Lau, Khartoum, dinner at the Palace, return to Rigl el Fula, Muglad, Lagawa and back with difficulty, last visit to Muglad, sad farewell to Rigl el Fula

POST SCRIPT **265**

The railway, Zacharia Bol and Francis Madeng Deng, Deng Mjok, Nazir Babu Nimr, Ian Cunnison, Christopher's visits, Abdel Rahman Babikr.

EPILOGUE BY CHRISTOPHER **268**

APPENDICIES

These are included as they may be of historical interest.
Handing Over Notes. My Sudanese successor was Mohamed Ibrahim Abdel Hafiz, who had been our Sub Mamur. I hope these were of some use to him!
I gave Christopher copies of No. 5, - Administration of Dar Messeria District and Council before he paid his visit in 1983. The D.C. told him that he wished he had this kind of documentation. So, with the help of the chap drilling for oil in Muglad who had a photocopier, he got them!

1.	**Governor General's speech at the opening of the new Council headquarters.**	**271**
2.	**My speech at the farewell party in Muglad.**	**272**
3.	**My handing over notes.**	**274**
4.	**Letter to Governor, Kordofan, 18th April 1954**	**278**
5.	**Administration in Dar Messeria District and Council 15th. August 1954.**	**285**
6,	**Letters sent to District Commissioners**	**296**

after the elections. By the Governor General, and Acting Civil Secretary

Farewell letters from the Governor General, the Prime Minister, Executive Officer, Dar Messeria Rural Council Achuil Bulabek, Omda Aweng/Akyor, Ngok Dinka and Malet Ayoun, a Ngok Dinka.

WHO WAS WHO   **301**

GLOSSARY   **306**

ERRATA. APOLOGIES TO:-
p..v. and Chapter 22 p. 238   Ian Cunnison (not Cunninson)
    Chapter 1 p. 9.   James Tiernay (not Tierney)

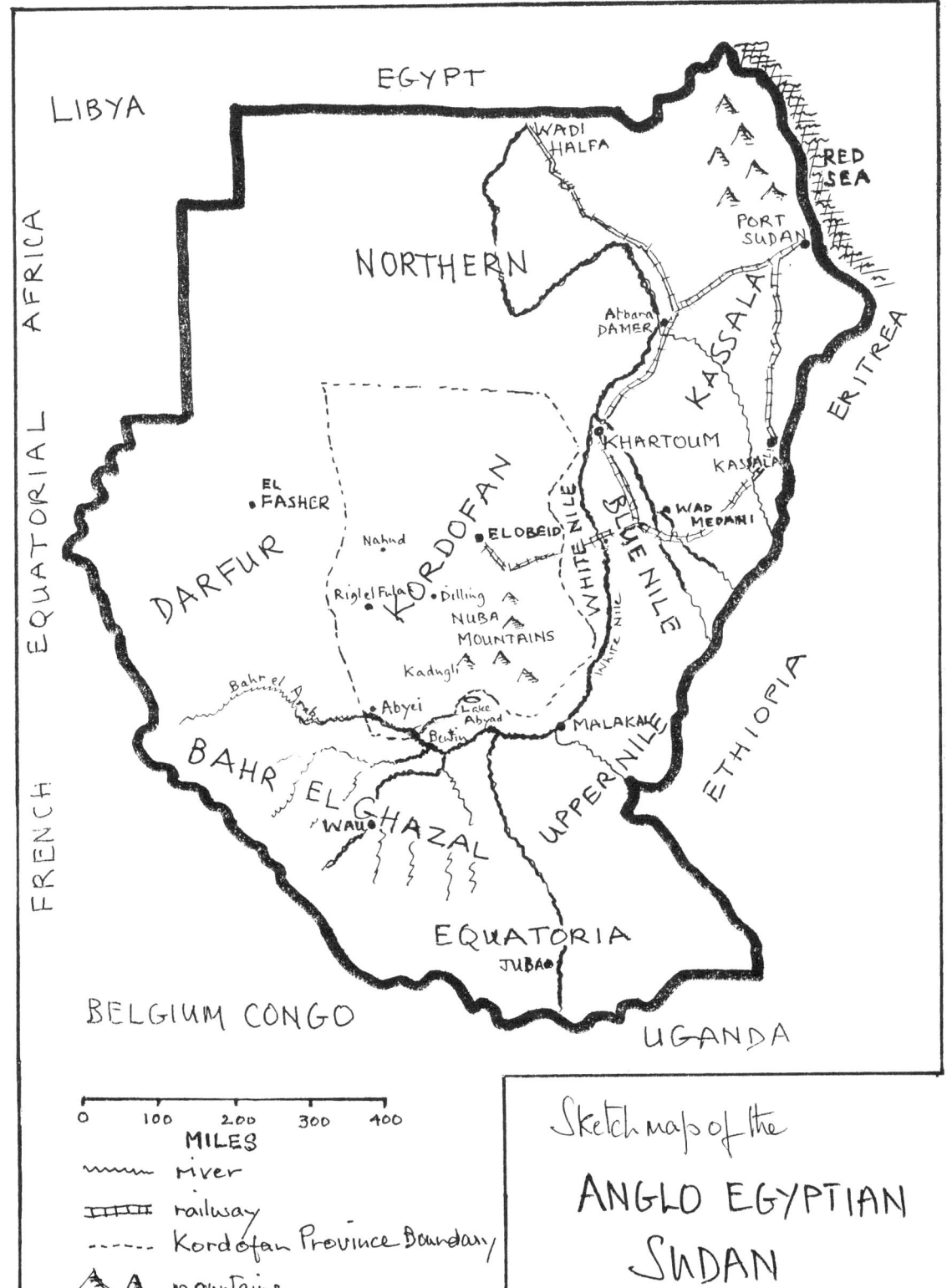

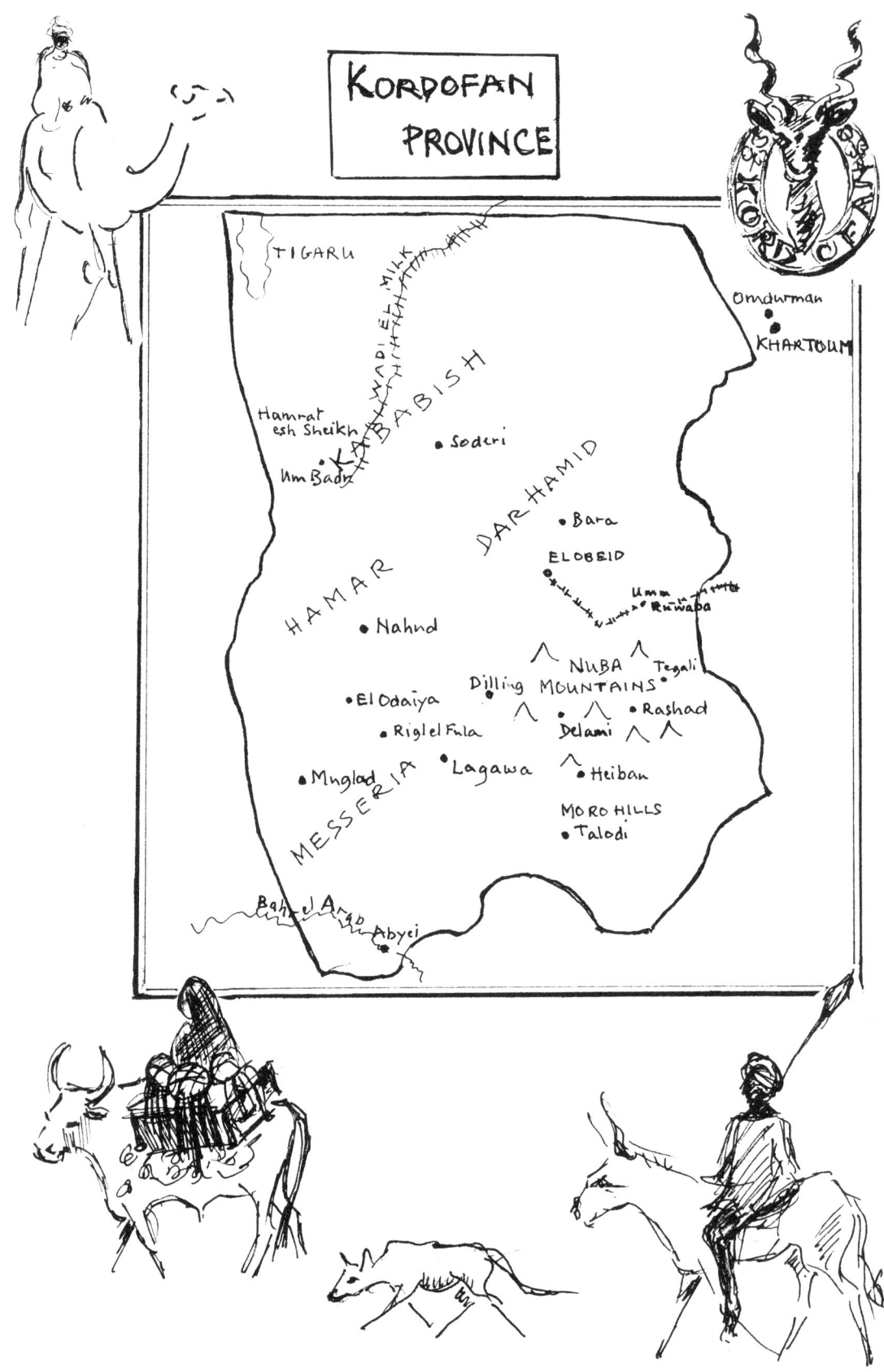

A SUDAN SUNSET

This is an account of the happy years we spent in the Anglo-Egyptian Sudan during the run up to independence. It is not an erudite book about politics or what might have been done. It is a simple story of how a District Commissioner and his wife spent their time and is mostly written from our letters to our families. At the time, Michael was in his late twenties and early thirties while Anne arrived in the Sudan when she was just nineteen. We have tried to avoid editing our letters so that their youthful freshness (!) is not spoilt. Anne has drawn the pictures.

Some time ago we happened to listen to the tail end of a discussion on the radio. One of those on the panel suddenly said, "We must remember we no longer have District Commissioners strutting through the tropics in their solar topees." We would hate our grandchildren to get the idea that we strutted anywhere. It is a travesty of what we actually did, but sadly a general modern view of how the British Empire was administered. When history is written, the era of the District Commissioners may well be recorded as a golden age for many in the African continent.

The Sudan today is a sad place, division where there should be unity; war where we tried to bring peace; poverty and hunger in a land with potential plenty. The sun set on our administration, we all did our best to make sure that it continued to shine, despite the impossibly short time table we were given. Those of us who served in and love the Sudan pray that the sun will soon rise again.

So, here is our tale so that our grandchildren will know what the first years of our married life were like. It also gives us an opportunity to record our heart felt thanks to all our Sudanese friends, particularly those in Western and what is now Southern Kordofan. Although we were 'set in authority' you welcomed us into your homes, your lives, your problems and your joys and in many cases our friendship still continues. To you all Thank You.

Blackbushe
England
to
Khartoum
Sudan
January 1949

AIRWORK LTD LONDON

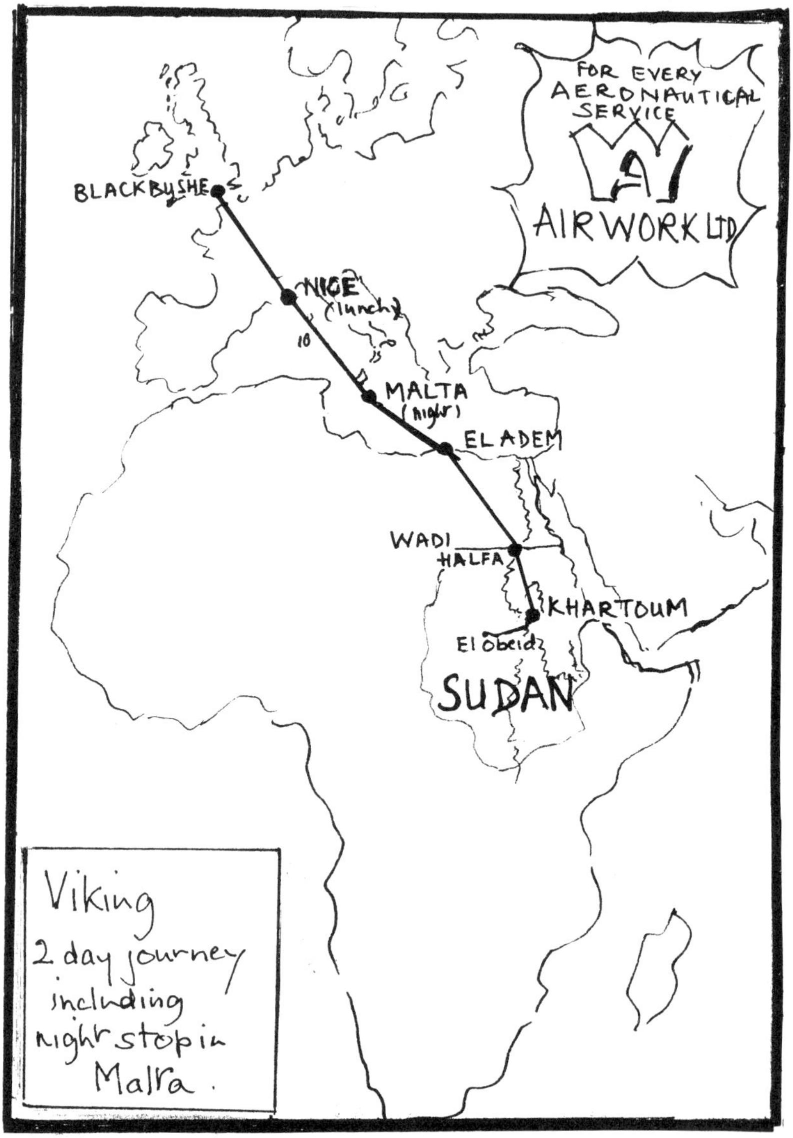

FOR EVERY AERONAUTICAL SERVICE
AIRWORK LTD

BLACKBUSHE
NICE (lunch)
MALTA (night)
EL ADEM
WADI HALFA
KHARTOUM
El Obeid
SUDAN

Viking
2 day journey including night stop in Malta.

Train 24 hours Khartoum – El Obeid.

1. HOW IT ALL BEGAN.

El Obeid, "the little white place" is the headquarters of the Province of Kordofan where a low white building housed the offices of the Governor of the Province, the Deputy Governor, the Assistant District Commissioner and the secretariat. I had arrived here after a long chain of events which had started with an early rise in a Youth Hostel in Oxford, a train to London and an interview with a selection board for the Sudan Political Service. Unlike another and very sticky session I had undergone with another august body, this had been a very friendly, if not light hearted affair. The Chairman was no less than the Civil Secretary himself, Sir James Robertson; they enquired what I was doing at the moment and seemed quite happy when I told them that I was actually leading a youth pilgrimage. The interview had ended when Sir James asked what "philuministics" was (listed as one of my hobbies). I explained that it was not very serious and meant collecting the tops of match boxes; then as he lit his pipe, I asked Sir James for his match box and took my leave as the board helped him collect up his matches from the table. I think that really typified the friendly way in which the Anglo Egyptian Sudan was administered.

Various negotiations followed, I was given a list of recommended clothing and equipment, which could be got from Griffiths and McAllister in Warwick Street off Regent Street, things like suitcases and a new tennis racket. I bought a dinner service from Stones in Haslemere, and selected pictures from the loft while my mother and father kindly parted with some spare silver which all went to G & A to be sent out.

I was told I should proceed to Cairo en route to the Middle East Centre of Arab Studies in Lebanon, where I would be for a year before coming on to the Sudan. My last Sunday at home at the end of September 1948 was Harvest Thanksgiving, but the day before I went down with a high temperature. I just struggled up the hill to Evensong, but that night was collected in an ambulance and whisked into Haslemere Hospital for an emergency appendectomy. I did not recover as I should and developed a rather debilitating jaundice. My main worry was what would happen to my new job. Out of the blue, a letter arrived from Sir James in his own hand saying I was not to worry, the job would be kept and I would come straight to the Sudan when I was fit enough.

So it was that I joined a group collecting for a Sudan Government Airwork charter flight at Cock Fosters Hotel in Egham at the beginning of January 1949 and flew off in a twin engined Viking early the next morning. We droned along for two days, stopping at Nice; a night stop in Malta; then el Adam in Libya, followed by a long haul across the desolate Libyan desert to Wadi Halfa. The Sudan at last and the day my pay would start. Then just two hours up to Khartoum, rather wondering what would happen next. A friendly face appeared, one Brian Dee who had been at my interview, he was 'personnel' in the Civil Secretary's office. He hoped I would stay with him and immediately enquired how the pilgrimage went off!.

Brian was wonderful, I would normally have been told what to do and go there by taxi, but they were on strike. I was also lucky in that three other probationers had arrived just ahead of me. They had already done the rounds and compared prices so were able to show me their comparative price lists. Brian took me to Vanians, the Greek outfitters for riding trousers, Bombay bowler and blankets. From there we went to Gamucian the Armenian hardware shop for saucepans, a colander, meat chopper and the like. Then to Mohamed the tailor for uniform, white dinner jacket and servants' kit. Next, I bought Thatcher's Arabic and a copy of David Copperfield at the Sudan Bookshop. Finally, to the government Stores and Ordnance in Khartoum North for trek equipment, including a chair, table, canvas bath and camp bed.

Brian's office was in the Secretariat, a large open building on the Blue Nile next to the Palace, with Kitchener on his horse in front. I got introduced to the Deputy Civil Secretary and many others, some of whom asked how my match box collection was getting on (the story had evidently got round). Then it was suggested I should get hold of some servants. An agent arrived and a succession of men in galabias (long white cotton robes) came in, each with his card and a sheaf of chits from previous masters, some laudatory,

Kitchener

some scandalous. From these I selected 2457 Ahmed Khalil Mohamed Ali, a Safragi, and 6576 Hassenein Mohamed Hassein (who answered to Mohamed), a cook. I contracted to pay the former £ 4 per month and the latter £ 4.50, I also had to give the agent Mr Pabasses 95 piastres comission.

I was reintroduced to Sir James with whom I then had dinner, and met his charming wife, Nancy. She told the party not to mind getting really sticky eating mangoes as we could always have a bath.

I was shown how to get to the Cathedral and called on the Bishop in the Sudan, Maurice Gelsthorpe, George Martin the Provost, and Uncle (no-one called him anything else) Harper the Archdeacon. Uncle Harper told me I must go and look at Gordon on his camel, children knew all about Lightening the camel, but not so much about Gordon. Later I was able to get to HC and Evensong on Sunday. Although it was an Anglican Cathedral only about 40% of the congregation were C of E, the others being Presbyterian, Methodists, Congregational, Armenian, Greek and Sudanese. Sunday was of course an ordinary working day, the rest day being the Moslem Friday, so services were early and late on Sunday.

Gordon

On one morning I went to the gallery of the Legislative Assembly which had just been inaugurated as the first step to self-government. For the first time the South was represented on equal terms to the North. The Assembly was run on parliamentary lines with a Speaker in a chair on a dais at one end, an interpreter and two clerks in front of him. The Members were on seats facing each other and speeches were made from their seats as in the House of Commons. At that time, independence still seemed a long way off. Twenty years from 1946 seemed to have a magic meaning, this from a speech made by General Huddlestone the previous Governor General to the Northern Sudan Assembly (forerunner of the Legislative Assembly).

I went to lunch with Sir Robert Howe, the Governor General in the beautiful white Palace on the bank of the Blue Nile and also had lunch with Duncan Cumming who was shortly to become the Governor of Kordofan. Finally Brian took me one evening to Khartoum station where I met my new staff who installed me and my newly acquired possessions onto the train for El Obeid.

The journey took a full 24 hours. The long white train had a dining car and first class sleepers at one end, then second, third and fourth class. The

The long white train

24 hours Khartoum to El Obeid.

Over the Nile at Kosti

1st Class sleeper
Panelled in mahogany
Lift up the chrome wash basin
to have a seat.

sleepers were extremely comfortable, panelled in mahogany with folding bed, basin, fan and a large window with tinted glass to keep out the glare. The track is only one meter gauge, so the trains trundle rather than run. After breakfast in the dining car we crossed the long bridge over the White Nile and stopped at Kosti. I met a young soldier, just come out and strolled with him over to look at the Nile, when the train gave a hoot so we rushed back rather quicker than we had come. It was only a false alarm.

We soon set off again and got into the kind of scenery which was to form a large part of one's life over the next few years. Sandy scrub, thorn trees and oosha - like a flowering cabbage without the flower, then the sight of camels, goats and shaggy sheep some white, some black, some brown with variations but all with long tails. There were also large herds of cattle looked after by little boys, some sitting on enormous bulls. I had dinner on the train, then again wondered what would happen when we finally arrived in El Obeid.

The answer was nothing. The passengers were met by their relatives and friends in a wave of hubbub but as it subsided, there I was with Ahmed and Mohamed, my suitcases and boxes. However, just as I wondered about finding a taxi but not knowing where it should go, a smart figure in Red Sea rig emerged full of apologies. "I am Geoffrey Hawkesworth, the Deputy Governor. I hope you will stay with me for a few days while you get settled in and you are just in time for dinner!"

So, I joined the dinner party and after eating a second dinner ending with jumbles and cream, slept soundly. Geoffrey had taken me for a pre-breakfast walk round the reservoirs and here I was in the morning, in my office in the Muderia wearing my new uniform for the first time. Kahki bush jacket with brass buttons, epaulets with one stripe to show an Assistant District Commissioner, shorts, stockings and Bombay bowler with the Kordofan Province badge, the head of a Kudu on the left hand side.

I sat with Geoffrey most of the morning trying to follow what was going on. I heard my name mentioned once during an Arabic conversation, "That was the editor of the local magazine, 'Kordofan'. He wanted to know your name and I don't suppose it will be the last time you will get a mention". (It wasn't). Then another call, the telephone nearly exploded with an outpouring of rage, I could just distinguish that it was a voice speaking in English. Geoffrey held the telephone about a foot away from his ear and muttered an occasional 'yes'. 'That', he said when it had finished 'was the District Commissioner'. 'What' I asked 'was he so cross about?' 'Oh he often feels that way'. This was my first introduction to David Evans, then District Commissioner of El Obeid. He and Ruth, like the Hawkesworths not only became firm friends to us, but our children as well.

I see from my letters home that I soon settled into the new routine, both in the office and in the tightly knit British community. After a week I moved into a room in the small Kordofan Club where I had little more than a camp bed, trek table and chair though I would suddenly find additions that Ahmed had bought, like a shaving mirror. It was here I had my first guest to dinner, Canon Arnold, a missionary who came up to take the Sunday services for us. Later I was able to move to a small three roomed semi-detached house known as the Darfur Rest House and later still to the ADC's proper residence opposite the Muderia, known as the Powder House. (As there had not been an ADC for some months it had been occupied by someone else). It had very thick walls and flat roof and had been the powder magazine for the Turkish fort, the gate of which formed part of the Muderia building.

Gradually I was able to build up some furniture specially made in the Prison workshops, I could not afford one of the expensive woods like mahogany, so it was all white wood painted light green for coolness. The only problem was that I had given very careful measurements for the armchairs so that they would not be too long but the prison added six extra inches to make them grander. However they lasted all our time. Unlike the Colonial Service, we all bought and owned our own furniture, which we took with us wherever we went.

In the office I found that I was responsible for going through all the correspondence and deciding whether it should be dealt with by the Governor, the Deputy or whoever, the Province transport four Ford 15cwt box cars (pick ups) and a lorry under the command of Onbashi (Corporal) Hassan, the government rest house, meeting new arrivals at station or air port and dealing with all visitors and generally being the air hostess for the Province. I was also very concerned with the Province Prison. This was under command of Hag (Pilgrim) el Nur (Light) Ahmed, a tubby jolly man who had originally served with Geoffrey at Rashad, one of the District Headquarters. He rapidly became my desert daddy (when one first goes to sea one usually acquires a sea daddy who takes you under his wing). Hag el Nur used to visit Geoffrey every day, give him an enormous salute and then come and see me. He would salute, then take off his hat and ask how I was, test me on how much Arabic I had learnt, correct any faults and generally instruct me on Sudanese custom. He knew no English but we soon, in spite of my limited Arabic, built up a lasting rapport.

Kordofan Province is the size of France but had a population of about 2,000,000 ranging from desert nomads, the Kabbabish, in the north to Nuba and Nilotic Dinka in the south. The province was administered in six Districts, Central District which included El Obeid and its immediate area, Northern Kordofan, Eastern Kordofan, Western Kordofan, Jebels (the Nuba Mountains) and Tegale.

The Kordofan Club

Settling in. 1949

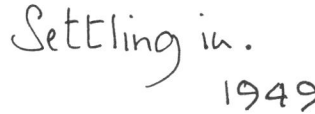

Started living in the Club,

had some furniture made,

then moved to the Darfur Rest House

The Darfur Rest House

finally to The Powder House

The Powder House

from the roof there was a good view of my office.

El Obeid was the railhead and the largest town in the western Sudan with a population of some 60,000. It had an enormous cattle market once a year known as the 'agdomia' when cattle were driven in from all over the province and sold to dealers who then arranged for their onward transport by train or on hoof to Khartoum and Egypt. The town also had the largest gum Arabic market in the world. Its buildings were low and with a few exceptions made of mud, the streets were of sand. The market (suq) was virtually contained in one long street and dominated by the two large general shops, Abu Nigma (One Star) presided over by a Greek Cypriot, Mr Lappas and its rival Thalata Negum (Three Stars). Behind the suq lay the mud houses of the merchants and wealthier Sudanese while all around were the grass houses, each in its own enclosure (hosh) comprising the 'Native Quarters'. The District Headquarters (Merkaz) was a stone built building on the edge of the suq beside the court and a new Town Council building. The Province Headquarters or Muderia lay a quarter of a mile away and round it were the dozen or so houses of the cantonment where the British had their houses. Alongside them were the headquarters of the local regiment, the Camel Corps, still with a British Colonel, second in command and Company Commanders.

Between the suq and the cantonment was the meidan (literally field),. The general idea was that in the event of an uprising, the British would be protected by the Camel Corps deployed on the Meidan and it was therefore important to keep the lines of fire open.

Fairly soon after my arrival I paid calls on the various important people with whom I would have to liase. The first was on the District Commissioner, David Evans; he explained that he was in the gradual process of delegating some of his powers to the new Town Council, but things were a bit delayed as the local taxes were in arrears. Until they were collected, the Town Council could not function properly.

Then came the Sudan Defence Force (SDF); I caused some amusement as having donned uniform again I treated it like a naval rather than a military one. The Political Service had developed from the army and retained some of its habits. I gave a nautical touch to my hat rather than a military salute and automatically tucked my hat under my arm on entering someone's office rather than keeping it on and saluting. However, I learnt that despite its name, the Camel Corps was now mechanised. I was a little puzzled by the army ranks but learnt that they retained the Turkish ranks used by the Egyptian army. The CO was a Miralae, the 2 ic a Kaimakan, and the Company Commanders Bimbashis; to make things even more complicated, Sudanese politeness demanded that one always referred to them by a rank senior to the one to which they were really entitled. So, the CO was called Sa'ta Lewa (His Excellency the Brigadier). Just to round off the hierarchy the GOC of the Sudan Defence Force was the Kaid. I learnt of the work of the Police under their commandant Yahia Bey, the Sudan Medical Service, (SMS); the Sudan Veterinary Service (SVS) the Education Service and the Public Works Department (PWD); its very important function included supply of water as well as buildings.

When I arrived in El Obeid, the Governor was James Tierney, but much to his wife's fury he was transferred to Equatoria. The new Governor whom I had already met in Khartoum was to be Mr D.C.Cumming CB, CBE, taking up his first job in the Sudan since the war. He had been in the army as head of AMGOT (Allied Military Government of Occupied Territories) with the rank of Major General and in charge of all the Italian colonies with his seat of government in Cairo. He had also been a rugger international at an earlier stage in his career. He arrived in El Obeid at night by train so there was no official welcome at the station, but we made up for it by having a levee in the Muderia the next morning.

Full uniform or suits were the rig of the day. The Political Service's white and gold levee dress with plumed hat had not been revived but I had to gird myself in my office dress - long kakhi trousers and tunic. I suddenly realised that I was short of brass buttons and a kakhi shirt and tie so had to send an SOS to the prison and a friendly Bimbashi.

So, imagine a hot day at nine o'clock; a long low white building like something out of PC Wren. In the front, a long verandah with steps down the middle leading to a dusty garden separated from an even dustier road by a low wall. A crowd is gathering, men arrive but not a woman to be seen anywhere. The men have a variety of costumes from colourful crimson Robes of Honour to gaudy palm beach suiting; they settle themselves on chairs and wait. A police Guard of Honour arrives and falls in with the Town Band behind. A small cavalcade appears, four mounted policemen escorting a green Ford limousine. Two of the policemen bear the colours of the sovereign powers on the tips of their lances. The new Governor leaves his car and salutes while the guard presents arms. The guard was trained by my predecessor who was a Royal Marine. He certainly did not let down the reputation of the Corps. While the Governor is inspecting the Guard, the Town Band bursts into its famous waltz which has been played every time that a Governor has inspected a Guard of Honour since Kitchener was here. It is believed that it was a well known tune but it is quite unrecognisable now. After the inspection the guard march past headed by the band. Two new additions have now joined the band, two policemen with bagpipes, presumably a legacy of one of the many Scots who have presided over the fortunes of the Province.

At last the Governor mounts the steps to the Muderia to be greeted by a committee consisting of the Deputy Governor, the Commanding Officer of the Camel Corps, a District Commissioner who happens to be in town and the Assistant District Commissioner whose main duty is to open the door of the office. The next part of the official reception follows swiftly on. The ADC (me) has a list of some 250 people in his hand, all split into groups of 10 headed by an 'Introducer'. The object is to arrange the groups outside the office door with the Introducer in front. Then, open door, insert group, whisper to the Deputy Governor who is contact man inside "Education Department" or "Notables, Pensioners civilian". The Deputy Governor then introduces the Introducer who introduces the Intoducees who shakes hands with the great man, who sits them on chairs and sits down himself. Then, general conversation for three minutes and the Governor says how nice it was of them to come and he's sorry they have to go so soon. EXIT through far door and repeat.

The first few batches were relatively easy, these were the government departments, the only difficulty being found in Posts and Telegraphs when Abdel Rahman effendi Khangi (P&T) tried to introduce Sudan Railways which should have been done by Abdullah effendi el Zein (Sudan Railways). Government departments were followed by Central District and then Notables as Listed. The Town Council provided a representative looking body including my friend Hag el Nur looking very military with MBE, Sam Browne belt and sword. Then came Bederia administration, the local tribe headed by Sheikh Hussein Zaki el Din, a grand old man of over 80 and ex-Nazir of the tribe. He wore a magnificent crimson Robe of Honour, First Class, a sword and on a chain round his neck the King's Medal for African Chiefs in Silver. He was complaining that he could not really get round without a stick. His two sons, the present Nazir and Wakil Nazir also wore robes of Honour, but not as grand as Dad's and anyway there did not seem to be much doubt as to whom the real boss was.

The most varied body was Religious Notables. Moslems headed the list, many wearing Blue (Religious) Robes of Honour. Then two Italian Roman Catholic fathers in plain white cassocks, they are in the middle of building a large and expensive looking school in El Obeid, a fine stone building they are improving by painting red! The Syrian Catholic priest came next, then Coptic Orthodox, the Rev Girgis Goda Gaddalla in flat hat and purple drape. Greek Orthodox followed, the Rev Father Athanassopanlos with long beard, bun and tall hat (he has a financial interest in a local firm of contractors, which has been responsible for a number of buildings including the mosque). The rear of the ecclesiastical throng was brought up by the Presbyterian American Mission, the Rev Robert.H.Molloy, a complete contrast to the others in a blue and white striped suiting rather like the bathing suit worn by William IV taking the waters at Brighton.

The procession wound on through Town Bench, Pensioners Civil and Military, Other Notables Egyptian and then Other Notables Sudanese. Some were having a round game, seeing how many times they could get introduced. A member of the Education Department would reappear as a Town Councillor or Other Notable. We had great fun sorting out the collection of sticks that got left outside the door. Dear old gentlemen got quite upset when they found their faithful object had been nicked by some unscrupulous stick snatcher, the most sensible old man did not bring his stick, but an elegant and unmistakable Queen Mary sunshade with an ivory handle. With a great sigh of relief we at last pushed in Foreigners - Armenian, French, Greek, Indian and Syrian and shut the door.

One of the functions of the Deputy Governor was the supervision of prisons. There were two in El Obeid, the Town Prison under the D.C and the Province Prison for long term offenders. Either Geoffrey or myself visited the Province Prison every Saturday morning; I would drive or ride across the Meidan to find the entire body of Prison Warders drawn up in three ranks. They presented arms (the first time I rode, the horse nearly took off), then after ordering arms one inspected the ranks. Inside the gate, a suitably surprised sentry called out the guard, so that had to be inspected, prison registers had to be looked through, then a round of each cell, ward (strong smell of Jeyes fluid) and compound. All the prisoners are lined up so that if anyone has a complaint they can say so and they are brought into the office later so that their record can be checked. The tour includes the workshops where the men do woodwork and the women basketwork (we still have one of their clothes baskets with animals round it). Then comes the kitchen and a taste of the prisoners' breakfast; the dispensary to make sure everything smells of Dettol; the wash area and the cells. One of the sad things was that certified lunatics had to be kept in prison because at that time there were no facilities for their control anywhere else. At one time lunatics who were not violent would be taken out and chained to trees outside the prisons where they could see what went on and talk to their friends, but one of the international bodies thought that chaining people to trees was too frightful, so now they had to remain locked up inside. In one corner of the prison behind a high wall was the gallows, where sometimes, early in the morning, I had to represent the Governor at a certain grizzly rite.

On other days it was necessary to visit the two model prisons about ten miles outside El Obeid at Turra and Ban Gedid, a good excuse to get out of town with one's tea. A sandy road leading through the usual scrub country but eventually we arrive at a patch of greenery which is the prison garden, but we leave it and go on another quarter of a mile to the bottom of a stony hill (jebel). Here are two groups of little round huts (tukls). One group to the left is for the warders and the one to the right, surrounded with barbed wire is for the prisoners. There is a guardhouse in the middle from which a small Guard emerges. This camp is for first offenders only. The idea is that they must realise the crime they have committed is wrong so they are sent to Turra. Here they live in healthy conditions and spend all day up the hill, hacking out the stone and rolling it to the bottom where it is carted away and used for building. At the end of six months very hard labour the lesson is considered to have sunk in and they are moved to the other camp at Ban Gedid.

Turra Prison Camp

Near the mens' enclosure is the boys'. Those with long sentences may be sent to the reformatory in Khartoum. If for some reason this is not possible or their sentences are too short they are sent to Turra, but not for stone breaking, they are taught bootmaking and do lessons in the evening. They are also getting quite good at PT.

Back to the green patch to find a similar camp, but this one has no gates; the prisoners are all on parole. There is nothing to stop them running off, but in fact they seldom do. Many of them are employed on building a new office and three houses for instructors in carpentry, building and gardening, all with stone from Turra. Nearby is a large poultry farm with ducks, geese, turkeys and one ostrich six months old which is quite tame.

On the other side of the road is the garden, which covers about four acres. Water, is of course the main drawback to any scheme of this kind; Ban Gedid was chosen as it lies in a small valley with a water table not too deep. There are four wells each of about 100 ft. deep; one has a centrifugal pump, the others have sagias worked by bulls which walk  patiently round and round turning a wheel geared to another vertical one on which there is a band of buckets going down empty and coming up full. The water is led off into a complicated system of irrigation channels which takes the water all over the garden. Most of the ordinary English vegetables are grown, then there is a large fruit selection including grapefruit, oranges, limes, lemons, bananas, paw paw and mangoes. There are obviously better gardens, but there was nothing quite like it near El Obeid. When the time came for their release, the inmates had all learnt some kind of a trade which gave them a better chance of a decent job than they had before their crime.

Ban Gedid.

2.   EL OBEID, THE FIRST YEAR.

My immediate task was to start learning Arabic, there was a great incentive to do this, apart from the frustration of not being able to understand what was going on; one did not get any rise in pay until successful in both the Higher Arabic and Law exams. The Province Inspector of Education recommended an Intermediate school teacher called Abdel Garda effendi; he came up to my house at 4 o'clock, but I also shared two sessions with Ivy Potter, one of the nursing sisters, as well. So, I struggled through a first reading book 'Kitab al Atfal' (The Book For Children). I would normally have come to the Sudan either having had a whole year at the Middle East Centre of Arab Studies in Lebanon, or having had three months at the School of Oriental Studies in London. However, I had to try and catch up on my own, though I had already asked if I could go to Lebanon for the next year.

I found that I was entitled to a loan of £E 60 with which to buy two horses, and a forage allowance with which to feed them and also pay the wages of a groom (scyce). Unlike my brother and sister, I had not been brought up to ride, though I had ridden Gossamer my father's horse who was a beautifully good natured animal. I had also ridden a horse belonging to Stewart Granger the actor who lived in Lynchmere, and had fallen off an enormous beast called Diamond belonging to Peter Dalglish our local farmer.

The Veterinary Department came up with a small stallion for which I paid £E 17. I named him Schweppes, as he appeared rather effervescent. I gingerly took him out for a few practice rides, but then felt confident enough to join a pre-breakfast ride on Friday morning with Geoffrey Hawkesworth, Tony Husband (one of the doctors) and the two nursing sisters Mary Pullen and Ivy Potter.

We had one or two good gallops but then he got frightened by another horse coming up and just shot off. I lost a foot from a stirrup and could not get it back as we dashed along under the thorn trees. I got him round in a left-hand circle but fell off. Schweppes tore off and went slap into the tall wire fence that goes for eight miles round one of the catchment areas. He reared up and then went rushing off into the distance; he ended up, a bit lame, at his own stable Tony Husband rescued me in his pick-up. I had landed in a soft pat of sand though I had collected quite a lot of prickles from the bushes.

I got one or two experts to ride Schweppes, including Gawain Bell, DC Western Kordofan and Tony Watson, the Province Judge who even rode him for polo. In the end I decided that discretion was the better part of valour and bought Westward, a docile grey, from another ADC who was being transferred to the Gezira.

I did try playing polo after a bit, at no 1, the beginner's place. This could be a frightening experience as it is an extremely aggressive game. One's captain used to shout instructions like 'Stay on the ball' as I was rushing round in circles. All I could do was to shout back 'I am only trying to stay on the field and I can't see the ball'. Most of the players were Sudanese SDF Officers who were extremely tolerant of my incompetence and it gave one a good chance to get to know them. Sammy Richardson, my predecessor came in from his District in Bara sometimes and said I was mad to try polo. The Christian Cemetery, he said, was put near the polo ground to make it easy for the SDF to bury all the British Bimbashis who had tried polo to please the Colonel. Half the tombstones had 'Died at Polo' written on them.

One of the highlights of the El Obeid scene was the races. There was a meeting soon after I arrived. My duty was to stand by the scales and make sure that all the jockeys were wearing their right colours. The weighing was done by the Greek grocer, Mr Lappas of Abu Nigma. Then there was a tote which I was surprised to see was under the command of the Chief Clerk of the Province Headquarters, Ahmed effendi Tahir and his minions. The rules were strict - no credit allowed, tickets 10 pt (10p) each.

The Governor arrived in his saloon; the Town Band was lined up to receive him. All the British and senior officials stood to attention as the band played the national anthems of Egypt and Great Britain, but the rest of 'the people' (nass) did not take an awful lot of notice'. Mind you, we knew what the tunes ought to sound like in the first place!

All sorts and sizes of horses took part, large, small, sleek, skinny, fat and flea-bitten. The British owned horses were well groomed with fine looking saddles but the next one would be an animal with a saddle like a Victorian arm chair with a hat stand in front, the bridle a piece of string, but the equipment made no difference to the results. All the races were flat and all except the last two were straight, so that all one could see was a collection of objects about half a mile away. A bell would ring; a bugle sound and some coloured figures all shouting

Life in El Obéid

The Mudería.
The old Turkish gateway

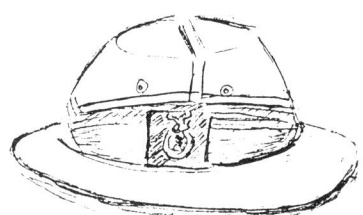

Bombay bowler
with the Province Badge

Tennis
Stiquet
Swimming

The Garden Fula

Polo

The Races

and doing a drum major act with their sticks (18 inches regulation size) would disentangle themselves from the dust and go flashing past the post. The race card started with the Police Race, then the Polo Scurry (owner ridden), Kordofan Maiden Race, Kordofan Open Race and ended with the Kordofan Derby, this was the best spectacle as they did a lap and a half going past the grand stand twice

Most of the townsfolk who were there would not pay their 2 piastres (pt) to go into the enclosures but hung about outside about four hundred yards away. What they saw, I can't imagine, except for one or two sportsmen who had the foresight to come on their camels.

The prizes were presented by the 80 year old ex Nazir of the Bederia, the local tribe. He had to present one to himself and was not sure of the procedure. Just as he had stuffed the cup inside his robes, an engaging little grandson came running out so proceedings had to wait while the cup was defolded and presented to him.

Later on in the year Westward came third in one of the maiden races; Scyce Abdul Rahman wore my racing colours of green and white hoops (my old house rugger vest) and I did come third riding in the Polo Scurry. I have two little silver ashtrays to prove it

The daily routine started at 6.3o with a walk or writing or Arabic before breakfast at 8.10. Mohamed the cook would then arrive with the grocer's order to sign, I would try and protest as I seemed to be laying in enough sugar and buckets of meat to victual a submarine, but one cannot really win. Then office from 9 - 2. Lunch 2.30 - 3. Siesta 3 - 4, Arabic 4 - 5, then a ride, possibly polo, tennis, stiquet and a swim.

In the Cantonment there were sixteen houses for the British, all much on the same pattern with dining room, sitting room and bedroom opening into each other. The whole house is surrounded by a covered verandah, part of which was covered in mosquito wire called the namlea. The little house (a bucket system), kitchen and servants' quarters are in the garden and if there is a guest room, this is usually detached too. The older houses, including the Powder House have flat roofs where one can sleep in hot weather, but when the rains come in June, so do the bugs, which means a retreat into the namlea. In winter it is cold enough to need three blankets. The only house with two stories is the Governor's which is of red brick; it looks like a cross between Lenin's tomb and a biscuit factory and is known as the Kremlin.

Also in the cantonment was the Kordofan Club. This contained a large central room for bridge and the occasional dance, a bar, three guest rooms and a large namleah (verandah with mosquito netting) at the back for table tennis. At the side were kitchens and quarters for the servants of anyone staying there and a squash court. At the back over a bridge across a small reservoir (the Garden fula) was a fine swimming bath built by the NAAFI for British troops stationed in El Obeid during the war. Further over were two mud and gum tennis courts and a stiquet court; this was like a tennis court with a six foot wall all round the outside lines. The ball is served over a wire six feet high; the game is then played like tennis the ball being taken from the wall or the court. It is the only court I have seen but I believe there is one at the Royal Engineers base at Woolwich.

An important social event took place when all the British received invitations from the "Hellenic Community to a Fancy Dress Ball in the Hellenic Club, (Fancy Dress Not de Rigeur)". We made up a party and arrived to be greeted very warmly and shown to our table on the small dance floor. The piece de resistance was the ceremonial arrival of Mr and Mrs Lappas superbly dressed as Louis XIV and his Queen. We were entertained very well, enjoyed the dancing and were plied with plentiful drinks; though it was rather disconcerting to find them all on our grocers' bills at the end of the month!

Last but not least there was St Peter's Church, dedicated in 1932 by Bishop Gwynne, then Bishop in Egypt and the Sudan. It was small, plain and simple, but just right. I found that part of my duties was to make sure it was cleaned and also to ring the bell for services. I also became Secretary of the Parochial Church Council. Outside the church was a small lych gate with a notice over the gate, which read: -

ST PETER'S EL OBEID
THIS CHURCH WAS DEDICATED BY THE BISHOP OF EGYPT AND THE SUDAN
I WILL ARISE AND GO TO MY FATHER
ON THE 3rd MARCH 1932

The order of this was changed back to what it should have been by Ruth Evans. Almost single handedly she undertook the restoration, rehabilitation and redecoration of the church, which had over a period of time become rather shabby. In some places she even had to retile the floor. Next door was a bat-ridden empty room and we took the opportunity of cleaning this up so it could be used as an extra room of the Kordofan Resthouse for which I was responsible

When I first went to El Obeid, Canon Arnold the CMS (Church Missionary Society) missionary at Sallara in the Jebels 100 miles away used to come about once a month to take the services, but later we came within the orbit of the Chaplain at Wad Medani, Mr Logan. However, George Martin usually came down for festivals, leaving his own longsuffering family in Khartoum. Sometimes the American Presbyterian missionary in El Obeid would be asked to take the service. After he had said that he sometimes bowed his head in shame at

St Peter's Church El Obeid

THE KORDOFAN PRAYERS

These were written by Sir Douglas Newbold KBE, when be was Governor of Kordofan 1933 – 1938. He was Deputy Civil Secretary 1938-1939 and Civil Secretary 1939-1945. His prayer book was kept in St. Peter's Church, El Obeid for the use of the current Governor.

The prayers, adapted for the whole Sudan, were used in all the Anglican churches in the Sudan during the Condominium.

FOR THE PEOPLE OF KORDOFAN

ALMIGHTY GOD, the Fountain of all Wisdom whose divine providence ordereth all things upon earth, we pray Thee, in Thy infinite mercy, to preserve the peoples and races of Kordofan. Let the shadow of Thy protection be over them in town and countryside, in mountain, forest and desert. Guard them, we beseech Thee from all disaster, of famine, sickness, floods and bloodshed. Pour into their hearts and minds Thy most precious gift of understanding, so that they may bring peace into their feuds, justice into their councils, loving kindness into their homes, and may cast away the works of darkness in their lives, Through Jesus Christ out Lord. Amen.

FOR THE OFFICIALS AND GOVERNMENT SERVANTS OF KORDOFAN

Grant, O LORD, Thy guidance unto all those persons, of whatever race or creed, who are in any way concerned in the administration of this Province: replenish them with qualities of faith, patience and vision; guard them from all frailties of body and mind; and so direct their conscience that they labour, one with the other, for the greater happiness and uplifting of this Province; with malice towards none; with charity for all; with firmness in the right as Thou givest them to see the right; striving seeking, and with Thy help, finding the righteous decision in all problems and perplexities. Teach them, most wise Father, to lead simple and incorruptible lives, that they may be examples to the people among whom they dwell, and grant that before their service ends, they may be enabled to contribute, each in his own degree and craftsmanship, to the wider establishment of Thy Kingdom upon earth, Through Jesus Christ our Lord. Amen

the wrong doings of the British Empire, we preferred our own Lay Reader; to which office David Evans was commissioned by the Bishop on one of his visits.

There was therefore plenty to do. The day usually ended with a dinner party somewhere. These as well as being fun, were a very civilised way of learning about the Province, its future plans and policies, its agriculture, education, medical, and veterinary development. There was a common pattern to these parties, which I summarised in the Club Bulletin, a board that was taken round to every household by Hassan, the Club boy. This gave news of any visitors, Club functions and church services. Needless to say, when one of the Bimbashis who had been Club Secretary left, I assumed this office as well.

Duncan Cumming, the new Governor was a fairly formidable figure. Over six foot tall, a Major General and a rugger international, he had really come to Kordofan as a grooming to succeed Sir James Robertson as Civil Secretary. He was certainly the opposite of Geoffrey Hawkesworth. He, Geoffrey had started his career in Kordofan when he and his twin brother Desmond were both ADCs in the old Nuba Mountains Province. Apart from one session as DC Duem in the Blue Nile Province, Geoffrey had spent all his time in Kordofan; he knew everyone and everything in the Province, but he was diffident to the point of retiring. Duncan was larger than life and could be a bit frightening at first, but as the leave season started and people began to disappear for three months I had to work much closer to him.

The 80 days leave was an early tradition of the Sudan; it was felt that people needed to get out of the debilitating climate and before the special air charter, four weeks of the 80 days could well be spent in travelling. The other theory was that it helped the continuity of one's job, it was good for the no.2's to be left in charge and if they made a mess of things it could not be so bad that the boss could not sort it out on his return. In some of the colonies, leave was given much more sparsely, and DC s often found they had a new job when they came back.

As a new boy, I was not entitled to leave during my first year, so had to watch everyone else come and go. This did give me the opportunity to get to know Duncan well, his wife had not yet joined him and Geoffrey was not there as a buffer between us. To counteract the Major Generalship I used to tease him by being nautical and tell him that the coxswain had brought his barge alongside. Sometimes if there was trouble in a remote part of the Province he would say he would fly up in the Dakota and I had to remind him that, sorry, there was no Dakota but if he wanted to go in his car I would hire a lorry to take his baggage. I also had to organise his dinner and drinks parties; one of these was in honour of the Civil Secretary on a short visit. My main duty was to make a fruit cocktail for the Moslem guests; 1/2 pint cold tea, 1/2 pint orange squash, 1/4 pint lemon squash, 1/4 pint pineapple juice, 1 pint ginger beer, 2 squeezed lemons, 1/4 lbs. sugar, watered and stirred.

One of the anxieties of the community was the impending arrival of the baby of Gawain and Sylvia Bell (DC Western Kordofan). Godfrey Clark, the Province Medical Inspector had given permission for the baby to be born in El Obeid hospital, but in practice the responsibility fell on Tony Husband and the nursing sisters, Mary and Ivy. All seemed to go well at first, but then both mother and baby got chicken pox; the baby, a girl, had to go back into hospital. We had practised special hymns and an anthem for her christening, but she had to be baptised Amanda Jocelein by George Martin on Easter Day, still in hospital. The Bells had a party for her afterwards.

The main cantonment gossip was whether there was, or was not an attachment between Geoffrey and Mary. They had gone on leave at the same time, but there was a news black out. Then gradually some filtered through. Geoffrey wrote to Hag el Nur and included a message to me to say he had called on my parents. Then a letter arrived from home to say that Geoffrey and Mary had been to Lynchmere, my parents had thought she was his wife, but it turned out she wasn't (yet?). Then about a week before they were due to return, Ivy confided that she had had a letter from Mary to say they were married. Duncan went off to Khartoum to go on leave, catching the plane bringing Geoffrey out. Just before he left, he came in to my office 'Did you know Geoffrey was married?' 'Actually yes', 'Why didn't you tell me?' 'Sworn to secrecy'. However, the great day arrived and we all went up to the airport to meet the Sudan Airways Dove. Geoffrey was Acting Governor in Duncan's absence so Ivy had brought some white bandages with which to decorate the saloon. G and M looked very pleased with themselves until they saw the wedding car. At a reception given that evening in their honour (all organised before they arrived so that they could not refuse) by Tony and Ivy, their health was proposed by David. Geoffrey in reply said that when they saw the car they felt they had run into the very thing they had tried to avoid.

As summer advanced it got hotter, but the dry heat was not so debilitating as it was beside the river in Khartoum or the Red Sea in Port Sudan. Even so, everyone began to pray for rain. Bob Molloy, the American, tried when he took one of our services but nothing happened; David Evans tried the next Sunday and we did have a shower. In the interregnum between Duncan's departure and Geoffrey's arrival the Province Prison received an official inspection from the Visitors. David Evans was acting Governor, but Rex Harrison was asked to come up from Dilling and sit in the Muderia. It was up to me to arrange a tea party for the prison visitors. So, I took Rex out to Ban Gedid for the tea party, showed the Visitors round and they enjoyed the tea. Mohamed had made a cake with pink icing for the occasion in which he said he had put 25 eggs, I did not believe this, and negotiated them down to 10. As we went over to the workshops afterwards there was a deafening chorus coming from the building next door. I asked what it was and Hag el Nur explained that we really must have rain for the crops and fruit, so the prisoners had been organised into continuous shifts to pray until the rains came. This did the trick; there was a colossal down pour the next evening. Overnight the dust settled, the whole landscape turned green and the desert really did bloom as a rose. The dusty roads became little rivers and everywhere, there were deliriously happy, naked little boys flopping in and out of the puddles.

Ramadam came, when Moslems fast from dawn to dusk. The test is to hold a black and white thread up, if you can tell the difference no food or water shall pass your lips until, in the evening, you cannot tell the difference again. Although the Christians do not fast, one has sympathy for those who do and have to be tolerant with tiredness and general exhaustion.

The end of Ramadam is marked by the Ramadam Bairam, three day holiday or Eid. I asked Geoffrey if I could go and see John Thompson, normally the ADC at Kadugli in the Jebels, but at the time standing in for Rex Harrison at Dilling. The journey would normally take four hours, but we were caught by a flash flood and took three hours to get ourselves out of a wadi (a normally dry river bed). In the end, we had to spend the night in a small agricultural station.

I borrowed a horse from Zachariah effendi who was the agriculturist in charge; he also lent me his scyce, Ismail Abdulla as a guide. At first I walked the horse, but Ismail said we would never get there and made me jog, the horses are trained to go at a pace between a walk and a trot, extremely uncomfortable at first until you get used to it. As we went, the scenery changed, more mud, more trees less sand and greener all the time. At last grass tukls began to appear, then houses, then Dilling meidan, like a village green and we finally trotted through the gates of the DC's house to be rapturously greeted by John. He had been out with a complete hamla (mule train) the day before and left a policeman up the road to help us in. He had just come back to report that there was no sign of us and we must have gone back to El Obeid.

I stayed in Dilling wearing John's clothes for two days and had a very relaxed time during which we visited the new teachers training college which had only just been founded. Dilling may be thought to be rather out of the way for this kind of establishment. The advantages were that Dilling was small and the trainees were less likely to be the target of political agitators than they would in one of the large towns; there was also an adequate water supply. I returned to El

Obeid with no trouble, bringing with me a missionary, Miss Drinkwater, who was going on leave, four mission children and their baggage. I had enjoyed Dilling so much that I told Geoffrey that if I could be transferred there, I would forget about Lebanon, only to be told that a new ADC, Robin Young, was expected and he would go to Dilling!

I was able to pay another visit to the Jebels, but not until December. I went with Hag el Nur with about eight in the entourage on the back of the pick up. I stayed in Dilling with Robin Young, who took me out to visit Canon Arnold in the CMS mission at Sallara. My log records that I was not very impressed with Sallara although the small brick buildings and the church were attractive

The next day we wound on another 100 miles to Kadugli where John Thompson held sway. On Friday John Thompson also took me out to see the country. I found the Nuba Mountains most entrancing, this was quite unlike the flat rather monotonous country round El Obeid. The word 'jebel' means mountain, actually they are rocky out crops and the Nuba villages cling onto the sides like hornets nests. Each family has a small enclosure, you step into this over a sill, all round are circular huts with grass roofs in which the grain is stored, and then there is a larger hut which is the families' sleeping quarters.

A new rain grown cotton industry has started up. 'Sea Island' cotton is rain grown, unlike the larger industry in the Gezira, which is irrigated, but it still needs very careful inspection and control. This is done by the Inspectors from the Agricultural Department. The cotton has to be brought into a centre like Kadugli where there is a ginnery. The cotton is bought at a fixed price and then cleaned and ginned. Finally it is baled and transported up to the railway by enormous lorries and trailers, mostly driven by Italians.

I had an amusing morning with John in his office listening in to the various cases that came up before him. Although I still had to pass the Law exam, I had already, as a Magistrate, sat as one of the members on a major court, but I had not yet had experience the run of the mill cases which were the DC's normal round. Cases are tried in Arabic, but the Magistrate writes down the evidence in English. A small group of Arabs were accused of illegally selling some old rifles to some Nuba. The Nubas' Arabic was not very good (rather like mine) and came out in a series of grunts.

Q (from Magistrate) Have you seen those things before?
A (from Nuba).   Yes.
Q   What have you seen before?
A   Gun.
Q   Which one?
A   That one.

Magistrate's notes	Witness Koko Tia. Sworn. I recognise the Rifle before the court labelled as exhibit A.
Q	Where have you seen it?
A	Bought it.
Q	Who from
A	Arab
Q	Do you recognise him.
A	Yes, Arab, that one.
Magistrate's notes	I purchased the said exhibit from the Arab, Mohamed Fulan whom I recognise as one of the accused.

    I took the opportunity of getting up early on Sunday morning to pay a quick visit to Katcha, the other CMS mission. Roland Stevenson, a celebrated linguist who had just received a doctorate, ran this. There were 200 boys in an elementary and an intermediate school. The new Chaplain, Jim Donnelly was just going to celebrate Holy Communion in Arabic for the first time, I was able to stay, but then made a dash as Hag El Nur was waiting.

    The road to Talodi ran through the Moru hills, colourful with poison trees . We stopped at a place called Dorein, where Nuba were getting ready for a stick fight. They fought with sticks about three feet long with a leather hand shield, their only protection was their own hair caked in a milk paste done up into spikes. The encounters were "to-morrow", which could easily mean next week, so reluctantly we had to go on to Talodi, which lies to the south of the hills.

Stick fighters ready for action, their hair caked in a milk paste, their hands protected by a leather shield.

    Talodi had been the Headquarters of the old Nuba Mountain Province. I slept at the former Governors' house where the King and Queen had stayed when they were Duke and Duchess of York. In the evening we inspected the suq and the grave of an Egyptian Mamur killed by a rock, it had his tarboush on it.

Up at 6.30 to see the prison, merkaz garden, some dams, and a quick whirl round the town. Breakfast at 9.30 and off again at 10.15. At first the going was flat, but then we climbed back up into the hills through a delightful series of little villages. Heiban was most attractive, all tree lined with neems, poison trees in flower and frangipani. I made a quick call on the SUM (Sudan United Mission) run by Australians. Then on through Abri and Delami where we stayed the night. We had tea with the Mamur, who holds the MM and the Sudan DCM, he was a mine of information about the Mountains and the Nuba. The rest house here was famous as it is covered in murals all painted by one of the local policemen. One room had a train going all the way round, another had well known characters, such as 'The DC drinking', 'Nuba wrestling, 'DC on trek' (in an old Ford). This policeman and Barbara Harrison, the DC's wife, used to go to art lessons at Dilling school and go off sketching together. We started home very early in the morning and I was back in the office by 9.30 having shot quite a lot of guinea fowl on the way.

So, my first year in El Obeid rolled on. After the leave season our social life became more active. Duncan had brought back his charming American wife, Nancy, who treated me as part of the family. Geoffrey and Mary had both settled into the Deputy Governor's house. A new nursing sister, Wendy Morris-Higgs replaced Mary. At Christmas, families came out to join their parents, including the Cumming's daughter Ann and their friends from New York, Mr and Mrs Abbott Moffat and their two daughters. Traditionally all the D.C.s came into El Obeid, so I found my spare time very occupied in arranging our Christmas programme which included a Service of Nine Lessons and Carols, a dance, Christmas dinner at the Cummings and a mounted paper chase.

Grave of Egyptian Marmur.

England to the Sudan 1951

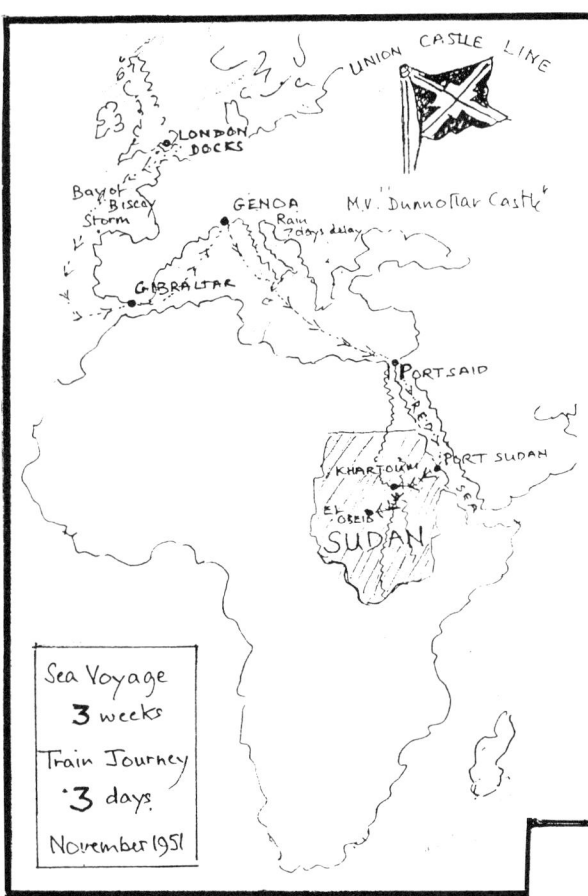

UNION CASTLE LINE

LONDON DOCKS
Bay of Biscay Storm
GENOA — M.V. "Dunnottar Castle" Rain 7 days delay
GIBRALTAR
PORT SAID
PORT SUDAN
KHARTOUM
EL OBEID
SUDAN

Sea Voyage 3 weeks
Train Journey 3 days
November 1951

M. V. "DUNNOTTAR CASTLE"

FIRST SALOON

NOVEMBER 11th, 1951

Music

*

March	On The Quarter Deck	Alford
Suite	Four Indian Love Lyrics	Finden
Intermezzo	Cynthia	Crook
Selection	Merry Widow	Lehar

Bandmaster: ROY MALVERN

Sailed from London docks
2 am Sat. November 3rd 1951

Ports of call
Nov 7th: Gibraltar
9th: Marseilles
11th/14th: Genoa
  (rain delayed us, perishable cargo to unload)
18th: Port Said (not allowed ashore)
20th: Suez Canal
Nov. 21st M's birthday
  Port Sudan
  Red Sea Hotel
Nov. 24th Train to Khartoum
  + straight onto El Obeid
Nov. 26th Arrived El Obeid
  (3 hours late)

DINNER

HORS d'ŒUVRES
Mixed Olives   Smoked Salmon
Spiced Anchovies   Salade Parmentier
Julienne de Betterave   Rollmops Hollandaise

Consommé Aurore
Crème Crecy

Fresh River Trout, Ecossaise

Jerusalem Artichokes à la Crème

Breast of Turkey, Chipolata

Roast Shoulder of Mutton, Red Currant Jelly

Petit Pois, Francaise

Potatoes: Browned   Vapeur

Salade de Saison

SWEETS
Pouding Diplomat   Pears in Jelly

SAVOURY
Soft Roes on Toast

Dessert   Coffee

JAMES E. BRADFORD   FREDERICK J. MORLEY
CHIEF STEWARD   CHEF DE CUISINE

The Dunnottar Castle

3. MARRIED LIFE BEGINS, ANNE'S FIRST VISIT TO NAHUD.

At the beginning of 1950, I said goodbye to my friends in El Obeid and went to Khartoum, staying on the way with John Phillips who had been in the Jebels and was now D.C. Wad Medani, and Peter Stern (from Lynchmere) who was working in the Irrigation Department in the Gezira. After a few days in Khartoum where I met Ralph Daly, we went by train, Nile steamer and train to Cairo where we joined Brian Walters and Philip Bowcock. Then by ship to Lebanon for a year at the Middle East Centre of Arab Studies (MECAS). The course lasted for a happy year, during which the four Sudanis travelled in our Ford V8 through Lebanon, Syria, Jordan (which then included what is now known as the 'West Bank') and Iraq. This however, will have to be the subject of a different effort to this one.

The really important event happened after I had returned home having been nearly two years away. I met Anne and before my leave was up in the middle of February I had proposed to her. We wrote to each other every day for the next six months

On my return to Khartoum, I had to take the Higher Arabic Examination so I was there for two weeks staying with Philip Bowcock who had been in MECAS with me. I was all set to go back to Kordofan when I was suddenly told I had to go to Dueim in Blue Nile Province instead. I protested and sent a telegram to Geoffrey Hawkesworth asking him to help. Fortunately the Secretariat changed its mind and I shot off to El Obeid before it could change it back again. This time, I was accompanied by Abdel Rahman Babikr as Safragi and Mohamed as Cook. Very soon I was re-installed in the Powder House opposite the Province Headquarters. While I had been away, John Haggar had done my job, lived in the house and used my furniture. He had now departed to MECAS.

So, I soon settled into the routine again. Duncan Cumming was now in Khartoum, Geoffrey Hawkesworth was Governor and John Rowley had come in from Bara as Deputy Governor, so I knew them all well already. This was not a very long tour as I had taken most of my 1950 leave in l951. The time went quickly; meanwhile wedding plans were going on at home.

I had an interesting week visiting Ralph Daly. He was now Executive Officer of the Kabbabish District Council in Soderi, Northern Kordofan. The Kabbabish are the largest camel owning tribe in the Sudan, and I had met most of the hierarchy from the Tom (pronounced Tome), the Nazir's family, on their visits to El Obeid. Ralph's DC, Peter Lumsden came up to Soderi and he took me on up to the north where the tribe had taken the camels. The Kabbabish move north in the rains, almost to the Libyan border, so long as they can find grazing. The men who go with them live quite happily on camel's milk and nothing else for as much as six months. Peter and I were entertained to supper, sitting round a campfire eating a boiled sheep from a cauldron. The Toms were excellent hosts, continually presenting one with choice pieces. Fortunately it was dark so one was able to toss anything which, to European eyes looked doubtful, over one's shoulder where it was instantly eaten up by an expectant dog. I left Peter and returned back to El Obeid via Western Kordofan, staying a night with John Hunter who was the A.D.C in Nahud, the District headquarters.

September soon arrived and there I was going home again on an Airwork Viking for an extra special leave. Anne and I were married by my father in our own church of St. Peter's Lynchmere on October 6th. So it was that we arrived back in El Obeid before Christmas having got married and had a honeymoon extended by a relaxed three week voyage out to Port Sudan in the Union Castle line's Dunnottar Castle. This was followed by a 48 hour train journey from Port Sudan to El Obeid. I carried Anne up the steps of the Powder House to be greeted by Abdel Rahman who had come on ahead to get the house ready.

Anne settled down very quickly and began organising the house, especially the bedroom; there had not actually been one except for a very hot and stuffy little room, really part of the veranda. I had only used it as a dressing room as I had slept in the veranda or on the flat roof. So, a new bedroom had been built on while I had been away. Anne's mother had asked me what colour my curtains were, that was the first time I realised that I had not got any! Anne also started Arabic lessons at which she was joined later by Jane Hook, the new wife of one of the Bimbashis, Hilary Hook, who has later achieved fame on the television.

Amongst the responsibilities I had left behind while I was at MECAS were the live stock. Buttercup, a sheep, had been given to me during 1949, but she had not been eaten as she had been pregnant with Daisy. Then there were the Muscovy ducks, Rachel and Rebekka. Unfortunately Rebekka had been lost while I was away, she had eaten some wet concrete which had solidified inside her and she could not be saved. Rachel was joined by some turkeys given to us for

October 6th 1951

The Powder House
from Anne's watercolour

Our sheep.
Buttercup & Daisy

Christmas. One had arrived from one of the oldest merchants Sheikh Omer el Tenai with a label round its neck which read 'Mrs Tipps one fine turkey for Christmas'. I had sold Westward, my original horse, but was very happy with Turveytop a roan stallion. We were looking for a horse for Anne, but then the Hooks were transferred to Darfur, the province to the west of us, so we bought Brown Willy from Jane. Brown Willy had originally belonged to Pricilla Hext, wife of Jack, an Inspector of Agriculture, not only a Cornishman but nephew of the Governor General, Sir Robert Howe; Brown Willy is a peak on Bodmin Moor, which Pricilla could see from her bedroom window. Anne described him in a letter home as 'so sweet natured, very handsome, a bay stallion with long black mane and tail, a perfect lady's hack'.

Apart from our first Christmas together and welcoming dinner parties, two things stand out on the social side of life. The first, a Friday visit to Peter and Nancy Lumsden in Bara. They had a small swimming bath at the end of their garden which had been filled up from a sagia by a polite camel and his keeper. After a bathe and an excellent lunch we listened to records on their wind up gramophone. The second was an invitation to tea by El Obeid's venerable merchant Sheikh Omer el Tinai, he who had given Anne the turkey for Christmas. We did justice to orange juice, tea, cakes, toffee and coffee, and then the real entertainment began. The old man handed round his "shehadas". These were testimonials written by pretty well all the Governors, Miralis, D.C's and famous people who had lived or passed through El Obeid, testifying to Sheikh Omer el Tinai's honesty, efficiency and such like in his various contracts. These were suitably received with polite admiration, to be succeeded by whistles of envy when they were followed by his bank accounts!

The Moonlight Sonata

I had always hoped to be appointed outside El Obeid to be ADC Kadugli in the south of the Nuba Mountains. I had been most attracted to the Nuba on my brief visits. However, Geoffrey sat me down one day and told me that Donald Rae, the ADC Messeria was resigning and I was to go to Nahud to replace him. I was disappointed, but Geoffrey pointed out that the job, although under the DC Western Kordofan, was usually given to a fully fledged DC. There had been a certain amount of friction between Donald Rae and the Nazir Umum, Babu Nimr. Babu was a Member of the Legislative Assembly, the son-in-law of Sayed Abdel Rahman, head of the Mahdi family and of the Umma party; and so the job could

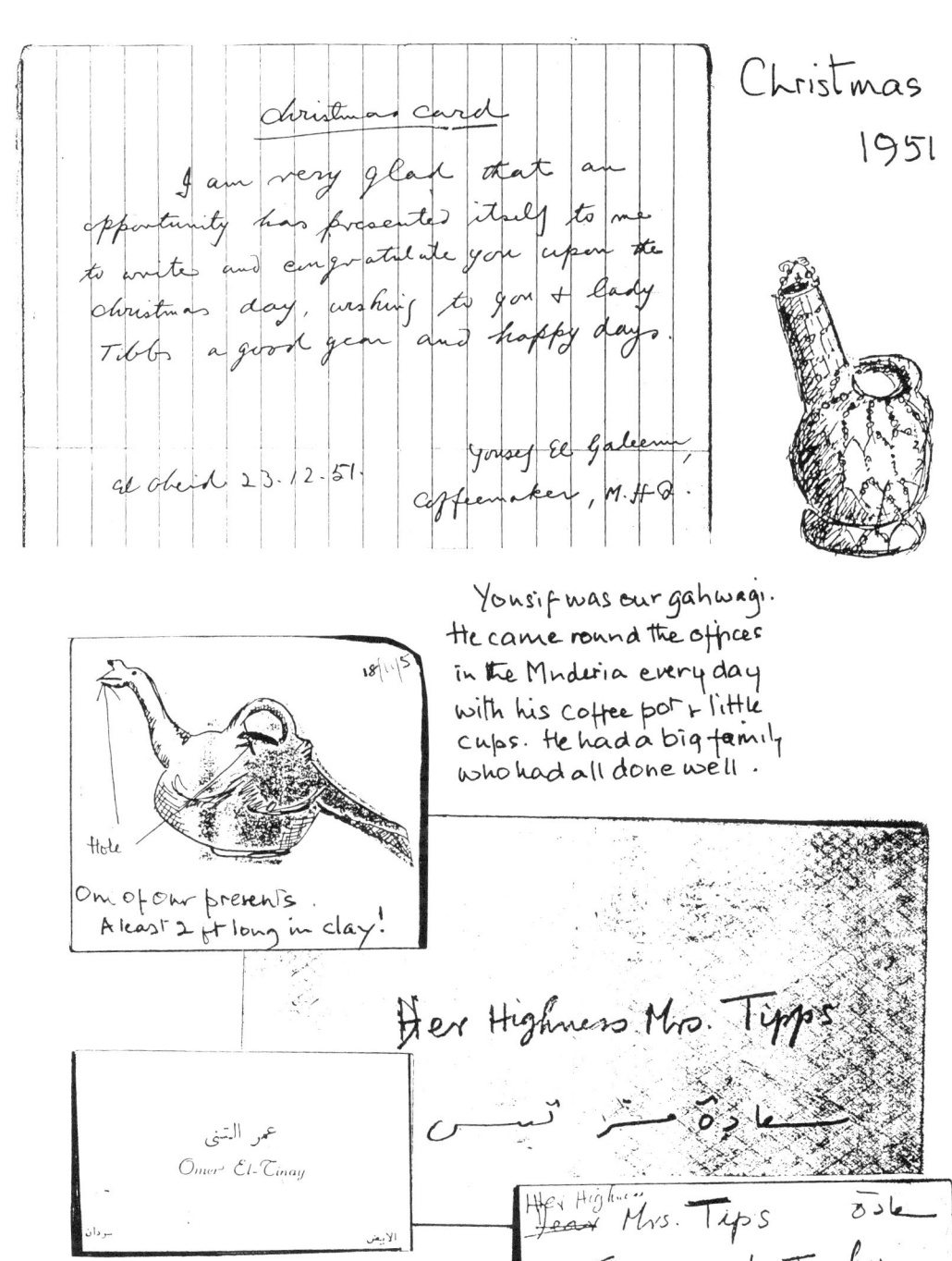

Christmas 1951

Christmas card

I am very glad that an opportunity has presented itself to me to write and congratulate you upon the christmas day, wishing to you & lady Tibbs a good year and happy days.

el Obeid 23.12.51.

Yousef El Galeem, Coffeemaker, M.H.Q.

Yousif was our gahwagi. He came round the offices in the Mudiria every day with his coffee pot & little cups. He had a big family who had all done well.

One of our presents. At least 2 ft long in clay!

Omer El-Tinay

Omer El-Tinay was a leading merchant in El Obeid. His tea parties were famous. As a finale his guests would be shown his flourishing bank statements.

Her Highness Mrs. Tipps

Mrs. Tips — One good Turkey for christmas — Happy christmas.

have political repercussions; at the same time Babu would need very careful handling. This was later emphasised by the Civil Secretary when I next saw him, he (Sir James Robertson) had been DC Western Kordofan and knew Babu well. "You are" he said "to make friends with Babu". As so often happens in life an initial disappointment turned out to be the most interesting and fascinating three years that I have ever spent and all the better because we were able to do everything together.

We were getting ready for our first visit to Nahud together when everyone was stunned and saddened by the news of the King's death. All flags on government buildings were lowered to half-mast and we paid a visit to the suq to get our mourning armbands. All the Sudanese staff came round our offices the next day to shake hands and offer their condolences. Later we had two memorial services. The first was an Arabic requiem mass in the Syrian Catholic church. The second was in our own little church of St. Peter when George Martin, the Provost, came down to take the service. It was packed with all Christian denominations and many of our Moslem friends.

One of the Public Works Department (PWD) staff, Freddie Ricks, was retiring so on a Friday afternoon in February we went to the auction they were having of their furniture. We were able to buy a cupboard, six small tables, one larger one, a kitchen table, three pastry boards, a trek table and a water softener for £E18!

When we returned to the house at 3.30 everything, beds, bath, tables, chairs, food, pantry box, kitchen box and all the other trek impedimenta had been loaded up on one of the Muderia lorries. A crowd had collected to see us off. Actually we were half an hour late as John Hunter had asked us to bring his new wardrobe, but it was far too big to fit in so we had to leave it behind.

We headed west, for 140 miles up the road which leads to Fasher, the capital of Darfur. Very sandy, straight and known as the 'Aly waty' (up and down) road, It was fringed with tall dry grass and bushes and scrubby trees of all shapes and sizes. We passed a few camels and donkeys and then an enormous number of cattle all heading back to El Obeid. For about two miles there was a stream of them, hundreds deep on either side of the road leaving a cloud of dust like an evening mist for several miles after we had left them behind. Then we ran into a swarm of tree locusts, we found ourselves driving through a black cloud, billions of

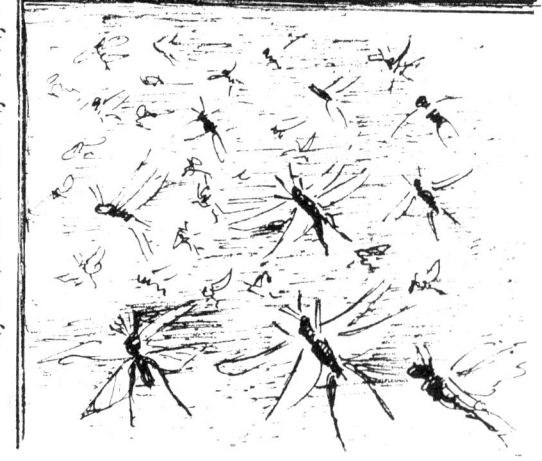

them flying at a level just above the lorry so only a few got into the headlights or onto the windscreen. The swarm covered about a mile and then suddenly, there we were under a clear full moon.

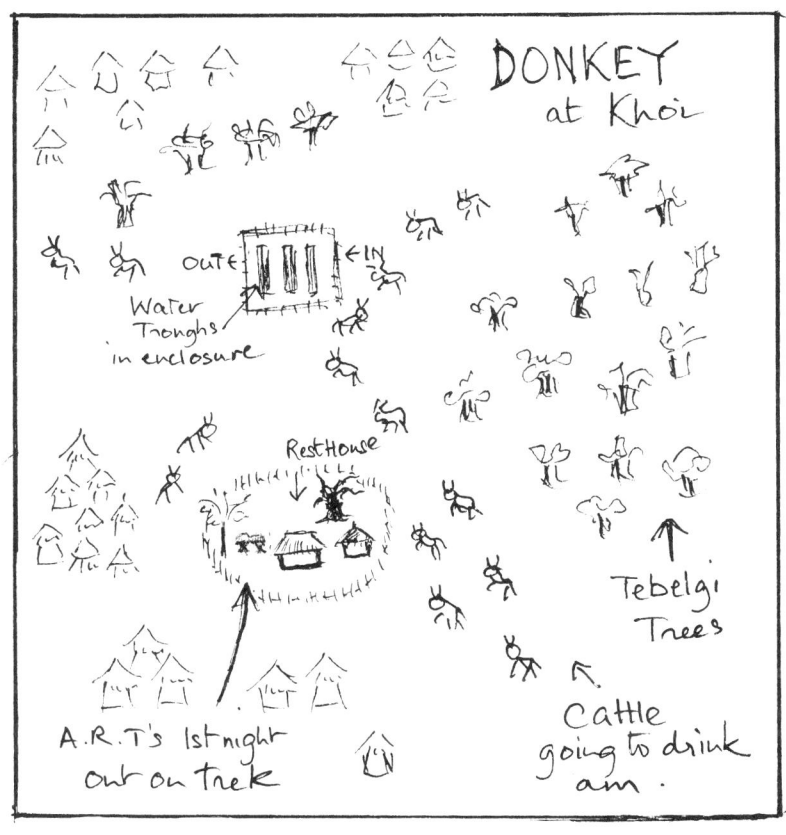

Khoi Rest House

We stayed the night at Khoi, about half way, in the 'Donkey' (water yard) rest house. This was Anne's first trek and experience of the PWD's standard accommodation. Two stone and thatched tukls (round huts) joined together by a grass roof, the sides are open. Outside was a concrete slab, the mustaba (patio) where our chairs were put out.

We had a bath, in our canvas trek bath about 3' square and 6" deep, displacing quite a lot of water onto the floor. This exercise over, we were able to have a drink. The supper had been laid on the trek table and we had soup, fried chops and potatoes with cauliflower followed by savoury of cheese and eggs on toast. So to bed outside under the most beautiful tebelgi tree with its branches silhouetted against the great round moon. In the distance there was the sound of dancing, but when that stopped, silence except for the crickets and every now and then a night bird, a braying donkey or a dog barking, which usually started off a whole chorus.

Quite a breeze got up in the night and we woke up to find our beds covered by a lot of prickly leaves which had blown off a nearby thorn tree. At 5.30 we were woken up by a hum of lowing cattle getting nearer and nearer until they were all pouring past us into the yard where the drinking troughs were and then out again when they had their fill. Luckily we were protected by a wire fence. By about 7.30 most of the cattle had drunk and had been succeeded by donkeys, camels and the local people coming to fill four gallon petrol tins at 1 piastre (1p.) a time. We went round to look at the pump. This was the real 'donkey' (sic) named after the donkey engine which drove it, (plural dwank).

We departed after breakfast and stopped for elevenses under an enormous tebelgi beside the road, whereupon a chap appeared with a great watermelon he kindly gave to us. We shared it with the servants there and then. There were small monkeys in the trees and masses of brightly coloured birds of all descriptions, some marabou storks, a few ground squirrels and an occasional fox.

We arrived in Nahud just after 12 and are staying with Peter Hogg. Just after we arrived there were earsplitting noises from the veranda, we could not think what they were but we discovered that it was one of Peter's servants damping down his ironing by filling his mouth with water and spitting it out as hard as possible onto the clothes. It is quite a common habit, but not one that we encourage. Abdel Rahman shakes water out of a bottle.

The next morning I went to the Merkaz (District Headquarters) to be introduced to the staff and had talks about the job with Peter. We then saw Donald Rae, John Hunter who came in from trek while we were there and Robin Crole, a probationer who had been attached to Nahud to learn the ropes from Peter.

Tebelgi tree

Anne's impression of Nahud was far better than she had expected. She was particularly struck by the large number of green trees, bushes and old tebelgi trees. Donald kindly allowed us to roam around our future house while he was at the office. Anne thought she would be able to make it very nice, though it was not at its best at the moment. Donald was a rather eccentric bachelor, only 34, but looked older. A Scot, he was in the Indian Army and had a good military bearing with a little moustache to match. He boomed out with a very powerful voice which was quite deafening.

Anne wrote…,

He is very keen on shooting with the result that as you walk into the house there is a terrific crackle and something hits you on the leg. You stop abruptly, thinking the floor is giving way, then you look down to see you have trodden on the dried skin of a poor animal, most of its fur worn off and curled up, dry and hard. It's very difficult to walk without stepping on a sea of them. You sit down on a chair and hurriedly spring up again having sat on a python's backbone, an elephant's tail or a crocodile's jaw full of teeth. In rising so rapidly you hit your head on a spear or a flywhisk dangling from the wall, and knock over a lion skin shield leaning on a chair. The furniture is all very dark and there is nothing except the absolute minimum. In the bedroom there is only an iron bed surrounded by rows of tin boxes. All the windows were shuttered up to keep the heat out. (Many people did this, we never did, as we preferred to have light and whatever breeze there might be). Donald's servants were all Dinka he had brought with him from his last District in the south.

Donald kindly entertained us to dinner. We gingerly tried to avoid stepping on the crackly skins, but actually, the floor is not much better because his servants have polished it with old gear oil, so your shoes are inclined to stick to it and if you don't leave your shoe behind, there is a squishing noise as you pull them after you. The place settings for dinner are of the family silver, but one course may be served in a silver dish and the next off a retired enamel plate with chips all over it. Donald though is quite charming and very helpful, he feels it is time he was settled in life and wants to study to become a Chartered Land Agent.

We left early, got back to Khoi at noon, had lunch leaving again at 1.30 and got back to El Obeid at 5pm rather battered from the aly wati road. It was worse than ever and we had to go slowly so as not to break a spring. The Hawkesworths were in their garden and heard us, so asked us to tea. By the time we got home the house was in order, the silver out, everything dusted, unpacked and our bath ready.

Maribou storks

Sunset on the Nuba Mountains.

4. OUR FIRST TREK TO THE MESSERIA
With Donald Rae

Kasha Rest House.

Anne's Letter....
15th March 1952. Jebel Kasha

It is just dusk, the stars are coming out and we are sitting on the top of Jebel Kasha, one of the smaller Nuba Mountains, lighted by a hurricane lamp, the big round moon not being quite sufficient. It really is a most delightful place. The Jebel consists of quite a high hill covered by boulders which make all sorts of nooks and crannies, little ravines and valleys amongst which, bushes and old gnarled trees grow. Clinging to the craggy peaks are the little round huts which are the Nubas' homes. All round down below stretches a greeny coloured plain, turning lovely shades of blue and purple in the distance. Rising out of the plain are the irregular shapes of the main Nuba Mountains.

To reach the rest house our lorry had to climb a precipitous track up the side of the hill, winding its way between boulders and turning sharply round the hairpin bends. As soon as we arrived, dozens of Nuba men and little boys rushed onto the scene and started to unload the lorries, much to our servants' amazement and almost embarrassment as they watched my expression at seeing all these bare bodies buzzing around! Nearly all are completely nude, or perhaps have a little painted decoration on themselves, or a string round their waist, some beads here and there, or perhaps a monkey' skin flapping over their behinds! Most picturesque, especially their fantastic hair styles.

The rest house consists of two round grass roofed rooms joined by an open grass shelter where one can sit out of the sun. We are not sitting there now, but right outside. Donald has just turned his wireless on and we are listening to Sandy at the theatre organ from the BBC. So extraordinary right out here in the wilds!

We left El Obeid this morning. By 9.30 everything was loaded up and our three servants all very happy at the thought of a jaunt, were assembled in the back of the lorry. We shook hands and said goodbye to the crowd gathered by the gate (mostly the neighbours' garden prisoners who had helped load up) and got into the front seat. The driver, a uniformed policeman clicked smartly to attention, shut the door and then got in himself, and away we went.

The scenery we passed was not very unusual, the red sandy track, on each side, bushes and trees, mostly not very tall except for the old gnarled tebelgi trees which are quite beautiful. Their trunks are feet thick and in some places are hollowed out and used for storing water in. It is getting near the end of the dry season, so most things are a bit lifeless, except now and then there was a patch of green where there was water. Except for vivid coloured birds of all descriptions, apart from ground squirrels there was not much wild life. We of course passed the usual herds of sheep, goats and cattle, pedestrians and camel travellers, but not a single lorry or motor vehicle

We arrived at Abu Zabad for lunch at 1.30 having driven about 100 miles, stopping on the way for elevenses under an old tebelgi tree. On all occasions when we stop, before we have had time to get out of the lorry, there are two chairs ready for us to sit in and in a few minutes fresh lemon juice, tea, or whatever it is arrives.

Donald was waiting for us at Abu Zabad. We had lunch and went on again in pursuit of his lorry. We drove for about another 20-30 miles and arrived here, stopping en route to look at a stone quarry, various building and bridges. The country is much nicer, shady trees and then all the Nuba Mountains in the distance. We crossed an enormous lake, practically all dried up now and lucious grass all over it. As soon as the rains come it will be covered up until next year.

While all was being unpacked we strolled round. Nuba appeared from all directions plus their dogs, sheep, donkeys and goats which all run loose amongst the rocks. One sweet sight was a pitch black little boy (completely nude) with a minute baby kid, snowy white. Black and white whisky advert?

We were very lucky as a sibr (party) was going on. We walked over to where a sound of beating drums was coming and soon we were in the middle of it. We were surrounded by dozens of black bodies all specially oiled, painted and decorated for the occasion, rings in their noses, spikes of glass sticking out of their chins, in fact objects of every description stuck in all parts of the anatomy. The women particularly had special mud and oil packs on their hair done in all types of fashions, thousands of plaits (minute ones), cock's combs or just a mass of oiled fuzz. They all wanted to shake hands with us. I really don't know how many hundreds of black hands I've shaken lately. They were all particularly intrigued with me as I suppose that most of them

A night on trek.

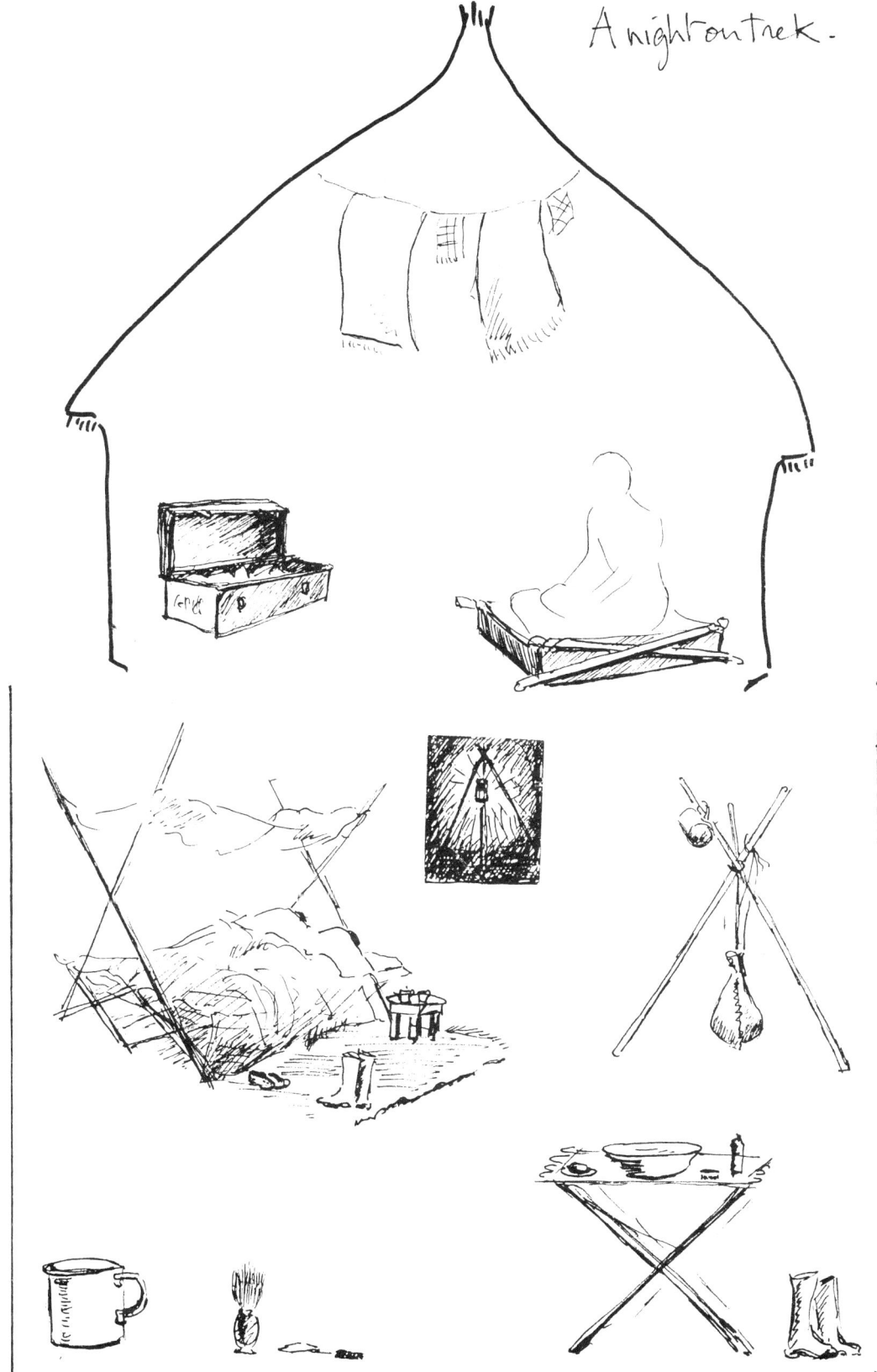

have never seen a white woman before. One old man wanted my white shell necklace to keep, but I would not give it to him, he had a beautiful string of dates round his neck.

We were ushered round by a six-toed man (one toe like a chicken's back one sticking out at right angles). He was called Abu Sita (father of six). He saw that we had the best view of everything when they did some wrestling and stick fighting. There was one great wrestler a champion, wearing a monkey skin round his behind, any clothing they do wear is round the back rather than the front! The women did some rythmic dancing. Their tattooed oiled bodies gleaming in the sun, they paraded round in a circle doing short small steps swaying their hips and raising their bosoms up and down in time to the beating drums. Their expressions were priceless to watch. Sometimes the men danced too, then it became a more lively performance with much stamping of feet and leaping in the air with shrieks and yells and much dust flying in all directions.

We came back to find tea ready waiting for us, now we have had it and also our bath. Lit by the light of a hurricane lamp, this is quite an amusing performance. There we sit in our canvas collapsable, having overflowed half the water in a lake round us. I don't think one could ever enjoy a bath so much or feel so refreshed afterwards.

Dinner of roast partridge or guinea fowl, both of which we, or rather Donald shot en route, is about to arrive, so I'll stop.

March 16th Jebel Kasha

It is 6.30 in the morning and I am sitting on a chair beside the wireless listening to tuneful English music while everyone else, the servants I mean, rush round packing up as we are off at 7. The wireless and myself have caused considerable curiosity and a crowd of Nuba has gathered a few yards away to scrutanise both, one or two have ventured in beside me to have a closer look. I have just completed my toilet by powdering my nose, applying lipstick and brushing my hair which was too interesting for words. The eyes got larger and larger!

We had a very good night sleeping right outside in the open, perfectly lovely, the full moon was a great golden ball amongst the twinkling stars, all just melting away when the sun came up from behind the hills this morning at about 5.30-6, a beautiful sunrise. Its so lovely with just the little round houses perched on the hillside about one, and then in the early morning hearing the chatter of the women as they go by down the hill to get water, carrying the jars so gracefully on their heads.

March 17th Lagawa

We left Jebel Kasha yesterday morning at 7oc. and had a lovely drive amongst the mountains for about 30 miles until we arrived at Jebel Tima where we spent the day. This time instead of the village being on the top of the mountain it was nestled at the bottom. The steep rocky slopes rising abruptly straight up behind. Some people had their homes on little shelves and terraces tucked into the hillside.

We had breakfast at 10 o'clock when we arrived at the resthouse, two tukls like the other one; then for the rest of the morning we lazed about, it being quite hot and the two men slept. I didn't feel at all sleepy, so finished my sun dress and read. We had lunch at 2, then at about 3 we went for a walk round. We saw the Sultan's house which he proudly showed us; mud with grass roof, spotlessly clean, then we saw the wells and his garden with banana trees. At 4 oc we were off again

The well at Tima

We arrived here at about 7, stopping at various villages en route. In one, we went in to the chief's house and had some cooling orange squash.

Lagawa is quite big, a town in fact and we will stay here until tomorrow. This rest house consists of four small mud huts and a larger one in the middle, all enclosed by a thorn hedge. I am sitting in the middle one where we have our tables and chairs and have our meals, except for dinner which we have outside. It's too hot to have the others out.

At the moment, Mike and Donald have gone to the office for the morning, so I am having a nice peaceful morning writing, reading and sewing! Before breakfast we drove out 24 miles to a village where a well was being dug. Donald wanted to view its progress. We sat in the back where the servants and the luggage usually go and it was very pleasant buzzing along. Nice country with the mountains in the distance.

I have just done the hissab (Housekeeping accounts) with Mohamed as I do every morning. Tonight we are going to have Christmas pudding, the second one you gave us which we have not eaten yet! I thought it would be useful to have hot with brandy butter to-night and then eat cold. A.R. has just come in with an armful of things, a bottle of orange squash, a tin of Blue Bird toffees and some tins of fruit, peaches and pineapples from someone to Sa'ata Sit. I've no idea who he is, some old Sheikh in the town I expect. Donald will know. Isn't it kind of him, I will have to go and thank him

The further south we go, the hotter it gets, though it is not at all unbearable. I don't mind it at all, though I have an everlasting thirst, drink pints and just drip!
6.30 pm.

Just come back from the suq, where we had to go and see various shop owners. Lemonade, fizzy, chocolates and sweets were of course stuffed down our throats and chairs brought forward for us to sit on.

Someone is going to El Obeid, so will send this with the driver, so I hope it will get to you. Hope you are both well, see you soon, we leave El Obeid by Dove on Sunday week (30th) and stay a few days in Khartoum before we fly on the 3rd.

28th March Between Keilak and Muglad.

I wish you could see us now! We have just driven about 40 miles through what seemed the darkest depths of Africa on a very dark night. In and out, up and down, an awful road or rather track. Every few yards there was a khor ie. anything from a deep steep sided ditch to a wide sandy bottomed river or stream, all dry now, but later on when it rains, a rushing torrent. If Donald had not got a guide with him we would not have been here yet. As it was we got off the track several times. After plunging through thick bamboo we came to an abrupt stop and had to retrace our steps. We arrived here about half and hour ago. It is just a clearing and round about under the surrounding trees are the glowing fires of the baggara (cattle owning nomads) who have brought their cattle to water at the spring and have made temporary grass houses.

We have washed and tidied; the servants have put up our trek tables and chairs, so we are having a drink and listening to an opera on the wireless while waiting for our supper to arrive. It is being prepared on a large campfire a few yards away; mutton to-night, a whole sheep, one of three we have been given, is being roasted. No sooner had we arrived than an old Omda (chief of a tribal section) appeared out of the darkness followed by a procession of people with a pail of milk, a dozen eggs, jars of water, dozens of angareebs to sleep on (we of course have our camp beds) and bringing up the rear a sheep led on a string. They are all now sitting cross-legged on the ground around us, mostly old men, listening to the music with great enjoyment.

A small group of mostly bare children are watching all our movements with their goggling eyes gleaming in the dark. It is very dark night and the moon has not come up yet. Hurricane lamps hanging from tripods light up our encampment, making everything else around look pitchy black.

We have got our beds on one side of the lorry, while all the servants and the considerable crowd of others travelling with us, are on the other side. They include the guide, Donald's head accountant, two policemen, the driver, driver's assistant, marassla (office boy), someone's wife, a baby and several others!

Mahmoud (our seconda) is being very busy as A.R. has gone to bed. Our police driver from El Obeid is ill and we had to leave him behind in Lagawa. It so happened that Donald Rae had an extra driver Anderea, a Dinka, with him. He was driving our lorry when we got stuck in a khor, he let the clutch out too quickly. AR fell off and hurt his back, not seriously luckily, just bruised. We've given him two asprin and I have rubbed him with Germolene.

This is the place renowned for lions and anyone who wants to shoot one comes here, so we shall probably hear them tonight, I hope so.

We left Lagawa early this morning and arrived at Lake Keilak at 10 o'clock when we had breakfast. The lake is vast but of course is mostly dried up now; though there was still enough water to make an attractive landscape with the Nuba Mountains misty blue shapes in the distance.

We slept and then had lunch, not forgetting to mention the usual stream of visitors, (including an old Omda with

Lake Keilak from the Rest House

two sheep for us, also a tray of orangeade) who called in on us. We were in the rest house, which has just been built. Anyway, at 3 oc. we were all ready to leave when the fan would not go round in the lorry engine, so that had to be mended. However, that finished, it was discovered that the coupling of the transmission (to the back wheels) was broken. Luckily, another was found to fit it, but it all meant that we did not leave until 5.30 and would not have time to drive all the way to Muglad as planned. Hence, we are camping here on the way, and had to do that bad road in the dark. I am very glad as it is such fun camping out like this with no rest house or cover at all.

We had a lovely night last night and we did hear lions, lots of them it seemed, roaring quite close, also hyenas. It was quite an experience going to sleep listening to them and watching the glow of the fires around being kept alight all night to keep them away. I woke in the night once, and the night sounds I heard were the snores from the servants, a gurgle from a baby, a dog barking, lions roaring and hyenas howling. Quite a mixture!

Musa Shwein

We were up before 6 and off again. We stopped at another watering place about 30 miles further on and had breakfast under a lovely shady tree, while cattle, cows, bulls, goats, sheep, dogs and children ran around and got water from the well. The great excitement here was that a dear old man, an Omda called Musa Shwein after waiting up for three nights had succeeded in shooting a lion in the night, one which has taken ten cows and numerous sheep recently. How he did, we can't imagine as he seemed half-blind and his gun looked pre-historic! but there it was, an enormous creature with a terrific mane and I really hated seeing it lying dead and what's more the old man has insisted on giving me the skin as a very special present! We protested and said we had not got time to wait for it and he ought to keep it for himself, but he was quite determined sa'ata sit should have it and within half an hour the skin was in our lorry! I had to be delighted and thank him very much and say how kind he was.

We arrived here at 10 am having got held up a bit with the lorry again. We also stopped to watch some monkeys, dozens of them in an enormous old tebelgi tree. There was a little gazelle there too, of whom we took a photograph and hope it will come out.

We are staying the night here in a stone rest house built recently, and then going on to Abyei about 110 miles tomorrow. The town is rather flat and dull. Mike and Donald have gone to the office to do some things and I am writing on the veranda. Tea has just been laid outside and I've just had to rush out and stop a mother goat from removing the entire tablecloth, tea and all. Then she followed me inside.

March 21st. Abyei 10.30 am

We left Muglad at 7 yesterday morning and travelled in the back. Mike shot three guinea fowl; Donald got five and an enormous bustard.

We arrived at Tebeldia at about 9.15 where there is a nice thatched rest house under a vast tebelgi tree, a well and that is all except for passing travellers with their laden bulls resting under the tree. We stayed here until 3oc, and then off again until we stopped for tea at Antila, a dry lake with lots of shady trees all round and two wells. Mike dropped his sun glasses down one, but luckily a man was able to climb down and came up wearing them. It was only 20ft. deep and not much water at the bottom. We drove on again in the back, which was lovely and cool as the night was falling. We saw quite a few gazelle and an ostrich, in fact a pair of them.

We arrived here in Abyie at 7.30. The rest house is an old white washed two roomed building with a grass roof and lots of low stick beams inside, very hot, rather smelly and full of bats! The new rest house is in the course of being built. Mike and Donald are outside sitting under a tree as there is no office, attending to a stream of people and their wants.

We slept outside as usual with all our mosquito nets up for the first time, not that there are any mosquitoes at the moment, but the flies in the early morning are irritating. The last time I slept in a mosquito net, I must have been in my basinette in the West Indies. We felt as though we were in a four poster last night.

As soon as we arrived last night, everywhere I looked I was confronted by tall black naked bodies carrying all our stuff from the lorry! The Dinka tribe find wearing clothes a bore, though they sometimes carry some on the end of a spear over their shoulder. They are all exceptionally tall, mostly well over 6 ft. with incredibly long legs. They love smoking and it is a priceless sight to see a stark naked body walking along puffing at a large pipe, perhaps wearing a necklace or a ring on his toe and occasionally just a hat! Nothing else.

We have been presented with yet another sheep from the chief of the tribe, this morning. Our meat bill is nice and low lately! (Note. Sometimes one had to decide what was hospitality and what was some form of bribery. The general rule was that if you could eat it, it was hospitality. For a guest to refuse traditional hospitality would cause great offence; we have to remember too that a sheep will also feed all the people travelling with us).

We went out to see the brick kiln before breakfast and were passed by lots of reddish or coffee coloured bodies, perhaps with a black face and two black legs. They love covering themselves with dust from the bricks, or if they can't get that, just wood ash, making them look like grey ghosts. It also keeps the flies off.

In the evening we went out to the river, the Bahr el Arab which is about two miles from here. The river is quite wide and there is an iron ferry which is propelled over by the ferryman pulling on a wire roipe. We crossed over and back for the ride and exchanged greetings with some of the other passengers. There is a creek beside the rest house, unusually it is dry for the first time for eight years. Last years rains were exceptionally low, that is why everything usually full is dry.

We stay here for today, then start home early tomorrow, Saturday. We hope to be in El Obeid by Monday night if we travel most of the time, somewhat exhausting but we must get back to pack up. We will have done over 1,000 miles by the time we're back I should think.

This time in two weeks we shall be nearly in England! Did I tell you that we Dove up to Khartoum. The Dove being the plane. It will cost about £4 more, but it will only take an hour or two instead of the tiring 24 hours by train and it also gives us an extra day and a half in El Obeid before we leave. We should have had to leave on Saturday's train otherwise. So, we shall have about three days in Khartoum and we hope we will be staying with the Evans again. We are looking forward to getting our letters in El Obeid, not having had any for 10 days. We have not heard about Peter (Mike's sister's fiancee), or the Audrey/Brian wedding.

I'm so glad we have been able to do this trek as now I know what it is like. I must say I am thoroughly enjoying it, though it will be nice when we have more time and don't have to rush round like this.

March 23rd Between Muglad and Lagawa

We are now wondering when we will get back to El Obeid after all. The lorry has broken down, battery run out, so all we can do is sit and wait in hopes that someone will come along in the not too distant future! It has of course had to do this at least 50 miles from any village or water in the driest dullest country. Luckily, the only tree with a few green leaves (the rest are bare and parched) is within walking distance from the lorry, so here we are sitting under the six green leaves surrounded by dry thorny bushes towered over by an ants nest; luckily uninhabited. We can't sit still for too long as the shade moves round as the sun does, so we are continually shuffling our deck chairs about. We have enough water and food to last us three days by which time if not before something will have appeared. The battery has been put out in the sun in the hopes that it might charge up again. What a hope, I say, though I admit my knowledge of batteries is nil. It really is funny and we can't help laughing though it is extremely annoying. However I'm taking the opportunity to do some of my correspondence.

We left Abyei yesterday morning at 6.30, had breakfast under some trees and then lunch at Tebeldia. Then, after a sleep we went into Muglad and stayed the night in the rest house where we were before. We went out to tea with the Mamur (Chief Executive Officer of the Rural District Council) a dear old man called Ahmed Abu Gasim. We had an excellent tea of brilliant coloured rasberryade, tea and cakes of vast sizes but very good. Tea was interrupted by the Sudanese present saying their prayers on a leopard skin as it was the hour of sunset.

We are now on our own. Donald has work in Muglad, so he has stayed there. We will see him after our leave when Mike takes over from him in Nahud. He has been very kind during our trek with him and a very generous host. We will both have one abiding memory. A necessary adjunct to any rest house is of course the loo, usually just a deep hole in the ground surrounded by a grass screen. We will always have the vision of Donald's purposeful after breakfast walk with his hat on and the Times tucked under his arm!

We went to bed early and started off before 7 oc this morning, drove 50 miles, had breakfast under some trees, drove a few miles on and here we are.

As I write, what do we hear but the distant buzz of a lorry coming! Hamd illa Allah (Thanks be to God). Yes here is one, the servants have rushed from the bushes into the middle of the track waving violently and it has stopped. Mike has gone to see the driver and everyone again has their heads in the bonnet examining our lorry's internal organs. I shall continue writing as I have no doubt it will be some time yet before anything else happens.

March 24th. Dilling

Well, we eventually got off yesterday after the wireless battery of the person in the other lorry had been fixed in ours and we'd been towed, pushed and pulled until our engine had started. We didn't dare let it stop until we reached Lagawa some 60 miles on, which meant we drove for three hours in the hottest time of the day without stopping except to put cold compresses on the engine when it got too hot, which it did frequently. We got to Lagawa at 3.45, had lunch which was very welcome as we were quite hungry by then. Our police driver, who we had left behind in Lagawa as he was ill, was all right again and so we are now being driven again by him after a series of other drivers. We went off again at 5.30 and drove through the mountains, up and down round and round over boulders, down precipices and arrived at Jebel Tima (where we had spent the day on our way). We spent the night in the rest house in the village nestled in the bottom of the mountain which rises steeply up behind. A lovely place.

The Rest House. Tima

We did not have a very peaceful night as when the dogs were not snuffling, growling, snarling, yelping and barking all around our beds in the rest house enclosure, the baby in the tukl 20 feet away from us on the other side of the hedge was yelling. Someone was snoring, another coughing and the goat baaing, all from inside this small mud grass roofed hut. It was lovely waking up and seeing the sunrise from behind the hills which surrounded us. We left at 6.45 having been presented with eggs and glasses of very strong sweet tea, which we had to drink with the Sultan. We have now just had breakfast, at 10.45 here and are calling into see the Jack Hunters who live here and then we have 100 miles more to El Obeid stopping for lunch en route.

2.30pm. Just had lunch under a tree, cold guinea fowl, green peas, dried fruit and evaporated milk. Hope to be in El Obeid by 6. Just longing to get my hair clean, it is long, straight and sticky and sticking out at right angles caked with sand and dust.

5.30 Home! Going to dinner with the Hawkesworths.

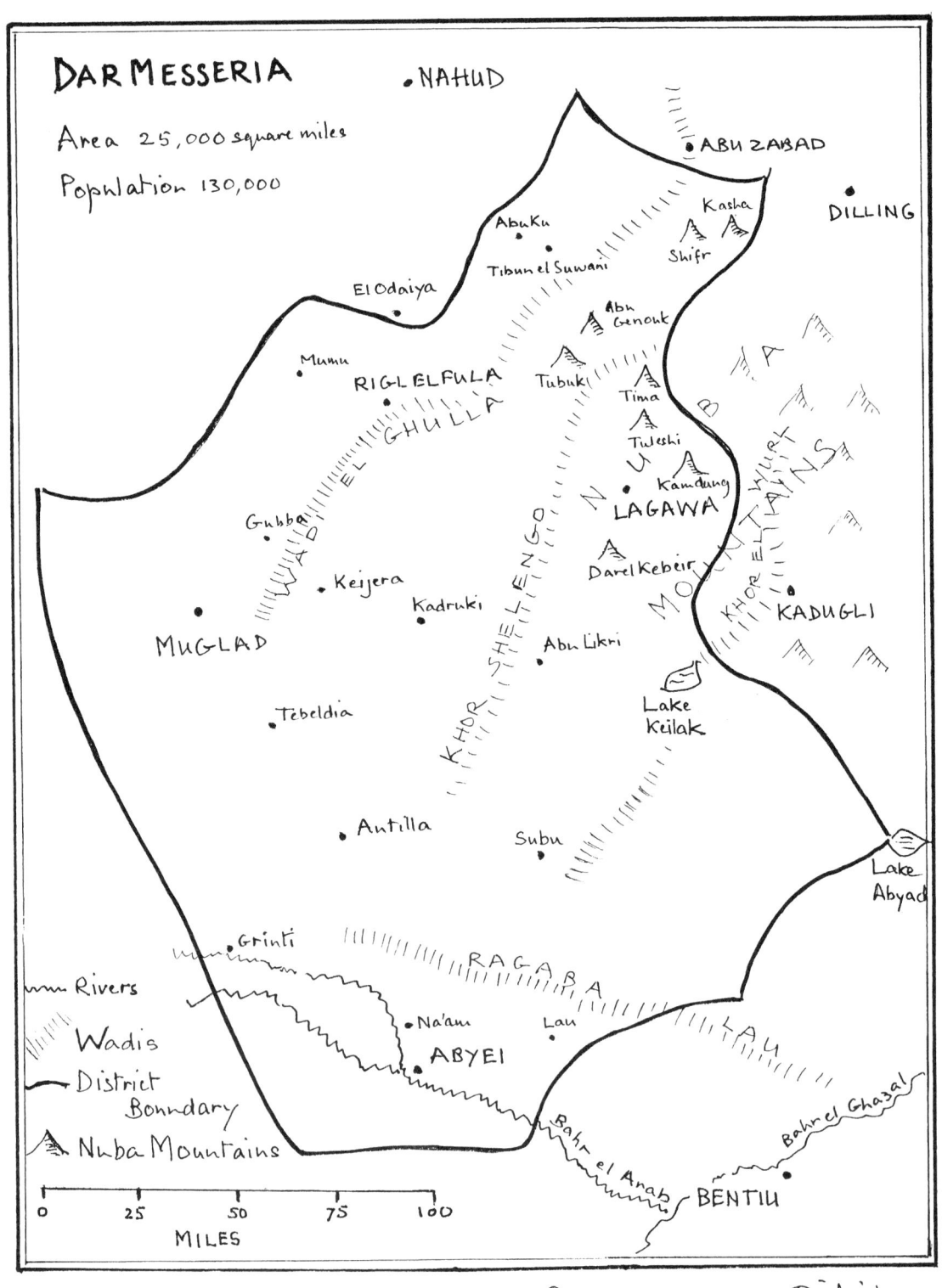

Sketch map of our District.

5. WESTERN KORDOFAN – A.D.C. MESSERIA AND THE MESSERIA TRIBE

Having been up to Nahud to see where we were going to live, the next excitement was that we had to go to Khartoum as I had not yet taken the Law Examination. This was important because until ADCs had passed both the Law and Higher Arabic Exams they did not get any rise in pay, nor could they be promoted to DC when their seven years as ADC was completed.

The departure of the train from El Obeid was always a social gathering. Abdel Rahman went down early with our luggage and had stowed everything in our sleeper, Mohamed came down to see us off, Yousif our garden prisoner came down with Anne's dressing case, then of course the driver had to come and drive us. The Chief Veterinary Officer was leaving the Province with wife and two small sons so all the British contingent were there to see them go, while one wife was going to Khartoum to see her husband who was in hospital. So we rolled along gently in the long white train and had a restful 24 hours, although I was frantically revising with my nose in the Sudan Criminal Code.

In Khartoum, we stayed with David and Ruth Evans. David had been DC El Obeid, but was now Director of Public Relations. We always enjoyed staying with them and they were most hospitable. Anne had fun shopping for both herself and all her El Obeid friends. Ruth was very kind; not only helping Anne with the shopping but she also drove us to Khartoum North to get a bedroll and other trek kit for Anne. We will always remember the evening when she took us sailing on the Nile. We embarked from the Blue Nile Sailing Club, which was the old gunboat Melik. The Nile was very peaceful and a flight of geese came over just as the sun was setting.

It so happened that the Chief Justice had recently visited El Obeid and knew that we were coming up, so asked us to drop in for a drink. The day before we left, we duly did and were greeted very hospitably. Another young looking man was also there so by way of conversation Anne enquired whether he had come up to take the Law Exam? Great guffaws all round and it was explained to her that she was talking to a Judge of the High Court! (Despite this I did pass!)

It was then time to be introduced to our new responsibilities. Anne has already described our tour of the Messeria country with Donald Rae in the middle of March. Donald was an excellent guide and host; his obvious love was the South, he said of the Messeria "the truth is not in them" but he had done a lot to build decent rest houses all over the District, which made it much easier for us later on. It seemed as though he would do a sweep into the Bahr el Ghazal Province (to the south of Kordofan), find Dinka who knew how to build and drop them off at various places having given them a few bags of cement. Donald would mark out the foundations, give them some money and disappear. For the next three years we constantly came across rather bewildered southerners, who when asked what they were doing so far north would answer plaintively 'Mr Rae brought me here'.

We went on leave in April, returning at the beginning of July. Most of our friends were on leave so we had to stay in the Grand Hotel for five days which was not only rather expensive, but also the weather was extremely hot and humid. However, we were able to make good use of the large bath. We stocked up on groceries, the

Keeping cool in the Grand Hotel

things we were not going to be able to buy in Nahud; this cost us £85, but fortunately we had some unexpected back pay from a salary award and we got 5% discount for cash.

John Hunter came back from his leave with his new wife, Mary, just before we did. They stayed with Gawain Bell, now Deputy Civil Secretary. On their way out to dinner, they dropped in to the large Khartoum grocer, Gamuchian. The story goes that John casually told Mary to buy all the stores she needed for the next nine months! The poor girl was quite confused having no idea in the world what lay ahead of her, or even about housekeeping.

An Armenian friend, one Nubar Epipane, took us to the Gordon Cabaret, Khartoum's hot spot one evening. He also insisted on taking us to the train. We had a bit of a panic when I found I had lost £5, but remembered I must have left it in a shop where we had bought a bottle of orange earlier in the day. This was confirmed by a telephone call, it was still sitting on the cash register, so we just had time to collect it (£5 was a lot of money in those days. We had been worried about our bill in the hotel, but it was less than we had feared, £ 16 for 5 days!).

Jebel Kasha

Wali Rest House

The Muglad Show 1952. Nazir Sereir, Anne, Nazir Babu.

Muglad. The Suq

This was a non sleeper train, but we had a 1st Class compartment to ourselves, the seats folded into four bunks and so we were very comfortable. Things could have been different. One of our friends is reputed to have once had a pleasant journey with a mixed bag of passengers from different backgrounds. One puffed a strong cigar, another reeked of a cheap scent while the occupant of one of the upper bunks tried his best to aim his expectorations through the open top of the window.

So back to El Obeid; Gordon and Daphne Hickson, who were going to relieve us were already there. So we lost no time in the great pack up of all our furniture, slightly delayed as Anne caught a feverish cold and had to have a day in bed. So Abdel Rahman, eight prisoners and myself packed and bound up the furniture in bits of sacking. We were observed by the storks from their nests in the trees all round the house. One nest looked very colourful, trimmed with branches of crimson bourganvillia that we had cut off our shrubs, ready for the journey. The babies inside were squeaking with joy at the thought of how lovely it all looked.

The great day arrived, with the help of twelve prisoners; everything was loaded into two large lorries, except for our trek kit and personal belongings. General post took place, we moved out into the rest house, the Hicksons moved into our house while Abdel Rahman and co. set off to Nahud in the lorries. Needless to say, the rains then started, swooshing down in buckets. All we could do was to hope that a tarpaulin had, as promised, been draped over our loads.

Loading up

Early the next morning everything imaginable that was left was stuffed into our lorry; lampshades, our best pots of geraniums, shovels, coats, macs, our new wireless, an enormous box with wire netted front with our three turkey hens, their husband and Rachel, the duck. Finally Buttercup and Daisy were hoisted up, they sailed along quite happily, chewing anything in reach but ready at any time for a mouthful of grain out of the only thing we could find, which was my uniform Bombay bowler.

We splashed up the 140 miles of the aly-wati road, taking twice as long as we should. Just after Khoi we came across a lorry with its entire engine in bits across the road. Needless to say, this was one with half our worldly possessions on board. It had broken down 18 hours before but we were assured that spares were on the way from El Obeid. We were at least able to rescue Abdel Rahman, he was very bedraggled as all his personal baggage had been on the other lorry.

We eventually arrived in the evening rather than the afternoon, delayed again as we got stuck in the sand and had to dig ourselves out. Donald Rae had kindly moved out of the house into the resthouse next door, so we were able to move what furniture that did arrive, straight in. Mohamed and a gang unloaded the one lorry, but we have chairs with no seats, a dining room table with legs but no top and a wardrobe with no bolts and hinges to put it together. Anyway, the Hunters have been here a week and had dinner all ready for us. Donald saw us in and then departed off on his final leave

Gradually everything got sorted out. Anne is pleased with the house, we have our own mud stabling and out buildings, some mature trees in the garden, while in addition to the male prisoners the women come in and sweep our drive. Anne wrote in one of her letters ...

'...the sweeping brigade has just filled our front drive waving grass brooms in all directions to remove hoof prints and other marks that might look untidy. A small black object brought up the rear, crawling as fast as he could with the solitary tuft of hair on the top of his head bristling in the effort to catch up mama. He was eventually picked up and had his breakfast while she held him with one hand and swept with the other'

. The Hoggs had not yet returned from leave, so I got down to learn what I could about the new job.

Peter Hogg was District Commissioner, Western Kordofan. It was the largest District in the Province, stretching 700 miles from the Northern Province to Bahr el Ghazal Province in the south; the distance from Inverness to Penzance. This was one of the most prestigious of all District Commissioners' jobs in the Sudan. It had been held by the present Civil Secretary, Sir James Robertson and many eminent members of the Political Service.

John Hunter was Assistant District Commissioner, Hamar, with special responsibility for the northern half of the District, inhabited by the Hamr tribe. Although they owned camels, they were on the whole settled and reliant on agriculture.

I had special responsibility for the southern half of the District with the title, Assistant District Commissioner, Messeria. This was in the days before the time when nobody could do anything without a job description, but later on I summarised it as ..."being multitudinous and all embracing. Keeping in touch with the Nazirs, officials and tribes people by constant travelling by lorry or animals for two or three weeks a month and often longer. Seeing court cases as a First Class Magistrate, conducting Magisterial enquiries, settling disputes, inspecting native courts and hearing appeals from them, explaining and propagating the policy of the Sudan Government and Rural District Council".

When I joined the Province Headquarters in El Obeid, I had been told to read the Civil Secretary's confidential letter to all D.C.'s. This had said that the next few years were going to be difficult for the administration. The Legislative Assembly was now functioning, but there would be continued efforts by the political parties for self government and ultimate independence or union with Egypt. With increasing sophistication in many areas, there was inevitably going to be more requests for information, statistics and returns of various kinds. While these were important, D.C.s should remember that their priority was to get out and about, getting to know the people in their District and explaining what the government was doing and what was going on. If by any chance this meant that returns were not always completed, this letter could be quoted in one's defence. Looking back now fifty years and several jobs later, I still hold Sir James's letter to be the best and most fundamental managerial instruction I have ever seen.

As I read through the Messeria section of the District files, the task and the distances seemed formidable, I would be looking after an area of 25,000 square miles. Most of this was the territory of the Messeria tribe. They are cattle owning Arab nomads, some 90,000 of them. Also within the area there were three other ethnic races. In the south on either side of the Bahr (river) el Arab, lived the Ngok Dinka numbering 30,000. Over on the western border near the Nuba Mountains (Jebels) District were the little pockets of Nuba and Dagu living in the hills, about 10,000 of them. The Nuba were the original inhabitants of this part of the country while the Dagu are of West African origin.

THE MESSERIA

The Messeria claim to have their origins in Arabia, to have migrated west through North Africa to Wadai in what is now French Equatorial Africa and are the descendants of Mohamed Messeria. The Sultan of Wadai did his best to extract tribute from them, an unpopular move, so they then migrated east in about the year 1775. They are part of the Baggara group; baggar being the Arabic for cow. They have been defined as "an Arab who has been forced by circumstances to live in a country which will support the cow but not the camel. He treats his bull just as he treated his camel, so differing from other cattle owning people in Africa" (Henderson). The difference is not only in the use of bulls as beasts of burden, but the whole cattle culture, forced to migrate with the seasons for pasture, also to escape fly. There is no emotional regard for cattle and they are not used as tokens in bride wealth. However, cattle do equal wealth, three bad cows are better than one good one, as chances of survival are 3 - 1.

The Baggara migrate in family groups known as feriks and their lives revolve almost entirely around their cattle. They live on their milk and meat, while nearly all their household goods are made from leather. The cows have names (often colours) and answer to them.

Six seasons are recognised during the year. Kharif (rains), Chelawy (autumn), Duret (harvest), Shita (winter), Seif (summer) and Seif Hannam (hot summer). During the twelve months of the year, the tribes migrate through four zones, each with different vegetation, rainfall and soil. From north to south these are Barbanusa, Muglad, Gos and Bahr.

Barbanusa (ebony) is waterless in the dry season and therefore free from fly in the rains. In the season known as the kharif (July – September), this is where the Messeria would be. Water from the rains would have filled local watering holes. Although the barbanusa provides grazing it is not good because the grass is 'masikh' which means it is without salt and the cattle lose condition.

Muglad is flat, well wooded plain of heavy clay impervious to water. During the rains water drains off into pools which form watering points. Also in the muglad are sandy pockets called atamir which produce good millet crops. In the season of chelawy (September – October), the herds come south to the muglad for salt grazing. Just to make life more complicated this type of geological zone also gives its name to the town of Muglad.

Goz is the large area between muglad and the bahr (river), it is mostly consolidated sand, but with some clay, waterless, except by the pools left by the rain.

Bahr (river or sea) are the pastures round the Bahr el Arab and its tributaries. The move south to the bahr would start in shita (December). This was into the territory of the Southern Nilotic tribe, the Ngok Dinka. They numbered 30,000 centred on Abyie, and had their own Chief Deng Majok Kwal Arop.

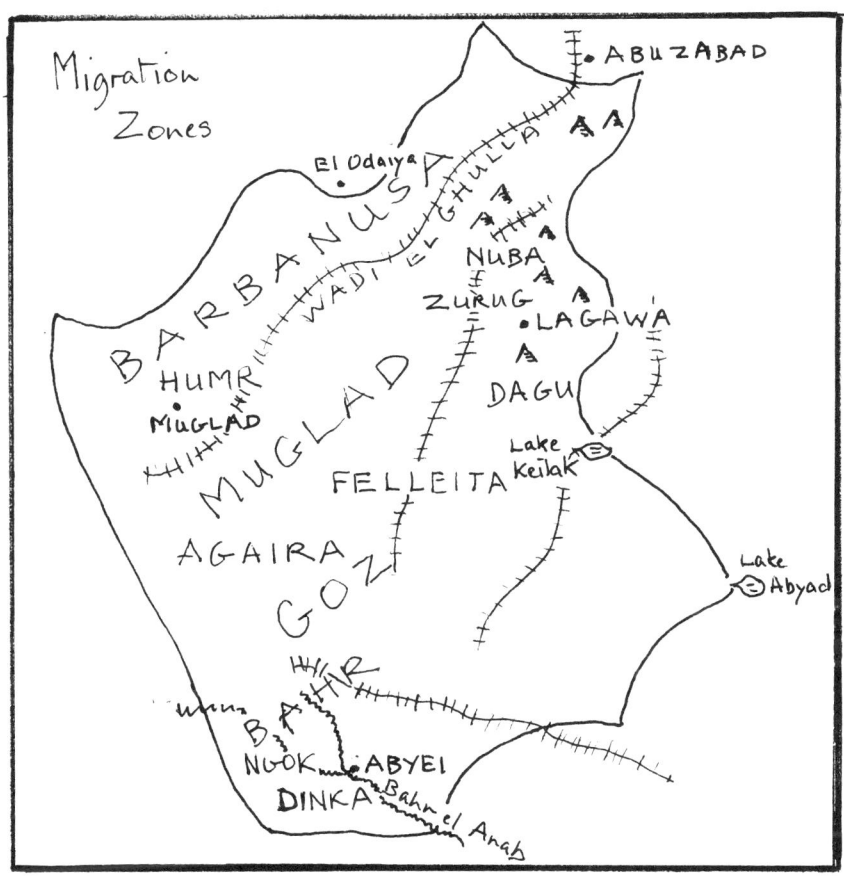

The feriks would stay in the south through the season of seif (summer) until the cold winds signalled the trek back to the north. In rashish (May-June), the cattle would be brought back to the muglad to manure the group's cultivations. In the rainy season (July/September) most of the feriks and the cattle are on the barbanusa so as to escape the fly; some go even further onto the northern goz. Some of the family will stay on the muglad so that the cultivations can be looked after.

At harvest time in October, the cattle go back to the muglad for salt on the way south. By December the feriks have come together again and go south all the way to the bahr. The ground is still wet but as it dries the herds have to concentrate on the larger pools and well centres. By April the south wind begins to blow and the trek north begins. May sees them back on the muglad to manure the cultivations.

The southern migration took the Messeria Arabs right into and through the Ngok Dinka and Nuer territory in Upper Nile Province. I knew from my time in Province Headquarters that there was the danger of friction between the Arab Messeria and the Nilotic tribes. There had been a serious affray the year before when Messeria had killed some Upper Nile policemen and justice had to be done, not without some difficulty. This arose from the Messerias' favourite sport, hunting giraffe on horseback with spears. This was a fearsome chase, with horses going full speed through the scrub, the poor giraffe was claimed by the first man to get his spear in, after which the girls would be clamouring for him. However, the real ace was given to the parallel and even more dangerous pursuit of elephant hunting, again with spears. The sportsmen had a great respect for their prey, which was why the elephant had been adopted as the badge of the Messeria Rural District Council. The carcasses of course provided a valuable source of meat, which was dried to preserve it. The areas where this was allowed were prescribed and strictly controlled by licences authorised by the Game Warden. This particular trouble had arisen when the police had tried to stop unauthorised giraffe hunting. Egged on by the girls, the young men persisted in ignoring the policmens' orders, and there was a skirmish with fatal consequences.

The traditional pattern of migration had begun to change. Some of the family would stay behind to look after gum gardens, others to tend cultivations of millet in the muglad, while rain grown cotton was beginning to be cultivated in the south of the District. Over in the east, one of the tribes, the Zurug, were beginning to settle round Lagawa to cultivate cotton for the government ginnery. Amongst the Zurug were pockets of Nuba and Dagu living on their rocky hills, about 10,000 of them

By far the most important person in the Messeria was the Nazir Umum, Babu Nimr. I had met him several times as he passed through El Obeid on his way to Khartoum. He was the 'Supreme Head' of the Messeria tribe and was influential not only in the tribe, but as a member of the Legislative Assembly and as the son in law of one of the two great religious and political leaders, Sayed Adbel Rahman el Mahdi. There is no hereditary system of succession for Nazirs. In the days before the present government, might was right. Leaders changed, quite often after open battles. Babu therefore was unusual in that he was the third Nazir from his family in a direct line. Before the Mahdyia the Nazir was Ali Massar. His nephew Ali el Gullah, who, with most of the tribe supported and fought with the Mahdi succeeded him. He stayed in Omdurman with the Khalifa Abdullahi, who took over after the Mahdi's death. He only returned to Kordofan after the defeat of the Khalifa's army at Omdurman in 1898. Ali el Gullah remained Nazir until he handed over to his son Nimr, Babu's father. Nimr died suddenly from pneumonia in 1924 when Babu was only 13. Despite his age, it was the general wish of the tribe that Babu should succeed and one of his uncles, Gabr was appointed Regent,

At the time of his succession Babu was strictly Nazir of his own section, the Agaira. But, with government backing, the other half of the Humr, the Felleita, united with the Agaira in 1937. Later, the Zurug agreed to join the confederation and Babu was created Nazir Umum, (Paramount Chief).

Under Babu therefore, there were three divisions of the Messeria tribe, two Humr (Red) and one Zurug (Blue). The two Humr Nazirs were Babu's brother, Nazir Ali Nimr Ali el Gullah of the Agaira and Nazir Sereir Hag Agbar of the Felleita. Both were centred on Muglad in the west of the district. Ali was tall, handsome and generally known by the British D.C.s as Prince Charming. Sereir had succeeded his father Hag Agbar who was still around at an advanced age, but full of life. At the age of 80 he had just married a new teenaged wife.

Over to the east at Lagawa was Nazir Izz el Din Humeida of the Zurug (blue). I had been warned that the Messeria were past masters of intrigue. I was aware of this from my time in El Obeid, where two of the Zurug's previous Nazirs had been exiled. They were Mohamed Fagir, dismissed in 1915 and his successor, Mohamed Dafaala, The latter's downfall occurred when it was found that he had financed his pilgrimage to Mecca from his court fees, which he was unable to pay back. He was one of Geoffrey Hawkesworth's regular visitors, bearing juicy stories about the present Nazir and his unsuitability. Sometimes I had to entertain him to keep him away from Geoffrey. When the Zurug elders had met to discuss a successor, they chose an outsider, Humeida Khamis who was recorded as being a surprising success. It was his son Izz el Din who was the present Nazir, no doubt well aware that the sons of both previous Nazirs were only too ready to step into his shoes if opportunity arose.

Next in the hierarchy under the Nazirs were the Omdas, elected by their people and responsible for between 8,000 to 2,000 souls. Further down were the khashim bets or extended family groups. Finally were the feriks, the smallest family groups which migrated, together with their cattle, according to the season of the year.

To make my life more complicated, I also had to look after the southern Nilotic tribe, the Ngok Dinka, which had their own Chief, Deng Majok. They were not part of the Rural District Council. Then over in the west there were some outlying jebels with Nuba and Dagu who were not in the Nuba Mountains District, but in Western Kordofan.

The policy of the Sudan Government so far, had been to work through the existing native administration. So it was the tribal hierarchy that was responsible for law and order within the tribe. Certain court powers were delegated to the Nazirs and Omdas who were allowed their own tribal police force. Their other important function was the collection of taxes. It was the duty of the District Commissioner with his supporting staff of A.D.C.s, Mamurs, Sub-Mamurs, police and prisons to ensure that all this was done.

With the advance of democracy, things had to change and at a fairly rapid pace. So far as we in a District were concerned, the manifestations were 'separation of the judiciary from the administrative' and 'advancement of Local Government'.

So, imposed on and interdigitated into the tribal structure came two extra layers. No longer was it possible for the migrating Omdas to try misdemeanours. Their magisterial powers passed to static Court Presidents at strategic centres round the District. However, the Nazirs were allowed to retain their powers to hear cases on appeal from the lower courts.

Local Government had arrived in the form of the Messeria Rural District Council, of which I found myself the Chairman. Unlike most Districts or sub Districts where there was an acknowledged centre, the government headquarters for the Messeria was in Nahud, seventy miles north of their territory.

There were only two towns of any consequence in the Messeria area, Muglad in the west and Lagawa with its cotton ginnery, in the east. Both had permanent suqs (markets or shopping centres), a dusty square, where the merchants had shops rather like open-ended garages built with mud walls and tin roofs. There were small government offices, houses for officials, a school, a mosque, police lines, a prison and a bucket system for sanitation. On the outskirts were the grass houses of the 'Native Lodging Area' (N.L.A). Down in the south, Abyei had about five shops, a school, a RC church, a police office, a small prison and little else, though round it were scattered the luaks of the Dinka. Abu Zabad and El Odaiya were just outside Messeria territory, though our Council had an office in the former.though there were other important looking names on the map, these amounted to little other than a cluster of grass huts.

The Nazir Umum lived in Muglad, but a District headquarters here was not agreeable to the Zurug part of the tribe. For their part the Humr would never agree to it being in Lagawa. In any case the 120 miles of road between the two was quite impassable for six months of the year. So, it had been decided that a new headquarters would be created at a place called Rigl el Fula.

Rigl el Fula was about hundred miles south of Nahud and forty miles inside the Messeria dar (territory). It was at the apex of a triangle about 100 miles from Muglad and Lagawa. (The latter as the crow flew, but not yet as the lorry could go). It had the advantages that it was acceptable to both sides of the tribe and there was already a government deep bore, pump and water yard (known as a donkey). Also, it was to be on the railway line when it was extended west from El Obeid. Historically, Rigl el Fula had from 1820 to 1870 during the time of the (Turkia), been the headquarters of the Nazir Ali Messer, who was the uncle of Babu's grandfather. (This was the time when the Sudan was ruled by the Khedive of Egypt, then nominally under the authority of the Otterman Empire).

My future task was to give effect to these new developments. It was clear that we would have to spend a lot of time on trek, bumping along sandy tracks or squelching through the mud. (There were of course no made up roads). However, the Mechanical Transport Department (MTD) provided us with a 2 ton Commer lorry known as a 'TFT III' (truck fitted trekking), not the most comfortable of vehicles and infirnally hot, but never mind. We also had our Police driver Segeir (a nick name 'Little Hawk), who drove, maintained the lorry and made sure that it had its regular servicing at the MTD service station in Nahud.

While I was absorbing my new duties and reading the various files, Anne transformed the house. Back in El Obeid, Frank Lorimer, the new Deputy Governor, had shown me a long letter from Peter Hogg who was bringing out his family, about his "logistics." One of the advantages of Nahud is that it has its own airstrip and the planes land here on their way to and from Fasher. So, one morning everybody who was anybody in Nahud went out to the sandy runway to greet the Hoggs. Peter, Joanna, William (2), Margaret (8 months) and nanny Heather Dew. The last, a farmer's daughter, well built and good-natured, with this wonderful name (which would suit a bottle of whisky admirably).

When Peter was settling down to work on his first morning back, I thought I had better pay him a call and tell him officially that I had arrived and what would he like me to do. He roared with laughter and with a mischievous twinkle in his eyes said "My dear Michael, I haven't got a thought in my head'!"

The Hoggs' arrival.

Nahud.

Sketch showing D.C's houses

Rough plan of our house & garden

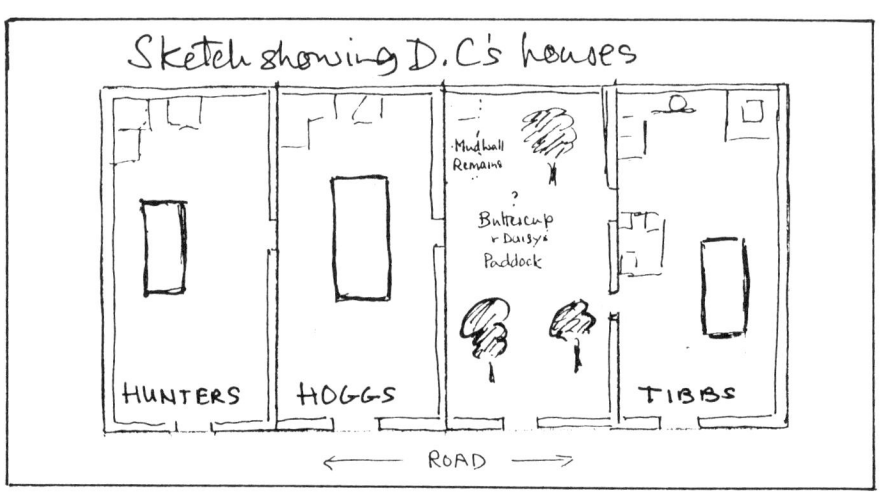

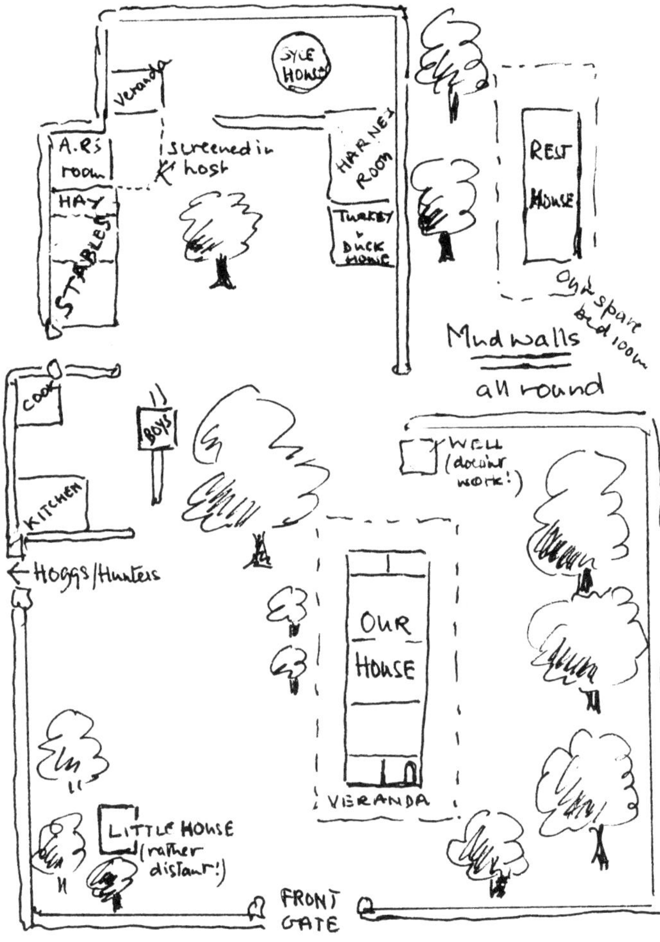

6. LIFE IN NAHUD

Nahud lay in a dusty hollow in the middle of an everlasting plain of desert scrub and red sandy soil. A few miles outside the town to the east a rocky mound broke the monotonous flatness, El Nahud, the breast, from which the little town took its name. Although the streets between the mud houses were of deep dusty sand they were lined with tall evergreen neem trees cooling the unremitting glare of the sun. The houses and shops were of mud, the houses of course enclosed by tall mud walls, actually mud bricks, baked in the sun until quite hard. They remained so until the rains came when they were inclined to dissolve and had to be renewed once the rains were over.

The three houses for the District Commissioners, also built with mud walls were together on the east side of the town centre. The largest, the D.C.'s house was in the middle. .Originally it had a thatched roof, but this was replaced some years ago with a corrugated iron one held up with steel girders. Its plan followed the basic pattern of all houses built by the PWD, though the three basic rooms were larger than usual and there was also a detached rest house. The Hunter's house, a smaller version with its garden, was.to the north; ours was to the south. Between us and the Hoggs was a vacant plot about the size of a tennis court. There used to be a house here, but it had fallen down. The Merkaz (District Headquarters) was only a hundred yards from where we lived. Here were our offices, the Police headquarters, the Prison Officer's office and the prison.

We soon settled down to life in Nahud. With the Hoggs's arrival, the little British community of three British families was complete. John and Mary Hunter were already there

Anne...
We have enjoyed settling into our new house, though it does not have the exceptional character of the old Powder House with its very thick walls and flat roof. There are three main rooms with a verandah all round. In El

Nahud

The front veranda, with sweeper and follower.

Buttercup and her twins

Rachel

William with Heather

Angustus the ram

Dindy

Obeid we had a water supply which came out of taps, here we have taps connected to oil drums on the veranda, which are filled up daily by prisoners. The house used to have thatch over the tin roof but Donald has removed the thatch and painted the tin with Hawke's white paint so he could collect rain water in a stone tank at one corner. (This did fill up nicely once but the public health inspector immediately drained it as it was breeding mosquitoes). We now have to get used to living without electricity. The garden is bare and sandy but we have big shady trees and all round is a greyish white mud wall about five feet high. This also encloses the servants' quarters, the stabling, outbuildings and a rest house where our guests can stay.

Inside, the house has been transformed with our light painted furniture, pictures, chintz curtains in the bedroom and bits and pieces. The black tiles on the floor now gear oil-less, shine with polish. Our tubs of bourganvillia brighten up the verandas and the hanging earthenware pots look decorative but wait to be filled with flowers.

We are particularly pleased to have our own stable yard so that all our live stock is close by. They each have mud wall buildings newly white washed inside. The horses have arrived with syce Abdel Rahman and an escort of two camels carrying their fodder, a 140 mile walk from El Obeid. Buttercup and Daisy, the turkey cock Dindy, with his harem of seven wives and Rachel the duck are all feeling very much at home. They all provide good entertainment for the Hogg children who come round to visit them. A Hogg problem at the moment is that Peter's nob-nosed goose, that he rescued wounded some time ago, will persist on removing the eggs from Joanna's hen each time she started sitting. (Eventually they asked us to let it loose on the lake at Rigl el Fula).

M...

The problem for Anne and myself was, that we had to drive sixty miles south to El Odiaya or 100 miles south east to Abu Zabad and beyond, before we entered our territory at all. Inevitably, we spent most of our time on trek rather than in our house. Not that we worried too much about this, but after continuous trekking for two or three weeks, in every month, one was glad to get back. In the office one had to collect one's thoughts, write reports and think about Messeria problems against continuous interruptions from police, citizens waving petitions for which they had paid good money (3 piastres) and wanted satisfaction, the Prison officer and worthies just dropping in for a chat.

We tried to organise things so that one of us D.C.s was always in Nahud if the other two were out. So, I had to take part in the 'town ride'. Once a week, the D.C., the Nazir, the Omda, the Police Officer and Public Health

Inspector would ride round the town at 7 am. Most of us on horses, but the Omda had a magnificent donkey which scuttled along at a great speed, he anticipated his masters every wish and was almost an extension of his personality. Quite often I had to do the early morning prison inspection, hear any complaints and make sure the register was being properly kept.

In the evening we often played tennis on a gum court in an old quarry in the middle of the town. This was one of the sights of Nahud and everyone turned up to watch and cheer, especially when Hassan Effendi the Mamur managed to hit the ball with a magnificent forehand to send it right out of sight over the suq (shopping centre). Fortunately there were dozens of small boys who thought it a great joke to go scurrying after it.

Sometimes it was rather nice not to be energetic and settle down to enjoy reading the latest batch of letters, only to be told that the Police camels were ready for inspection. I was not a great expert at this, but fortunately the police Sol (Warrant Officer) could usually point out any sores needing attention that I had missed.

Mary Hunter and Anne shared the distinction of being newly arrived brides but Mary was also a recently qualified doctor. Fairly soon after our arrival Anne went over to see how her unpacking was progressing and found her in a rather bewildered state enveloped in clouds of white mosquito netting, trying to make two single mosquito nets into one double one before going out on trek that evening. Ahmed, their safragi, had unpicked the entire two single nets in error, so Mary had to start again from scratch. Anne sat down and joined the battle and by lunchtime the net was at least stitched together with large tacks, and that was how she had to take it.

Mary had not fully realised how soon her medical skills would be tested. Once John's parishioners realised she was a doctor, wives whose pregnancies had gone wrong or worse still those who could not conceive, queued up to see her. She also did duty in the local hospital acting as relief when the resident doctor was away. On one occasion she had to amputate a leg. A local gentleman had jumped off a moving lorry after he had seen someone who owed him 50 pt (50p) by the roadside. He slipped and the back wheel went over his leg. He was brought back to Nahud hospital, Mary was called out, so she had to saw off the leg while husband John administered the anaesthetic under her direction. On another occasion she had to deal with a bad camel bite, not usually on the curriculum of a British medical school!

Although hot and rather featureless, Nahud was a good-natured place with many interesting characters. We had a very warm welcome and received many invitations. One of these was from one of the Sudanese doctors who asked us to 'drinks'. The Hoggs and ourselves went and having had several drinks accompanied by fried potatoes, green stuff and cheese, we rose to go. This however was by no means the case. A terrific dinner was rushed in and we had to send messages back to our cooks to say we would not be in for dinner. Evidently 'drinks' meant dinner too. We had everything imaginable, anchovy eggs, cheese, potato, greenery, chipolatas, bread, chops, pasties, fried brains, vegetable fritters (Sudanese style) and fried blocks of ?, a special Armenian dish. All this was brought round, one after another until our plates were heaped high and it was an impossibility to eat even half of it. All rather greasy and smelling strongly of scented sesame fat. (We rather wondered what results there would be afterwards, but fortunately there were none). Actually it was a very enjoyable evening, especially as it was all outside in the garden.

On one occasion, Joanna and Peter were asked to a wedding. The bride was a Syrian, her father an important merchant in the town. The Hoggs wondered what they could do about a wedding present and decided to give a rather nice glass vase which had been one of their own wedding presents. The ceremony took place in the small Syrian Catholic church; this was followed by a reception attended by all the elite. The Moslem guests were of course teetotal but their susceptibilities were soothed as the bride's father who owned the gazooza (soft drinks) factory had tactfully put whisky in the bottles beforehand. The highlight of the proceedings came when the bride's father read out the list of presents "The brides parents, Two hundred pounds" (roars of applause). "The bridegroom's parents, Two hundred pounds" (more applause). "Mr and Mrs Christopholos, One hundred pounds " and so the list went on until at the end "……Mr and Mrs Hogg, this little vase!"

One of Nahud's features was the local lunatic; he was quite harmless, his only aberration being that he thought he was a lorry. He would go round pretending to collect loads at one place and deliver them somewhere else. On one occasion he fell over in the middle of the town. Some of the townsfolk went to help him up but he explained that he had a full load and needed a really substantial heave. In no time thirty strong men had gathered round and gave a good hoist. Our friend was soon up again; he started his engine, changed gear and was off with a grateful toot on the horn.

Abdel Rahman wanted his wife to join him. Relations having failed to find a suitable chaperone to accompany her to Nahud, AR was given leave to go and get her himself. He arrived back one morning, the journey from El Obeid having taken three days up a waterlogged road. Mrs AR trotted along behind him rather timidly and shook hands with us, a sweet little girl from what we could see under her snow-white drapery.

Anne described Zeinab's proper introduction, which followed a few days later…

Yesterday morning at 11 am sharp. Clap, clap, clap outside, there was Zeinab, Abdel Rahman's 17 year old wife. She was all dressed up in her pale blue with white spots robia voile tob with a blue satin dress underneath, very chic. She presented me with a large box of chocolates; most embarrassing, but all I could do was to accept and say how lovely. (Abdel Rahman told me afterwards they had racked their brains to think of something nice, as we had given them so much, unlike Khartoum, in Nahud there was nothing at all, so they got the chocolates). Very naughty of them indeed, as it must have cost at least 50 piastres (10/-), which was a lot out of their month's wages.

It was the first time Zeinab had been in an English house; she was entranced and looked at everything, even inside the fridge. I had to explain what everything was, including the bath and how it was filled with water and how we got in. She then enquired what the hand basin was for, so I washed my hands to show her. She loved the Christmas tree and all the Christmas cards and the photographs we have got about in the bedroom. I showed her our latest trek ones, with which she was thrilled and picked out everyone in turn. I showed her one photograph and asked who they were, so she said 'That's you and mufetish and……..giggle giggle', was all she could do, it was of course, Abdel Rahman. She asked me to give her one of us both so she could show it in her village on leave and also if I would take one of her, which I did; she even shed her tob and stood in her satin dress to pose. She insisted on ringing the big ship's bell (from H.M.S. Varne, M's last submarine) which we ring for meals or if we want A R. Luckily, he was in the suq, so he did not come rushing in. Zeinab sat in an armchair and sipped her orange leaning back in a most elegant manner with her legs crossed and stayed at least one and a half hours. She thought the photograph of my mother was very beautiful.

In September we were able to have a really relaxed week. It was the Eid el Kebir when the Moslems celebrate Mohamed's flight from Medina to Mecca. The Hoggs, Hunters and ourselves had a round of parties at one house or the other. M's main task was to build a turkey house. They had no secure accommodation and roamed at will laying their eggs anywhere, particularly in long grass where they were difficult to find. So, with the help of our two garden prisoners, Kumdung and Abdullah, M rescued some rafters from an old building from which he made a run. A hole had to be made into a stable we did not need, an old wire netted door had to be remade to fit the stable and finally an old manger made quite a good perch.

Poor Rachel has been egg bound, she has been waddling around with a dropped behind for a day or two. When it was nearly touching the ground we decided we must really do something about it. The vet lines were closed owing to the Eid, so having consulted "Teach Yourself Good Poultry Keeping" we held her hind quarters over a bowl of steaming hot water which she seemed to enjoy. When the water got cooler, we put her right in. For the rest of the day, we awaited the arrival of the egg. Nothing happened and Rachel continued to waddle around quite happily. The next day we were able to send her up to the vet lines with Kamdung and of course  on the way what should happen but the most enormous egg arrived, a prize effort.

On Monday night all the Inglese went to the Youth Club play. Shaigi our messenger had arrived on his bicycle to deliver a special invitation. There was a large audience including all our staffs. We were ushered to the front row of the stalls and sat in state on cushioned sofas. Unfortunately our particular one was a bit ancient, during the first act there was a loud crack and our legs shot up into the air in most undignified fashion as the back fell off so for the rest of the evening we were not so comfortable. The lighting was ingenious, two Tilly lamps on stands with shades to project the light onto the stage, during the intervals the shades were reversed, so the front stalls were blinded and it was very difficult to see anything until a long way into the next act. The play in very fast Arabic was quite amusing although Peter was the only one who could understand it all. Shaigi appeared as an ancient old man with a black beard and handcuffs, and there was some good singing by a chorus of little boys flashing their white teeth.

The main event was a visit by all of us to the great 'tent city' put up just outside the town. It is to some extent a 'return to the desert' to celebrate the Eid (Festival). Each of the 'tariqas', the various sections of Islam, had their own little encampment with tents made out of carpets, rugs on the floor and sofas and chairs. It was all very friendly. Everyone was, of course dressed in their best clothes and some had coloured sashes to symbolise their allegiance. There were constant processions while they went round singing 'Allah, Allah, Rubana, Allah, Allah, Rubana' ('God, O God, Our Lord'). We were escorted round each tariqa and had soft drinks and sweets while we offered our congratulations.

Life in Nahud

Heather (Nannie)   A, Margaret, William, Joanna and Peter Hogg

A picnic on Jebel Nahud

Abdel Rahman's bride, Zeinab

M & A

John & Mary Hunter with Mat Tima

Joanna Hogg must have a special mention. Nahud was not the ideal place for a young English family; it was hot and airless, dry and dusty. The water supply from the local wells was brown and brackish. All our drinking water came in a tank on a lorry from the 'donkey' (PWD water yard) at Khoi seventy miles away. There was a Greek grocer for basic provisions but very little in the way of fresh vegetables or fruit. Occasionally we were able to get some from Ban Gedid, the prison garden near El Obeid, though they were not exactly in their first blush by the time they had bounced up the hot track.

The logistics for the young Hogg family were indeed formidable, but Joanna seemed to take them in her stride.

Anne wrote that...

She was a tower of strength to the two new young wives, sharing her warmth and delightful sense of humour. We had such happy times together, whether it was exchanging recipes, solving dress making problems or trying out a 'Toni' home perm; our astonished husbands returned home one morning to find Joanna curling one side of my hair and Mary the other. 'Are Sa'ata Sit's hairs all right?' enquired Abdel Rahman, our anxious safragi, when my head was still in a turban after several hours.

There would always be a warm welcome and dinner waiting for us at the Hoggses when we came in from trek. On one important occasion during the rains we just had to be back from a long horse trek in time. It was Williams third birthday party; we played Ring a Roses and Looby Loo.

For an evening out on the servants' day off we would drive out to Jebel Nahud for a moonlight picnic. The hot dusty plain changed to something magical as we sat round a fire under the stars on top of this rocky outcrop in the middle of nowhere cooking a rum omelette.

Christmas saw us all in El Obeid, but Joanna and Peter gave us a lovely New Year party when we got back to Nahud. After dinner, we played charades. The highlight was a re-enactment of a recent local drama, when our ram, Augustus had upset William from his tricycle as he, Margaret and Heather were on their way over to see us one day. The Hogg's very dignified safragi, Abdel Latif, came into the room with a tray of glasses, to be confronted with Peter riding the tricycle, Joanna acting as Margaret, John as Heather while Anne was Augustus with two feathers in her hair (representing horns) at full charge. Abdel Latif's face did not move, but he reported to the servants' party going on outside that we had all gone completely mad.

These happy memories of Joanna and Peter, and many more since, will always be with us. As time has passed, our admiration for Joanna's competence in bringing up her children in such difficult conditions has changed to amazement that she succeeded so well. We were so grateful for her care and concern for us all. We are privileged to have been included in her family and to have enjoyed her sense of fun and her wonderful zest for life.

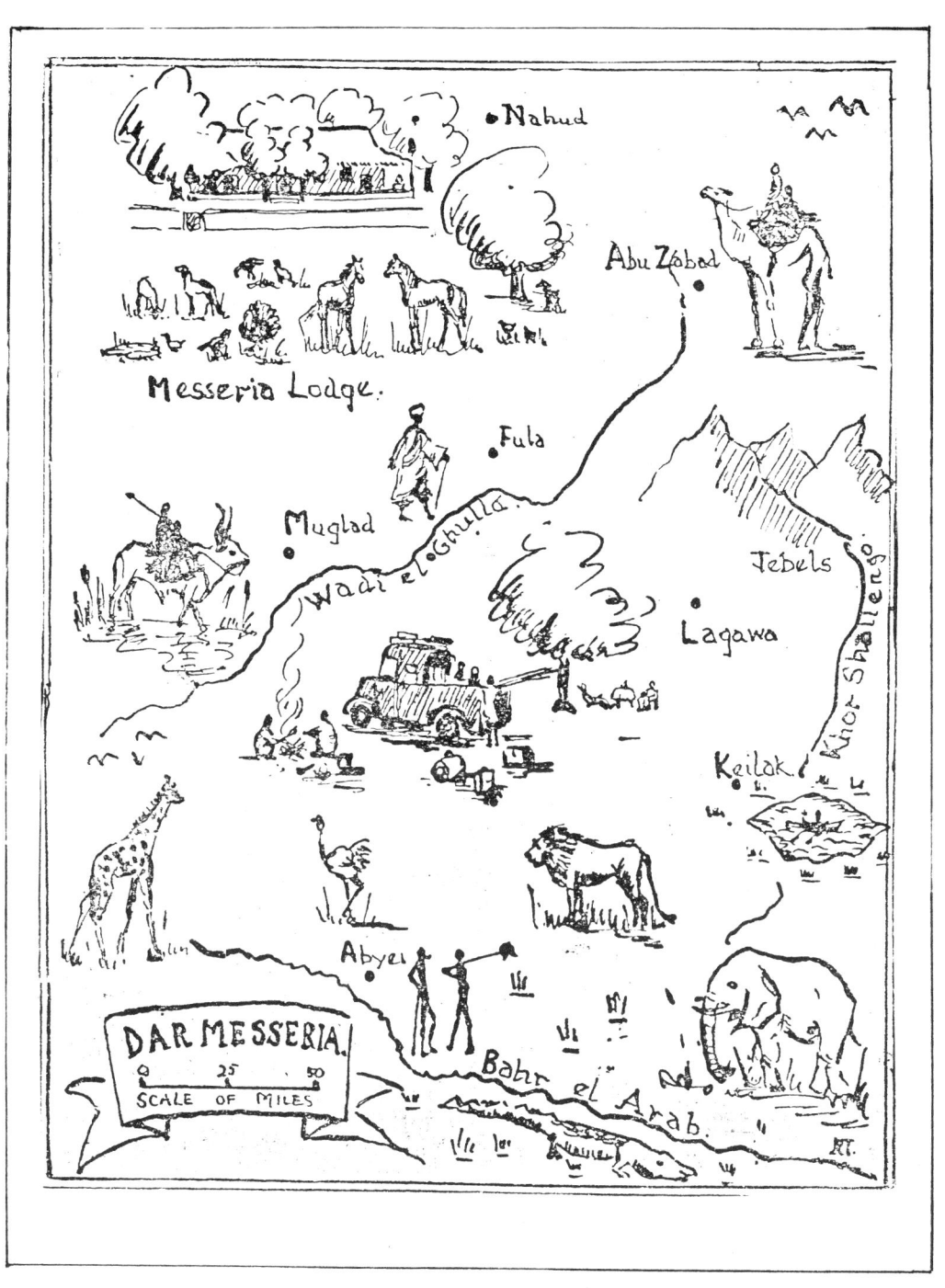

Our Christmas Card 1952

7. THE MUGLAD SHOW

One of the year's great occasions was the Messeria's Annual Tribal Gathering and Horse Show which lasted three days, our equivalent of the Horse of the Year Show. At the beginning of December, Anne and I had been down to see the Dinka in Abyie, then back to Muglad to inspect the final preparations and see that all was ready for our distinguished guests. We drove about five miles out with Nazirs Babu and Ali to the show ground, a vast cleared level expanse of ground, which also doubled if necessary as the airstrip.

We found fleets of grass houses going up . There was a settlement all round an enormous tebelgi tree for the British guests. Each house was labelled in English for its occupant. The Governor and the Hoggs had three roomed grass bungalows surrounded by grass walls; the Hunters and ourselves had two roomed houses, the rest had one room. Each had a kitchen and servants quarters behind. Right in the centre was a big grass hut, mysteriously labelled 'Publications Bureau'; it emerged that this was our communal mess.

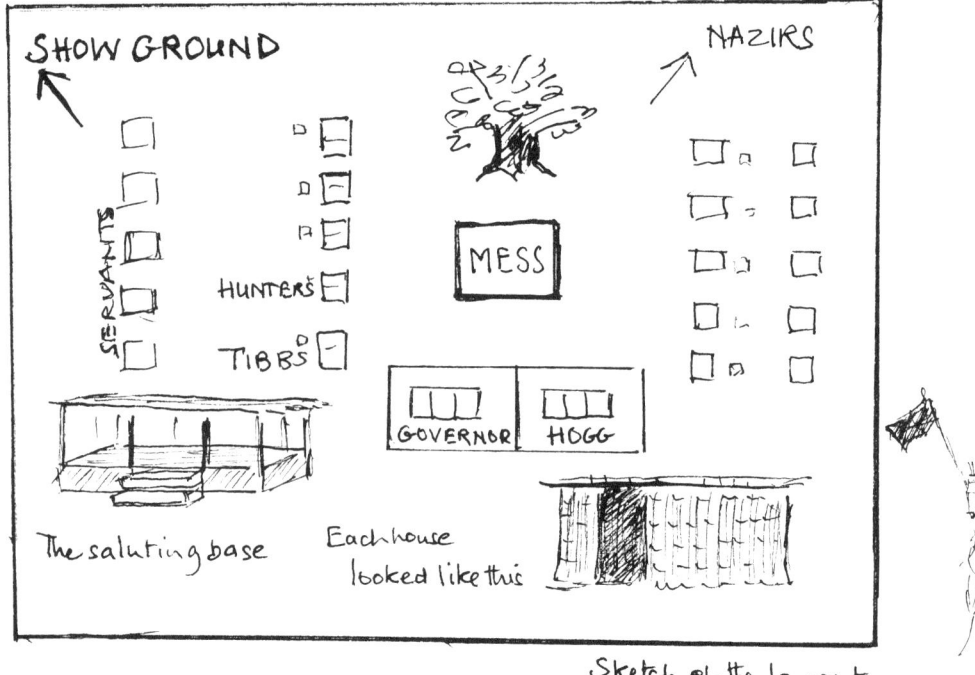

Sketch of the layout

A few hundred yards away there was the Nazirs' settlement, huts of every shape and size to suit their individual needs, according to how many wives, children and relatives they intended to put up. Babu of course had an absolute palace for himself and his wife. She had consented to leave her Khartoum residence and come for a stay in the country. The tribesmen, their horses, and spectators were camped under the trees on the other side of the showground. A raised platform of mud bricks with grass roof overhead had been put up as the grandstand.

Our horses, Turvey and Willy were in bouncing good form after their 160 mile trek down from Nahud. Syce Abdel Rahman came down in company with the Hunter's syce and horses and a police contingent. They had to guard the horses closely at night, as there were a lot of lions about.

We moved out into our grass residence on Tuesday evening. On Wednesday morning we went for a ride before breakfast, then at 8.55 a note arrived asking whether we would go and watch the 'proof' of the show. Five minutes later I was also told that I was expected to take the salute at the "proof" which turned out to be the dress rehearsal. So, Turvey was retrieved again while I quickly changed back into riding breeches.

Babu and myself, feeling like the Queen on Winston, set off to the parade. The mounted tribesmen were drawn up on two sides of a square behind the flags of their respective Nazirs and Omdas. We passed down the line with some exciting moments as I manoeuvred Turvey alongside the Omdas to shake hands. As we passed down, each Omdia yodelled while I shouted encouragement back. Half way down was Nazir Sereir of the Felleita. He had a white flag with red writing and a Union Jack in the corner; the effect was like a windblown white ensign. Inspection finished, we returned to the saluting base and each Omdia rode past in columns of four, dipping their flags as they went.

Peter Hogg and the Hunters arrived during the morning. We did not know what time the Governor, Geoffrey Hawkesworth was due to arrive, so we arranged for him to be stopped if he came too early. However, at about 4 o'clock we all went off to a place where the road widens.

About 1,000 mounted tribesmen were drawn up on either side of the road. A magnificent sight, two long lines of horsemen facing inwards with standards fluttering in the breeze as the sun set, a great red ball sinking behind them. We parked our lorry on a slight mound for a good view. We had almost given up when we saw a cloud of dust rising in the distance as the Governor's saloon came into view. Police outriders with the two Condominion flags got into place and escorted the Governor through the ranks. When he had passed, all the tribesmen followed on behind. We shot on ahead to join the welcoming party of Nazirs, Sheikhs and Omdas.

The British party in addition to Geoffrey Hawkesworth the Governor, the District Commissioner Peter Hogg, ADC John Hunter with Mary, consisted of the Inspector of Local Government, Geoffrey McComas, the Province Judge, Kevin Hayes, and two Agricultural Officers, John Smart and John Manton. Mohamed had arranged which cook would do which meal and reported to Anne who was doing what. Anne then told Abdel Rahman who told the duty safragi who was the cook on duty - any direct liaison was not countenanced. AR explained to Anne that the cooks had to be organised, but the safragis were able to do it themselves. Needless to say, under Anne's guidance all went without a hitch

The great day dawned. Everyone emerged from their apartments having had an excellent night, with the exception of His Honour the Judge, and perhaps his near neighbours. His bed had given away with a loud report in the early hours. Anne commented – "not surprising really". Kevin had a large robust figure, red face and bushy moustache, always jolly and exercising his singular ha, ha,ha, guffaw.

The horses arrived at 8.45. I rode Turvey, Peter Hogg was on Anne's horse, Brown Willy (usually very good but could not be guaranteed not to make eyes at any girl that took his fancy). Geoffrey Hawkesworth wanted a quiet mount and had Mary Hunter's, John was on his own. Ahmed Abu Gasim the Executive Officer mounted himself and Geoffrey McComas. We lined up behind

Ready to go.
John Hunter   Peter Hogg   Geoffrey Hawkesworth
                                         G/M.G.T.

the mounted police outriders with the Union Jack and the Egyptian flags and off we went down the line. Anne thought we looked very resplendent, she and party drove to the grandstand in the Judge's Super Humber Snipe. They sat in the front row of armchairs, behind them sat the important Sheikhs, very colourful in the deep crimson Robes of Honour with medals on chains round their necks.

Meanwhile the Governor and escort rode round the great arena. The horsemen were lined up according to tribe and Omdia, each with their respective banners. Each Omda rode forward to shake hands with the Governor as he went past. All went well, the horses behaved impeccably and we returned to the saluting base in good order.

The throbbing of the nahas, the huge copper drums which were the official insignia of a Nazir Umum, had been going since dawn. The deep resonant boom now rose to a crescendo as the great parade began. At the head of the procession came the red and blue banner of the Nazir Umum followed by Babu himself mounted on his prancing charger with all its trappings. He looked splendid in his scarlet Special Robe of Honour with its gold cords and tassels as he sat cushioned in a snow white sheepskin, which hung almost to the ground each side. As he raised his drawn sword in salute to the Governor, it glittered in the sun. He was followed by his escort of warriors carrying their long Baggara spears and wearing heavy chain mail, said to be of Crusader origin and handed down through the generations. (We inspected these more closely later and found it was very heavy indeed.)

Nazirs Ali and Sereir in their red robes headed their sections of tribesmen all in white robes with colourful trappings on their horses. Each Omda rode in front followed by their men in columns of four abreast. As they went past the saluting base all sorts of antics were performed; horses made to prance up and down, stand on their hind legs, buck on their front legs or pirouette. One little boy on a beautiful grey horse, quite enormous for him, made it dance on its hind legs. Some of the warriors were tiny boys perched up on top of their mounts, one was followed by a little foal and a dog, in fact several foals insisted on trotting in the procession behind their mamas.

1,019 horsemen rode past

After this they continued in sober lines until they past a large group of girls who shrieked and warbled. Here the horseman left their columns and charged the girls at full gallop waving their spears in the air and pulling the horses up on their haunches in a cloud of dust only two feet away.

Nazir Sereir M Nazir Babu
Sitting down. Geoffrey McComas
behind Judge Kevin Hayes

On and on they came until after an hour 1,019 horses and riders had gone past. Next came the races. The Agaira Omdias raced in the morning and the Felleita in the afternoon. The starts were the quickest we have ever seen. The horses lined up, the starter blew his whistle and they were off - just like that. The Nahud police band provided the music, two bagpipes, a big drum and side drum. Last year the El Obeid town band came out at vast expense, but there were no bagpipes and everyone complained. They were much happier this time.

The non-stop entertainment continued with the Muglad Elementary and Sub-grade schools sports.

In the evening some of us drove out a few miles to look at a fula (lake) to see if there were enough duck for a shoot the next morning. The ponds were one mass of white water lilies with yellow centres. There were only a few ducklings and other birds swimming about but beside the lake were two lovely golden crested cranes, with terrific gold crests on top of their heads.

The next day, some went for a ride before breakfast, others went duck shooting. This party arrived for a late breakfast dripping with muddy water having only got ten birds, but enough to replenish the larder.

Then, more races, this time the best Agaira horse against the best Felleita horse. This was followed by a horse show, best mare, and best foal. After lunch came the climax, the best horse of all. This was, to his great delight, Nazir Ali's horse, Barez, ridden by John Hunter's scyce, Mohamed Musa, who was thrilled to bits. The Governor presented the prizes. Nazir Ali got an enormous challenge cup and the no. 2 a hunting horn which was presented by Donald Rae last year. First and second paraded round, very pleased with themselves.

Nagara, the tribal dancing followed. Long lines of men and girls dancing a long conga to a lively drum beat which followed us as we all went off to a tea party given by Babu. This took place outside his grass palace. We all sat cross legged on mats and cushions in a huge big square, about fifty of us. As usual Babu with his stately manner was the perfect host. Anne sat next to the headmaster of Lagawa school, an extremely courteous elderly gentleman. He was most interesting and taught her quite a number of new Arabic words.

We thought it a pity that custom prevented Babu's wife being there. She had watched the races from a distance in the privacy of a saloon car. She and her companions were heavily veiled. All the sheikhs we knew were at the party so it took a long time to say goodbye to them all. On return, we had baths, drinks, dinner, then, bed for which we were quite ready after a long and eventful day.

We started Saturday morning by riding round a nearby lake with Peter. After breakfast we had lengthy discussions with the Nazirs about taxes, haffirs (reservoirs) and elections which lasted all the morning. Anne and Mary talked and sewed. We sent our lorry on ahead to Rigl el Fula, so travelled in comfort with Geoffrey in the saloon while he told us all the gossip from El Obeid. We had lunch on the way and got in at about 4, feeling a bit sick - our lorry is much firmer and rides the bumps better than a car. We stayed in the three out of four houses which had been completed and showed them round, this did not take long but we think they were quite impressed with what had been done..

They all departed the next day before breakfast and we were left on our own. I spent most of the day with a tape measure and succeeded in finding a good site for the new Council Chamber with two tall acacia trees in front to make an impressive entrance. (On Babu's next visit he approved the site "especially when the trees are cut down!"). I also laid out the first twenty shops. The sites had to be cleared and in the evening we marked the plans out on the ground so that the builder could start getting the foundations dug.

Nazir umum's Nahas

8. SOME TRIALS OF LOCAL GOVERNMENT
and the growth of Rigl el Fula.

From the security of the Governor's office in El Obeid, I had been able to view the advance of Local Government in Kordofan. Even from there one could understand the apprehension of the Nazirs who were worried about the erosion of their traditional powers. From El Obeid I had been able to pay a visit to Ralph Daly, A.D.C. Northern Kordofan, he lived in Soderi and had set up the beginnings of local government in the north of Northern Kordofan as Executive Officer of the Kabbabish Rural District Council. It all seemed incongruous that the largest camel owning tribe should need a Council. The tribesmen were always on the move with their seasonal migration, but Ralph had obviously persuaded them that local government was a good thing.

The Messeria District Council had been started off in 1949. By the time I arrived, the Mamur, Ahmed Abu Gasim was well established as the Executive officer and there were also two Assistant Executive Officers. They were Bukr eff Ali in Lagowa and Abu Gabr eff Hag Agbar, who was the brother of Nazir Sereir, in Muglad. There was also a small office in Abu Zabad looked after by a cashier, Hag Said.

I was the appointed Chairman of the Council and was due to take the chair at my first meeting in September. The idea was that Anne and I were going to El Odaiya and trek down to Muglad with our horses, accompanied by the Nazirs. Having got to El Odaiya, Anne did not feel well, for some reason we had not got a thermometer, but Nazir Ali was able to produce one and she had a very high temperature. So, I had to take her back to Nahud where she went to bed under the care of Joanna Hogg and Abdel Rahman. I had to return and trek on my own with Nazirs Babu, Ali and Sereir. They had already gone on and I caught up with them on the Muglad road at Sidr el Kebir.

The Omda, Adam Yousif was waiting for us and very annoyed that Anne was not with me as he had all the boys and girls out in their best clothes dancing for her. The arrival of the Nazirs was spectacular, the dancers separated into two lines and one by one the Nazirs galloped through at full tilt and fired their shot guns into the air; at the end of the line they pulled up, the horse reared up on its back legs, then full tilt again with another bang.

We spent the next two days visiting the feriks on the way down to Gubba. The first day we left at 7.30. On the assurance that we only had a short ride of 1½ hours, I did not have any breakfast. We went west. After 2 hours I was told our destination was 'near', after 3 hours it was 'quite near'. We eventually arrived after nearly four hours and I thankfully drank three pints of the frothy warm milk which was handed round to us in gourds as we sat in a circle on angareebs. Only two hours trek in the evening and the next day I took the precaution of having two boiled eggs before I started.

One of the advantages of this particular trek was that it gave me an opportunity to get to know Babu better. His real name was Osman but when he was small his grandfather used to call him Babu - a small child, and he has been called Babu ever since. He was only 13 when he succeeded his father Nimr, who died at an early age having been Nazir for only six years. Despite his age it was the general wish of the tribe that Babu should be Nazir but one of his uncles, Gabar, was appointed Regent. He was also very much influenced by the Mamur, an Egyptian by the name of Ahmed Mukhtar Khalil. It was from him, so it was said, that Babu learnt his art of mimicry, he could imitate almost anything from courting birds to dancing couples. He was a very agreeable companion.

We arrived at Gubba at 10 am on the third day and found the lorries had got down the road, so by 2pm I was in Muglad ready for the Council session to start the next day. However, I was told that the Zurug members from Lagawa had not yet turned up but I did find Ian Cunninson, the anthropologist there with what looked like mumps, though he said it was quinsy. He was being looked after by the medical assistant in the hospital.

On the Monday we decided to have the Finance Committee with a bare quorum but then, needless to say, the Zurug did arrive so we had to have it all over again. Lagawa is about 100 miles from Muglad but they had to go a round about way to Abu Zabad, 100 miles, Abu Zabad to Nahud 100 miles, here they left Nazir Izz el Din who was ill, then 40 miles to El Odaiya and 120 miles on. What dedication!

In the middle of the finance committee I spied a box car coming down the road, so excused myself and was delighted to see Anne beaming away, sitting beside Peter.

The Council meeting started at last on Wednesday morning. I put on an immaculate white uniform bush jacket and shorts for the occasion and went down before breakfast to see how the largest room in the office had been laid out. Ahmed Abu Gasim complimented me on looking so smart but said I should remove my A.D.C's stripes, it was very important that as Chairman I did not look like a D.C., the Members might feel intimidated. So, I had to go back and later re-appeared in shirt and tie; the first potential blunder avoided.

Most of the meeting concerned the establishment of the new Council Headquarters in Rigl el Fula. The question of a proper headquarters for the Messeria had been discussed as early as 1935 when the D.C.Western Kordofan was James Robertson (now Sir James, the Civil Secretary). He had suggested Kadorke. Paul Howell (D.C.Messeria) had, in 1948 suggested Rigl el Fula or Kigeira, but decided that Fula was more central.

The Nazir Umum, and Nazirs of the Zurug, Felleita and Agaira attended a meeting in Abu Zabad in June 1950 and agreed that the Council Headquarters should be at Rigl el Fula, the actual site depending on the location of the P.W.D. water yard. This was built in 1950 and in 1951 the Council had received a grant of £E8,000 and work was started.

When I arrived on the scene a large store had been built at Fula for building materials. Donald had also decided that it would be much cheaper for the Council to undertake the building itself, so he had recruited a master builder and also a carpenter who were each in charge of a small artisans' school. Houses had to be built for them to live in, also for the Executive Officer, Clerk and Accountant. There also had to be a rest house as it was not always convenient for us to use the one built by the PWD in the water yard.

Before the meeting in Muglad I had gone through the books with Ahmed Abu Gasim and there seemed lots of money left over from the original grant of £8,000. We explained this satisfactory state of affairs to the Finance

Committee. One of the problems of the Messeria was that Babu was not a wealthy man. He lived in a government house in Muglad and there was no way he could afford to build his own house in Fula and he did not really want to live in another government one. The difficulty was resolved by agreeing to give him a loan from the Council. We also decided that we should build a proper council chamber on the lines of the one that the Kabbabish had in Soderi (I had filched a copy of the plans)

When the full Council met they rather doubtfully agreed to the loan for Babu and very cheerfully endorsed the plans for the council chamber and our other expansion plans.

While I had been Councilling, Peter had been taking a Major Court. We left on the Friday, he back to Nahud; Anne and I back to El Odaiya to resume our horse trek

The minutes and financial decisions of the Council had to be referred to the Director of Local Government through the D.C. and the Governor. In the meantime, the work went on and by January the next year ('53) we had finished houses in Fula for the Executive Officer, the Clerk, the Accountant and a two roomed rest house. They were able to make the move in February. In addition houses had also been built for the staff in Lagawa and Abu Zabad

What I had not realised was that my predecessor, Donald Rae, had not really approved of the idea of a formal building with offices and a council chamber. He could see no reason why the Council should not revolve its meetings round the main centres as it had done in the past. Where he thought the officers were to work when they moved to Fula, I am not sure. The upshot was that a lot of the grant of £E 8,000 which had been specified for the Council's Headquarters in Rigl el Fula had actually been spent on the houses in Lagawa and Abu Zabad and on the very fine chain of rest houses Donald had built all over the place. To make matters worse, a series of accounts from the Public Works Department, eighteen months old, had been overlooked altogether and were not entered in the grants book.

It seemed, as the full horrors were revealed, that we had already run through our £E 8,000, were overspent by £E 4,000 and were only half way through our building programme. Fortunately, the amounts involved were (in those days) enormous.

There is a fundamental principle of overspending your budget or grant, if you are going to do it, it must be done on a grand scale. If you over spend by £50 you will be severely reprimanded by an accountant who will threaten to have the increase in pay due to your book keeper withheld, and in any case the deficit will be deducted from next year. If you overspend by £1,000, the

Chief Accountant will get into a tizzy, the auditors will be sent out and the whole affair will be reported to the Governor. If you commit a real enormity, then it will go to someone who can take the right perspective and sort it out. Here we were with a likely overspend of £E20,000, so the whole thing got onto the right level, that of the Director of Local Government himself

In February it was arranged that no less a personage than the Director would visit Fula. It began with the sort of delay and muddle which tries one's patience and of which if one gets too upset one should not be here because it is this sort of country. Peter Hogg went off to greet the D of L.G. in Abu Zabad. Joanna came down to Rigl el Fula with Anne and myself leaving her family under the charge of Heather with the Hunters next door keeping an eye on them. We arrived and had lunch in the rest house.

Ahmed abu Gasim had arranged a grand tea party for the important guests as we had expected Peter, Geoffrey McComas (who had been D.C. El Obeid but was now Inspector of Local Government) and Mr and Mrs Director of Local Government to arrive at about 4. A lorry turned up at 5.30, it was D. of L.G.'s cook who announced that the party had arrived at El Odaiya. The Omda had told them we had not been through. Peter rang Nahud and was told we had left early so he assumed we had broken down and rushed off to rescue us. So, it was not until 7 oc, that all the guests arrived for the Sherif's tea party. Peter had heard on the wireless that an Agreement had been signed between the Egyptians and H.M.Government about the future of the Sudan, so we listened to the news at 8 oc to see what our fate was to be.

We had not met the D. of L.G. though the others had known him for some time. He was Lawrence Buchanan with his wife Doreen. By the time we had finished listening to the news it was quite late, the timetable had gone haywire, so Anne being the hostess said we would sit where we fell. Dinner was on the sand outside the rest house and we sat at our battered aluminium folding tables, (a legacy from Donald Rae, they were Italian and liberated by someone after the battle of Kerala). As we started to sit down there was protest from Doreen who explained that as I was her host she should sit on my right; Anne should sit at the other end of the table with the Director on her right. So, we all had to get up again and reshuffle. Never mind that we had over spent our grant, perish the idea that the announcement on the wireless meant we should lose our jobs, the Honour of the Empire was upheld under the stars in Rigl el Fula!

The following morning I led a conducted tour of the rising city. About six houses had been completed, the Council building was rising steadily, we had chosen the site for our house, we had pegged out the shops and we had a town plan showing how the development would proceed in the future. After breakfast the men talked finance while the ladies knitted and chatted.

Anyway, so far as our grant was concerned the session was most successful, we got a loan of £E 11,000, a grant of £E 4,450 and were allowed to find £E 5,064 from our reserves and sale of materials. The Council (me) sold most of the surplus to the District Commissioner (me) for the central government buildings, the Merkaz and D.C.'s house. The person who really suffered was poor Babu, we were not allowed to make him a loan.

The Council meetings needed a lot of preparatory work, especially when the budget had to be discussed and passed. First the Executive Officers had to be consulted, then the Nazirs. Living so far away from them this was difficult and was one of the reasons we had to spend so much time on trek away from our home in Nahud. In the old days, the District budget was fixed through the D.C and the Governor. The Nazirs and Omdas were informed what taxes had to be raised and they were responsible for making sure they were collected.

Once the Councils started, they proposed the level of spending and they were also responsible for collecting what was due. Not all the money raised was theirs, a proportion had to go to the central government for running the country. This all had to be explained to the taxpayers, so one spent hours sitting on an angareeb (rope bed) just talking in simple terms how it worked. "That new donkey (water yard) had a very long pipe down into the water with the pump on the top, it has been built by the Public Works Department, so some of the taxes has to pay for it". "Ah, but why do we have to pay a piastre for every tin of water we take?". "Well you want clean water and there must be a caretaker, that is where the piastre goes, but you want another one at that place ten miles away, some of the taxes will go towards that. Then there are the police, they have to be paid for"...and so it went on.

The Nazirs were in a peculiar position, they were appointed by the Governor, so were paid from the Province Headquarters but we had to make a contribution equal to their pay. Much the same happened with the Court Presidents. Omdas, however were paid direct by the Council, as were the tribal policemen, ghaffirs of Council rest houses and reservoirs, drivers and gardeners. On the education side we were responsible for primary schools. Upkeep of reservoirs and digging wells were essential items and there was the all important question of transport and the upkeep and making new roads.

When I came, there was only one Council lorry which was getting very decrepit. By the time I left we had seven, one for each centre, one for the Nazirs, a small pick up for the Executive Officer while 'Decrepit' was very useful in bringing in stone for the building works. For some reason the Local Government Department in Khartoum never liked us having proper transport. We had to get our budget approved and every year it came back with our intended transport queried. Every year I had to write and explain that if we were going to be effective we had to able to move. Once Peter Hogg became Deputy Director of Local Government, things became much easier as I had a direct line to the top.

So, all these knotty questions had to be thrashed out, written out in the prescribed manner with full explanations and added up. We then had to get them through the Finance Committee and then to the full Council.

The proceeding were, of course in Arabic, but once the Dinka joined, we had sometimes to wait until the essentials were translated into Dinka. Being in the chair, one could never relax, especially at first, as the Messeria have their own pronunciation of some words (like north Yorkshire?) and some Baggara words were not Arabic at all.

The agenda had to be very carefully constructed. It was most important that the first item was controversial and if necessary could be accepted as a defeat for the establishment. Such a one was the construction of a road between Rigl el Fula north to Abu Ku. It soon dawned on the members that the people who would receive the greatest benefit were going to be the D.C. and the Executive Officer, in saving them about two hours every time they went to Abu Zabad. So, this proposal would be voted down, a victory for the common man and everyone was happy. The members, flushed with satisfaction would now be much more lenient with some of the other proposals.

Needless to say the most important items were the ones in a member's own Omdia or territory. A cattle owning Humr would reckon it was a ridiculous waste of money to build a reservoir which would help a Nuba on the eastern side of the District to grow cotton. A balance therefore had to be struck and the Humr member reminded that he had also asked for a reservoir at Subu on his cattle route, he was of course quite right in wanting to ensure these developments were economic, so the best thing was to withdraw both proposals. The member might then withdraw his objections.

Having reached the target expenditure, the Council then had to agree how the money was to be raised. Some of our income came from fines, market fees and traders' licences. The Dinka paid poll tax but the Messeria's wealth was measured not in money but in cattle so it was their animals that were taxed. At one time the D.C. and staff had somehow to physically count all cattle, horses, camels, sheep, donkeys and goats. A tremendous organisation had to be set up so that they could be driven past a fixed point and counted. Fortunately a formula had been devised under which it was assumed that a cow had a calf every year, one of these would replace the original cow, one would die or be sold, and one would be an increase. So someone who started with 100 cows would have 133 after three years or 111 after one year, so this was the number to be taxed. One then divided cows into piastres and there you were, more or less.

When the figures were announced there would be uproar. "The cattle had all died through disease, they had been stolen by the Um Borroro (West Africans), eaten by the merchants and the original figures were wrong anyway." "Oh dear, in that case we will have to postpone our new primary school, cancel those four wells and the lorry for the Nazirs; we will also have to consider a complete count of all animals." At this stage there would be some whispering and the Nazirs might ask for an adjournment. They and the Omdas would disappear for half an hour or so. When they came back a compromise would be proposed. The Nazirs would go through the list with the Omdas, and the amount required would be raised. Relief all round.

So the day would go on. As the tin roof above us heated up, some heads would begin to fuzz a little and more progress would be made. With any luck by this time to-morrow the road from Abu Ku to Rigl el Fula (as opposed to the road from Rig el Fula to Abu Ku) would be nodded through and they would not notice that item 32 was the same as item 1!

Gaiyaling Midday Stop.

9. HORSE TREK.

Anne's Account...

Off at last! Just as it was getting light this morning and we were having our early morning tea; a long line of bulls arrived to be tethered in a row to the rest house fence. El Odaiya, a small town about 60 miles south of Nahud was the assembly point of this trek. The bulls were a day late so we had a relaxed time with Nazir Sereir and Sheikh Mulah discussing plans for the journey. It is their two tribes that we shall be visiting so they accompany us. They are both great characters, Sheikh Mulah is an absolute charmer and concerns himself greatly over me. Nazir Babu is not with us yet as his daughter is ill, but he hopes to join us later.

Soon it was all hustle and bustle. Everything was packed up, roped up and heaved onto the bulls. There it stayed or fell off again depending how well it was balanced. The bulls wear sort of saddles with a wooden framework and padding made from plaited grass. There is no girth at all, it seems that the Baggara have special dispensation to defy the laws of gravity. It is not surprising the completed load sometimes capsizes. It was quite a performance to watch, especially when one bull put its head into our fruit and vegetable basket and started chewing a lemon, much to the concern of the little boy in charge. He shouted and hit the bull as hard as he could and he must have hurt his hand but the bull took no notice and went on to try a marrow.

All this time the sky was a leaden grey and we expected a downpour but luckily only drizzle set in, this is quite unusual.

Eventually the baggage was secure and it was time for the drivers to mount, no easy task with the balance problem. However, a few helping hands, a spear to lean on and the bull's horns to step on after his head had been pulled down to a suitable height, and the feat was accomplished. To remain on these precarious perches the spears were used as a leg to the ground. One snowy white bull had the appearance of a flying angel with our trunks and armchairs on board. An even loftier perch was to be had on the only camel, specially

Horse Trek
Some of the baggage.

The heavy kitchen boxes

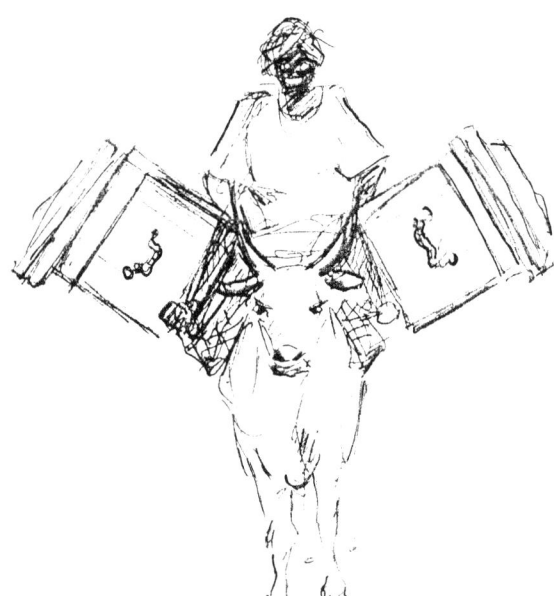
Ahmed with the pantry boxes and folding chairs

Having a leg up.

Hassen doing up our bedrolls

Our clothes

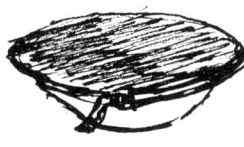
Our washing kit

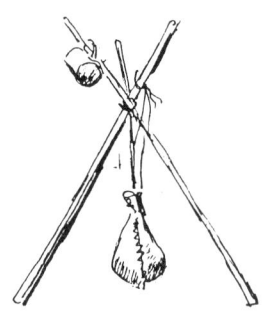
Drinking water

employed to carry the pantry and kitchen boxes, too big and heavy for the bulls.

Soon the cavalcade was ready to move off. By this time the Sheikhs' retinue had joined them as they lumbered off through waist high grass up a gentle slope out of the town, and over the horizon. After a few minutes the Nazir and Omdas arrived at the gallop on their horses. We mounted Willy and Turvey and set off after the rest of the party. The cavalcade now included 16 horses, 16 bulls, 10 donkeys, 1 donkey foal and 1 camel. Ali (our boy), Awad, (Mike's messenger boy) and Abdel Rahamn were riding donkeys, Abdel Rahamn the syce was on a horse, as was Sulum our policeman, such a nice person and help in general. We had to leave Mohamed our cook behind as he had a fever.

Led by the Omda of the first ferik we were to visit, we wandered along small paths in and out of trees. We soon passed the bulls going slowly at their own pace, buckets rattling, tins clicking and a cloud of dust rising from the path after them, not to speak of the buzzing flies about them. Usually one bull is trailing behind after the reorganisation of a collapsed load.

Willy and Turvey behaved very well indeed. They have got used to their girl friends in the party, in fact must be bored by them as they have ceased to stand on their hind legs waving and shouting at them as they did on their way here. They both look very handsome and fit and are obviously enjoying themselves. Turvey just fancies himself, as he is wearing the saddlebag made of coloured rope with long tassels bought by M in Aleppo. It is very useful for carrying macs, sunglasses, biscuits and sweets, sweaters and anything else we might want en route. M looks like a cowboy in his bush hat and mac (it is still drizzling).

After two hours riding, now 10.30, we arrived at Na'ama, a clearing with haystack objects scattered around. We had arrived at a small ferik; unusually half of the people were Felleita and half Zurug. Feriks are the family

Horse Trek

M

A

Abdel Rahman (Syce) and Willy

Our policeman

Abdel Rahman

based groups of the Messeria who migrate north during the rains with their cattle. The haystack objects are their houses made of a framework of sticks covered by rush mats, grass or skins, whatever is available.

On our arrival we found a place all prepared for us a little apart from the ferik. A clearing had been made, the grass had been cut and some trees had been made into a thick roofed shelter with extra branches inter woven and supported by poles. The ground had been hoed so it was sandy underneath; angareebs had been brought for us to sit on.

No sooner had we sat down than an enormous gourd full of frothy warm milk arrived, (they always boil their milk, but not for the same hygienic reasons that we would, I'm sure). Michael drank a pint or so, I drank some and then Nazir Sereir and Sheikh Mulah had some too, a loving bowl in fact. With the milk, arrived a great party to welcome us, we paid our respects and shook hands with all of them and then we were left on our own to have a belated breakfast at about 11.30, now laid ready by AR on our trek table

As it became very overcast and cloudy we put the tent up. 'We', of course did not include any physical action from us, except to say which way it should point. Our policeman, Sulum took charge, assisted by a contingent of Council police and various passers by. Having a 'head', but no temperature I had a short siesta before lunch.

Nazir Sereir and Sheikh Mulah returned for much talking while I sewed. My new pink plastic cotton reel container intrigued them.

After lunch we went over to sit under another tree to watch some dancing laid on for us. The drums had been beating all the morning and now the girls appeared. A group of small boys, goggle eyed stared at us, as did the surrounding crowd that had gathered.

Entertainment over, we found that all our belongings had departed and our horses were ready. So after fond farewells we rode off again in similar procession as before but with the addition of various presents, eggs, a chicken, a sheep and part of a bull.

It was a lovely evening with a beautiful sunset and it was very pleasant riding along in the cool, watching the surrounding countryside change colour and the shadows lengthen as the sun sank lower. All around us was the distant sound of drums, each with a different beat. This was to guide the cattle back to their own ferig. They all know their own call, so that even if the ferig has moved duirng the day while the cattle are out grazing, they will find their way to the next encampment.

We rode for about two hours and then we were told we should hurry up a bit; so for the last half an hour we cantered, about 20 horses thundering head to tail down the narrowest of paths. (Such a thing would never have been allowed in the Pony Club!)

At 6.45 we arrived at no-where in particular and waited for the bulls to catch up. They were not very long and soon we were having tea with Nazir Sereir and Sheikh Mulah while Sulum and his gang put up the tent. Sheikh Mulah is afraid of his life that something will happen to me. Peter Hogg has apparently told him that I am not to travel too far in case my fever comes back. (M's comment. However he is more impressed with her every day, what with her cooking and horsemanship. Peter seems to think that we are bound to come to grief and insists on sending the lorry to meet us at Abu Ku' to make sure we are all right.)

Monday September. 22nd.

Slept like tops, up at 6am and by 6.30 all the boxes were packed, tent down and bulls loaded up. We waited until the hamla (the baggage train), was under way, then took to our horses. A very enjoyable ride to Shelu past an extraordinary jebel (hill), a smooth bare rock with some grain growing on it in one place and four palm trees on the top. We went up a rise by the side of the jebel then down into a shallow valley with the Jebel Shelu rising all round, in the distance to the south, a view of the big Jebel Ganouk rising out of the flat plain. We found two small trees prepared. We decided to use one as our living room, the other as our bedroom with the tent in the middle

Until our chairs arrived, we sat on an angareeb (rope bed). Then our hosts rolled up bringing their contributions. First of all we had orange squash, then a bowl containing a mixture of honey and lemon (very succulent but rather rich), then more orange, a large bowl of milk, then in succession twelve people with their tea pots from which they poured small glasses of wet sugary, sticky and in some cases very milky tea. Fortunately, Sheikh Mulah diverted some of them. I managed to keep pace, though there was a little rhubarb when I refuse second helpings. Lady Tipps was caught with four glasses of plain tea, one glass of milky tea and one glass of orange. The four owners glared at her, waiting for their glasses back. She began by drinking half each of the small glasses, then an old man came forward and poured the remaining tea out of his glass into all the others, leaving Lady T with three glasses of plain tea, one big glass of milky tea and one glass of orangey tea. Eventually we said that we would drink the rest with our breakfast and return the glasses later.

Now, having had breakfast, all is peaceful except that small boys are trying to bang drums, which are only 25 yards away, they are removed every now and then but soon creep back again. We are surrounded by a flock of sheep, which the scandalised owners are trying to drive off. The sheep are having a happy time licking some toffee papers, which have not been cleared up (further hospitality from the day before). A committee has just driven a large white bull into a space a few yards away, so that we have a good view as they tie up its legs, push it over and slit its throat. It is then dissected, but fortunately, behind a bush.

Trays of tea, bowls of milk and round dishes with matting covers are carried to and fro, but they appear to be for the Nazirs and our servants' breakfasts rather than for our elevenses. A large leg impaled on a stick has just emerged from behind the bushes.

Sulum and another committee have erected a convenience for us out of sticks and mats. Our heads come out of the top, but that is all. Yesterday, the mat screen was not very tall and by the time we had mounted the throne made of branches inside, only our knees remained unexposed, we just had to hope that the spectators were more abashed than we were.

The country with the Jebels in the background, the green grass and the trees looked very homely. Little blue flowers with short spiky leaves carpet the ground while every now then there are patches of little red flowers. Not quite in tune with the pastoral scene, some of the trees have sprouted strips of meat (ex bull), hanging up in the sun to dry. We had a peaceful morning during which I made a lemon soufflé under observation from polite but amazed eyes which had not seen one before.

After lunch we went and talked for an hour or so and then returned for a sleep. However, scores of people came up to shake hands with us so we had to stay awake, then Nazir Sereir arrived for a long talk about the iniquities of his colleagues. We then looked round the ferik, a big one, little round huts made out of matting stretching out in all directions. When they move south again the matting goes too, leaving only the skeleton of sticks behind.

Nagara during Horse Trek at Shelu.

It was then time for the games. About seventy girls in lines of four or five were all dressed up in coloured frocks, bracelets, nose rings and tajes (beaded coronets). These are a web of silver chain which goes over the head with a large silver blob on the top and with large silver triangular dangles over the ears. Round the girls' waists are lengths of white cloth with long ends they flap up and down while they shuffle their feet. While this is going on, three lines of about a hundred boys and young men wind round and between the girls and the drums. They wear the brightest things they have, with ornaments like mirrors and yards of ribbon. One of them was draped in the Merchant Navy medal ribbon, 1914 - 18. How on earth did he get it? We went round and took photographs and then M beat the drums, tum tity tum te tum te tum. Everyone was very happy. After the dance, called the naggara (drums) they started the sufga (clapping). We sat by our tent while they closed in a very tight circle round us; the girls clapping and singing about their ideal young men while the boys leapt up and down in the middle. The circle got tighter and tighter and the crowd nearer and nearer, so we evacuated through the throng and broke them into six sets, which made it easier to see.

Tuesday 23rd September.

M's mother's birthday and he joined the navy twelve years ago! We had a good night except when a few thousand cows went past the tent. We got up at 6am and were off at 7.30, but not before I had got on a camel belonging to one of the Sheikhs and ridden round the ferik. Nazir Serier and Omda Abu Gasim came with us for about a mile to say good bye. At 9 o'clock we arrived on the El Odaiya - Abu Ku' road. We heard a lorry and up drove Babu Nimr, the Nazir Umum. He had stayed behind in Muglad as his daughter was ill but she had now recovered. We declined to go on to Abu Ku', our next stop in the lorry and 'ghaled' (spend the heat of the day) under a tree by a pond near the road.

Inspite of the fact that one can go for miles in the Sudan without seeing anyone, it is impossible to stop anywhere without someone rising up out of the ground. So it was only a few minutes before a delegation arrived to find the Mufettish (D.C, literally Inspector) on his bed and Sa'ta Sit (Her Excellency the Lady) in the kitchen (that is, the camp fire) where she was presented with four chickens and some milk. Later on, we went over and talked to the delegation, now draped round Sheikh Mulah's tree and talking higher politics, mostly directed against the Gelaba who inhabit the towns. (The riverain and towns people wear the long galabia or gown, which comes down to the ground. The country people like the Baggara who ride bulls and the

Kabbabish who are the big camel owning tribe wear a shorter covering that tucks up through their legs when they are riding). The caucus agreed that the Gelaba only wanted power for themselves and when they had it, they would not know what to do with it, would not be bothered to find out what the rest of the country wanted, which was to be left alone to stay as they were. M tried to explain what self-government meant and that things were not as bad as they feared.

Off again at 3.30, this time through settled villages surrounded by crops of tall dura (millet) stalks which Turvey and Willy kept on picking and went along chewing with long leafy bits hanging out of their mouths. Some of the dura was 15 feet high, so we were riding along green tunnels with only our next ahead in sight. We also went through heskanite which has small burrs, they stick to everything and are extremely itchy.

The reaction of the villagers to our cavalcade varied, some took a long look and went on with their lawful occasions as though a D.C and his wife rode past every day (the last time was eight years ago). Others rushed out with eggs and chickens, which were added to the collection already, suspended by their legs upside down from the saddle of a donkey.

Near Abu Ku' the sky clouded over, so having stopped for a moment to look at the new well being dug, we cantered the last two miles and clattered to a halt by the school where Babu was waiting with the Omda, Sheikh Hammad Mohamed Dafallah. We sank three orange squashes and then sat down to tea in the open. Mike, myself, Babu and Sheikh Mulah sat at a table while the rest of the company were on grass mats on the ground. As the hour coincided with sunset conversation was a bit difficult, as we did not know which of the guests were just contemplating and which were praying. Three iced cakes were produced, as soon as they were cut, a dust storm blew up so we had to beat a quick retreat into one of the classrooms. Our lorry (sent by Peter) had arrived, so its battery was borrowed so that they could listen to the news from Radio Omdurman, after which we escaped. We slept well in a newly built grass rest house,

Hyena

having read our mail which Segeir had brought with him. Mohamed (cook) also rejoined us, quite recovered. One of the sheep we had been given had been tied up between the rest house and the servants' hut, but in the morning all that was left was the track of a hyena!

Wednesday 24th September.
>Up at 6. M went off to the suq (market) and discussed a round robin which had been presented the night before. They want a dispensary and a donkey (i.e. a deep bore with pump and a water yard). We think that if they want an assured water supply, they should move the village to Tibun el Swani, about four miles to the east where the water supply is known to be good. Then a dispensary could be built there. However, the parishioners obviously think that the Government is responsible for the water table being as it is and they want water in Abu Ku'. By the time this session was over it was 8 am before we got off. This time we had some camels as well; they were late joining us as the drivers had gone off the night before and got drunk on merisa (native beer) in the suq (market). In the end we had eleven horses, eleven bulls, thirteen camels and seven donkeys. After about two hours we got to a wadi (valley) with a jebel (hill) at the end called Sheheit. We had a rest until 3 pm and then went onto Um Sesia, this was a space in a sort of swamp, full of mosquitoes which buzzed round us all night though we did not get bitten too badly.

Thursday 25th September.
>Lunch after a three hour ride, we found that the ferik had moved and we spent over half an hour trying to find it. When we did, we were immediately regaled with milk in gourds and a bed was produced for me in case I wanted to rest. We were persuaded to spend the night and were given a sheep and two bulls, one for us and one for Babu. A restful day with more dancing and singing in the evening.

Friday 26th September.
>We did not have a very good night. First of all, something seemed to be trying to get into the tent through the side. M rushed out in his pyjamas, tripped up over one of the guys and shooed a lot of cows away; then tripped over the rope again on the way back to bed. Then I woke up and said there was something inside the tent; there was, a large cow busily eating my trousers. Back to sleep again but woke up to the most awful row. Willy had got loose and attacked Turveytop who also got loose. Willy then had a go at Babu's horse and was finally caught after galloping through the camp like a mad thing making eyes (etc) at a girl friend. Poor Abdel Rahman (the scyce)

A Baggara ferik.

The ferik at Shelu.

Bull saddle

A shugag. tent made of matting

Swinging the boksa of curdled milk.

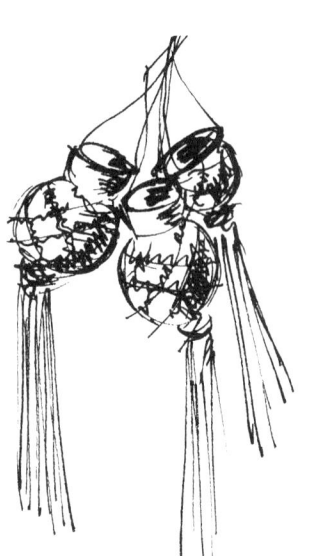

The bed with chickens underneath

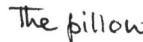

The pillow

Anne and some of the baggage train

Unloading before the storm

A senior Baggara wife on the move with her goods and chattels

Early morning tea

had gone to bed early with a headache but had to spend most of the night running after Willy, no-one else dared to try and catch him, he was that mad. Also during the night all the meat from the bulls which had been hung up on trees to dry, was eaten by dogs. Fortunately they were too busy to pay us a visit.

Off at 7, rode through the usual wooded country and then up the steep side of a jebel to find a ferik on the top. We had only ridden for 1½ hours, but having been three hours yesterday; they had added an hour to their estimate for luck. Everything was prepared for us under a very shady tree. We spent the morning gossiping, hearing complaints and explaining the political situation.

In the afternoon, Sheikh Mulah took us off to see a 'house'. Every wife (Moslems are allowed four) has a house of her own, made out of brush matting. The furniture consists of a large bed also covered with matting with a long leather pillow with two humps, one for him and one for her. The husband visits each house in rotation every night, (one in four), and there is a great outcry if the routine is broken. The small children and girls sleep in the bed with mother, but the 'teenage boys sleep outside. All the wife's pots and utensils hang from the roof in leather cases with long leather thongs hanging down from them.

A special Wedding House

In the old days, all the marriages were arranged by the family. In these days a boy usually sets his eye on a girl, but then the family takes over and all the negotiating is done by the two fathers. If the girl's father thinks that the boy is not good enough for his daughter, he may forbid the banns, or put the price too high. The Baggara do not actually trade their girls for cattle but a 'present' is often required. When the agreement is finalised, the bride's mother will let it be known that the girl expects silver bracelets for her wrists and ankles, a necklace and perhaps a taj (silver headdress).

The next step is the betrothal, which takes place before a fekki (Holy man). The boy (or his father) and the girl's father affirm the contract in public.

After the betrothal, the bride's mother will require two to four weeks to get the wedding preparations complete. She is responsible, but the boy has to pay for everything - bulls, sheep, flour, grain etc

A special house is built for the wedding outside the ferik; this is much bigger that the usual size and is divided down the middle by a curtain; the middle of the roof is left off. On the evening of the first day of the wedding celebrations, the bridegroom is put on a horse and surrounded by his friends and preceded by his female relations all singing and clapping, is led to the wedding house. He is then, saddle and all, lifted from the horse and tossed into the air three times. He is then carried into the hut and seated on an angareeb (rope bed). He spends the night with all his friends around him, but his uncles and father's old friends come in and give him good advice. While this goes on, the ferik's drums are beaten beside the house until 5 am. It is considered a bad thing for the bridegroom to have too much sleep; however, he may sleep from 5 till 7 am. Then, he is again put on his horse and led to a bed under a tree for the day.

Inside the Wedding House

The bride, in the absence of the bridegroom, is smuggled out of her mother's house and put in the bridal house. Once she is there, the roof is completed. In the evening the bridegroom is again put on his horse, led back to the house and tossed three times in the air. When he is let down all the bride's girl friends try and stop him entering and he has to force his way in. When he does, he finds his bride in the middle of the house completely covered up by a cloak. He rips off the cloak to find that she is bound up by a string of red beads. The girls all try and stop him, but when he succeeds in breaking the string of beads, he is married.

The bride and groom then sit on the bed together while the dancing and feasting start. They stay in the wedding house for two days, during which the bridegroom and his friends live on one side of the central curtain and the bride and her friends on the other. They do not see each other until the morning of the third day, when finally, they are left alone for another three days. The honeymoon now being over, the bride goes back to mother to get all her pots, pans, bed etc ready, and then after about three weeks from the wedding they set up house together without any further ceremony.

In the evening, we set off again past the veterinary camp. Once a year all the cattle not already done are inoculated against rinderpest. The District Council pays £E 2,000 a year to the Veterinary Department for this and any of the Messeria can have his cattle done. We did not actually see them in action as they were waiting for more supplies. We got to Duweika el Nuggar at about 5.30 to find the hamla had arrived first and that everything was ready.

Saturday 27th September.

M continues... I left Anne with Uncle Mulah and drove off to Abu Zabad in the lorry to inspect the ramp and bridge over the lake. The rains had done no good to it at all, got back at 2 pm. In the evening we had the usual discussions, dancing and singing. I was practising some dancing behind the tent in private, I thought quite unobserved, when there was a guffaw from behind a tree and a small girl came out. She explained that she had been away when we arrived and had now come to see what we looked like. She carefully examined us, the tent and all our belongings, and only departed after great persuasion. Mrs Mulah (no 4.) arrived with a selection of Arab dishes for Anne to try. We dug in with our right hands while she watched, but finally she was satisfied and said we could give the rest to our servants if we liked. Sheikh Mulah offered to give Anne a ring for her nose, but for some reason she did not want her nose bored, so she missed her chance.

Sunday 28th September.

Horse trek over, we left in the lorry with all our staff. We had been asked to visit a ferik 'beside the road'. This ended up with seven miles of driving through trees and uncharted bumps and dips. M spent the morning trying to explain self-government. –"How are the rains?" –" Good". –"How are the animals?" -. "Good". –"How is self- government?" –" Good." –"What is self-government?" –"We don't know, but if the Government is making it, it must be a good thing"...All they really want is to be left alone to look after their cattle and grow cotton in their own time and to be helped with water by provision of wells, donkeys and hafirs (reservoirs). 'Who shall we vote for in the elections?" is always a favourite question requiring a list of virtues. Heaven help the unwary DC who says 'Vote for X'. That is a candidate's job...

We got back today at 4.30, just in time for William Hogg's third birthday. We played Looby Loo, Ring a Ring a Roses and Hide and Seek.

10. MATTERS DOMESTIC.

Anne…

When the first Christmas catalogues plop through the letterbox in mid summer and Easter eggs and hot Cross Buns appear in January, we merely think 'Why on earth do they have to be so previous?'. I sometimes look back to our Sudan days when we did not see such things at all, except on the arrival of an exciting parcel from England. Sometimes after its journey by sea, train and lorry it arrived long after the event for which it was required. But even so, the thrill of opening the battered brown parcel and unwrapping the contents carefully packed by our dear family is something I shall never forget. I am reminded of it every year when we get our accumulation of Christmas decorations down from the loft.

There are those well travelled coloured geegaws and the folding Christmas tree made of strong wire, wood and what must have been the stuff undertakers' grass is made from (no plastic then). Little candle holders from Harrods made of fir cones, some Christmas crackers and on our first Christmas some over-dried holly and mistletoe. Not even a fir cone existed to be gilded, though now with more experience and imagination, I expect I would have made something from tebelgi fruits or loofahs, though in the great heat, Christmas preparations would still seem strange.

Although I probably had more time to read then, than at any other since, there was no library. So one of the events of the month was the arrival of the monthly volume from World Books. My mother wrote, "Would we like Punch and the Tatler?" "Yes please, if it is not too expensive to send, by sea of course". Thus we were able to enjoy seeing pictures some of our friends getting engaged or married (being at that stage in our lives); albeit a few months late. An extra was Queen, which has particularly good recipes though frequently the ingredients were not procurable.

Best of all were our letters from home. They arrived at very irregular intervals, usually by lorry, but sometimes by donkey. It was always wonderful to read the news, even though it could be a month old. No faxes then, or even a telephone.

Talking of food and stores; when I arrived, the bachelor establishment was running very smoothly under the direction of Mohamed in the kitchen and Abdel Rahman in the house. I am sure my arrival was viewed with no little apprehension and perhaps curiosity. Luckily they seemed to approve and all was well. Until I had learnt to speak some Arabic, the daily encounter with the rather imposing Mohamed was a mere enquiry as to what we might expect, (that is if I understood his kitchen English correctly). I was informed of all the groceries and meat necessary for him to buy in the suq. It did not occur to me at that stage that we did not personally require all those bottles of tomato ketchup or all those pounds of meat for soup stock. Even when it did, I realised it was cook's perks and some had hungrier families to feed than others

Those first days in El Obeid were simple. There was a large Greek merchant's shop called Abu Nigma. You want it, he got it, as regards most essentials, though at a greatly increased price after its train journey from Khartoum. It was on our return from our first leave, in the knowledge that we were moving out 140 miles to Nahud, that things became more complicated. On our way back through Khartoum a morning had to be spent in the dripping heat drinking fizzy gazoozers at the large grocers, Morhigs, while we gave our order for everything we might need in the next nine months. This needed careful calculations and later monitoring of the supplies in the storeroom so that one had not finished all the coffee in the first two months. We received a special freight allowance for these stores so they could come with us on the train to El Obeid. One year the bill came to £E 85 with 5% discount for cash.

On reading through my letters home there were requests for things we all take for granted, like khaki darning wool to mend M's socks, Thawpit and some egg cups. With no electricity, our wedding present of a smart electric iron soon became redundant, so in one letter - 'Please could you send a flat iron. M says there are lots in the Vicarage, and some beaded nets to keep the flies off the milk.'

Wherever we went an old iron cartridge box went with us, this was our medicine chest. Its contents when stocked up included bandages, cotton wool, and a large bottle of Dettol, castor oil, Zambuk, Germolene and calamine. We also had permanganate of potash in a small wooden phial complete with a sharp scalpel which unscrewed at one end. This was to score a cross in the flesh over the spot stung by a scorpion or bitten by a snake. I only had to use it once when M got stung by a scorpion, but what really cured him were the incantations of the holy man (Feki) who was with us.

The Medicine Chest.

Contents include

Dettol, T.C.P., Dressings, lint, gauze, cotton wool, elastoplast & Fermigan pad

Castor oil, liquid paraffin, ENOs, Epsom salts, Lixen - XLax

<u>In GLUCOSE TIN</u> Throat paint & lozenges (Victor-Negus) Optrex, Golden eye ointment

<u>In TOFFEE TIN</u> Burnol, Tannifax, Iodex, Germolene, Zambuck, iodine & Vick

<u>In SOAP BOX</u> Quinine, Kwells, Veganin, & phenobarbitone

Also Robinsons Groats, Glucose.

Snake scalpel with permanganate of potash, insect repellant

Thermometer, medicine glass, RED CROSS FIRST AID MANUAL

<u>In BROWN BOX</u> see over.

The Medicine Chest (cont)

Anne's Instructions with the guidance of Mary Hunter.

C.S.M. (Cerebrospinal Meningitis)

Symptoms: Sudden headache, irregular fever, stiff neck + rash possible.

Treatment: Bed in dark + quiet place — Plenty to drink — SULPHATHIAZOLE.
Dose — 6 tablets, then 2 every 4 hours. TOTAL 40 tablets.
(Crush up in Milk if unable to swallow)

Dysentery

Symptoms: Fever, diarrhoea, blood + mucous.

Treatment: Don't eat but drink plenty — SULPHUR GUANIDINE.
Dose — 6 tablets (3 gms) then 4 every (4 hours). TOTAL 40 tablets.

KAOLIN (also give for diarrhoea alone)

Dose — 2-3 heaped teaspoons in ½ glass of water as soon as diarrhoea commences — Fluids + no food for 12 hours then light diet (avoiding tough meat, veg etc) Plenty of fluids. Continue tabs for a further 2-3 days if symptoms persist.

Pneumonia

Symptoms: Fever, hot + dry, cough, pain in chest + hurts to breathe —

Treatment: SULPHUR MEZATHINE
Dose — 4 tablets then 2 tablets 4 hourly for 48 hours.
TOTAL 40.

Malaria

Symptoms: Irregular fever.

Treatment: ATEBRIN.
2 to 3 tablets 3 times a day for 2 days then 1 × 3 times a day until 30 —

In BROWN CARDBOARD BOX

- Sulphathiazole
- Sulphur Mezathine
- Sulphur Guanidine
- Kaolin
- Atebrin

A thermometer was, of course, essential. Once I took Abdel Rahman's temperature and it was 107; I thought the thermometer must have been in the sun so I took it again, but result was the same; he had malaria. For guidance, the box contained a Red Cross First Aid book. Luckily, being young and innocent I never worried about disasters and illnesses that could have befallen us out in the bush hundreds of miles from a doctor. We had complete confidence in our chest, though we were more than a little shaken when our cook, Beshir, died suddenly in Rigl el Fula through an unknown cause.

On several occasions I got struck with severe tonsillitis. As luck would have it, each time Mary Hunter, who was a doctor, was in reach and gave me penicillin, still then a relatively new drug. It was only years later that she told me how worried she had been about me on one occasion when she thought I was getting quinsy. The tonsillitis was due to the dust and sand in Nahud, a notorious dust bowl. Once on leave the family insisted that I saw Sir Victor Negus, a friend who was a well-known E and T specialist in Harley Street. I returned with instructions to gargle eight times a day with very hot salt water. I was also given special lozenges and some oil, which I had to squeeze into my tonsils with a spatula if I had a bad attack. (Having paid a modest fee to Sir Victor's secretary, he and his wife Eve, took us out to dinner and the theatre to see Dear Charles with Yvonne Arnaud)!

When we moved to Rigl el Fula; - no dust, no tonsillitis but M got very bad hay fever instead from all the grass!

I have been asked how I occupied myself as so much time was spent on trek and while M was doing his work. I spent many hours alone in a rest house, whether it was a grass hut, stone with a tin roof or simply an encampment in the open. The last was always entertaining. I sat in my deck chair, usually knitting or sewing as Michael held court nearby. I would listen to what was going on and try to understand what the witnesses were saying about the alleged murderer standing there bound with chains. Only occasionally would my curiosity get the better of me and I felt compelled to enquire "I understand what he did, but I am not sure how?".

There was always something to watch and people would gather round, intrigued at everything I did, a white woman was a rarity. During the longer stays in Muglad, Lagawa and Abyei where there was a government office, we would ride or walk to inspect wells, buildings or works before breakfast. M would then depart from 9 until 2. This could be a long five hours in great heat. Sometimes the only social event was the daily session with the cook discussing the possibility of duck for supper, if we had shot any, or how many guineafowl were left, or was it time to have another sheep (one of our many presents). We rarely bought meat on trek.

Sometimes I would go for a walk before it got too hot and chatter to the market sellers if there were any, though their different country accents were a bit much for me. Occasionally I knew a wife of a Nazir or Sheikh and would visit them. Otherwise I usually divided the morning into three.

The first part I spent writing letters, I kept up a large correspondence with family and friends. Having been taught at school to jot down lists for our weekly letter home I did the same, though instead of 'won lacrosse match, school concert, more chocolate spread please', the list might read 'the lorry got stuck four times, tribal dancing, presented with a leopard skin'. Rather than keeping a diary I sent my family a complete account of our activities, all now filed in date order by my meticulous father; hence the first hand information for this book.

The next part of the morning was dressmaking time. Abdel Rahman would have been in with a fresh limoon and would have been round flapping at any flies that had dared squeeze through the mosquito wire. I would usually be sitting in the 'Meat safe' area of the rest house. Dress making materials and patterns came from England. Although the markets were stacked high with materials, they were seldom of the type and quality I liked. I preferred the then fashionable Horrocks cotton (6 shillings –30p- a yard in London). Flimsy muslin for tobs and shiny satin and garish patterns were more to Sudanese tastes. I always had something on the go which was really time absorbing but frustrating at times when I needed a machine and someone to fit me but AR would help.

My dear great aunts had given me Aunt Ethel's Frister Rossman sewing machine for a wedding present. They had it converted from a treadle with a little motor on the side. It was crated up and joined our other wedding presents on their voyage in the Dunnottar Castle. In El Obeid where there were no curtains (bachelors don't have them), it came into its own. In anticipation of this, Harrods had been asked to send a hundred yard roll of pretty glazed chintz with our linen and dinner service. These went direct to the ship under the export system so we did not have to pay purchase tax. The electric motor had short use, as from then on, we had no electricity. I attached its original handle and when I had a lot of machining, our seconda boy enjoyed turning it.

For the last part of the morning when the heat of the day was at its height, nearly always over 100 degrees under a tin roof and not even a fan, I would revel in reading until I heard the familiar footsteps of M returning.

Lunch followed immediately and I would hear of the morning's work, then it was siesta time and hours sleep or read until it was cooler. Up and out, either on foot or horseback to look at cultivations, show the flag, or perhaps a tea party.

Luckily, it was considered polite to crumble up cakes one could not eat, often they were far too scented for our tastes. I am not sure that I felt the same when sometimes we had a tea party and I had joined the cook to make some special sponges and our guests treated them in the same way.

We were of course very lucky in having a retinue of servants. These were headed by the Safragi, Abdel Rahman (AR). He remained with us for the whole of my time in the Sudan and was a very faithful friend. Mohamed was a very good cook with great charm, though he had rather expensive ideas. Once we got to Nahud, he and AR fell out, we never really discovered the whole story but there was no doubt that Mohamed went very peculiar in the full moon. Unfortunately we had to part with him and Beshir took over. He was quiet and efficient and we were extremely sad when he suddenly died. The 'secondas' work with the safragis in cleaning, polishing and waiting. It was difficult to find one who came up to AR's high standards so we had a succession until Ahmed joined us. The horses and livestock were looked after by Abdel Rahman the scyce; he stayed with us the whole time M was in the Sudan. It may seem grand having so many servants, but life would have been impossible without them; there was no way that the job and the chores could be done at the same time.

Darkness fell suddenly and early, so back for a refreshing bath, change and supper. 'What! Changing for dinner in the desert?' some of our friends have asked. Well yes, always. Just think how you would feel after a long day in the shimmering heat on horseback, in a lorry, in a stuffy office under a tin roof, or in the house or rest house. Air conditioning was unheard of; in any case the nearest electricity was in El Obeid, two or three hundred miles away and more. When the day was over and the cool night arrived, one could not contemplate sitting down to a drink or supper in the sweaty clothes one had worn all day. One just longed for the luxury of a bath, even a canvas one three feet square and six inches deep, and the feel of something clean.

When we were engaged, my mother asked her friend, Mary Longe whose husband was a Sudan Governor, what I should have in my trousseau. The list included a number of long evening dresses. Obviously these were not suitable on trek but I had two pretty sea island housecoats, which with my long mosquito boots were a good protection from the bugs when sitting outside.

We had to put up with tremendous heat and long jolting journeys in a Commer lorry with the floor so unbearably hot, that I had to put my feet up on the dashboard or out of the window. Sometimes there was very limited water to wash in, only a jug of muddy brown liquid from the only source of water, such as a rapidly drying up puddle. Then there were the flies, myriads of mosquitoes and poisonous snakes hiding behind the 'bucket' or rustling out of the grass screen round the deep hole of the loo.

Wherever we went, we always took two 10 gallon tanks of drinking water with us. We also had emergency rations of some tins of food. We never knew when the lorry would break down and strand us miles from anywhere.

We were lucky in our weather, although it was very hot; it was dry heat unlike the sticky humid heat in Khartoum and Port Sudan. It was also unusual for us to experience the severe dust storms known as haboobs, even so, they sometimes happened. I wrote once from Muglad:-

"It was stinking hot two days ago 109 degrees in the shade and very close. Just as we began a tea party, it became dark, there was a great roaring and rushing of wind as a haboob arrived. Blinded with sand and dust and nearly blown away, we rushed inside, where we felt that the roof would take flight at any minute. After a few minutes there was a blinding flash of lightening and deafening crash of thunder and down came a torrential downpour, the like of which one never sees in England. All this rather disturbed our tea party as no one could hear themselves speak until the storm subsided. Since then, it has been deliciously cool and fresh. It was early for rain, so it was a nice surprise."

'Why?' I am asked by those who do not relish the idea of a primitive life style without modern assets, 'did I enjoy the life so much?'

I am a great lover of the out door life as our friends who join us in picnics in what some would consider adverse conditions, know. The experience of sleeping out in the open in the middle of Africa miles from any civilisation never ceased to enthral me. I will never forget the feeling of isolation and moonlight magic under the starlit sky. The security of our four poster bed of mosquito netting gave me complete confidence that the lions prowling and mewing around us would not have us for supper.

The everlasting lookout for game made every journey interesting. It was exciting to come upon an ostrich or warthog and follow it along the track, or catch a glimpse of many types of antelope, or see a magnificent kudu standing on guard. Occasionally one got a glimpse of a lion or a civet cat with their eyes glinting in the headlights. Once a cheetah kept pace with the lorry for about five minutes before she went off into the bush. Best of all, was to drive along with giraffes cantering effortlessly along beside us.

I did not mind the huge monitors and lizards, which used to visit us in rest houses. I liked to watch the bats flitting around, although when a thick black crowd flew out of the grass loo one evening, I was a little put off. Some of the old grass rest houses became completely alive at night with creepy crawlies and we lay listening to a creaking concert of tiny movements. We were glad of our canopy of mosquito netting to catch what dropped down from above. On one occasion our canopy could not protect us when we encountered a plague of earwigs which got into our socks, shoes, inside our shirts, even into our sponges, in fact everywhere.

Little animals we did not mind were the mice who lived in the rest house in Lagowa. This was built of mud with a central dining hut and four thatched sleeping huts round it. At one time the roof had been raised, leaving a mud shelf all the way round the hut. During the night this provided a highway for the mice who quite enjoyed curling their whiskers as they looked down on us and wondered what on earth we were.

The resident mouse who looks down on us from his ledge above –

I love wild flowers. These were scarce in the dry sandy soil, so it was a high light to come across a cactus, or even better a poison tree. These had strange grey trunks out of which grew a profusion of brilliant pink flowers. It was also a joy, after miles of barren scrub to come across a wadi with large leafy green trees after miles of barren scrub.

I will always remember the thrill of the first drops of rain, the delicious smell from the damp ground which followed, and the miracle of the dry bare earth becoming green as one looked at it. Then too, carpets of tiny brightly coloured flowers would appear and everything was transformed.

The happiest memories we have are of the people we met, all so friendly, hospitable and generous. Although I came to know the sheikhs and notables very well; I also had the great advantage that I was able to talk to the women and get to know them, something which for a man was impossible. In return they were very curious about me and wanted to know all about our home background and customs. In many cases they became great friends.

A Poison Tree

THE TTO

(Drawn by M)

An essential member of the staff was one's marrasala (messenger). These boys had left school at 14 and were in complete charge of the TTO (Tibbs Travelling Office). The marrasala collected this rather battered brief case at 8am every morning and he remained in attendance all day. He controlled the flow of visitors, ran messages and sometimes translated my Arabic into Arabic of baggari that the petitioner could understand. When going on trek it was useful to take records about the places we were going to and the people one might meet. Any letters were written in a copybook so that I had a carbon copy.

I am very grateful to Shaigi, Mahmoud, Awad, Hassan and finally Ahmed Matta. All were excellent and guided me through some potential administrative disasters.

AND A QUESTION OF STICKS

At large District Offices, such as Nahud, there was a Police post with a guard, which turned out when the D.C. arrived in the morning. I was always amused at the different kinds of batons, aids or sticks carried by different DCs. The military men like Ralph Daly, who was a Guardsman, had leather covered swagger sticks, some DCs carried walking sticks, while at the other end of the scale the more basic ones like Donald Rae swished a flywhisk. I did wonder about my naval telescope, but thought this would take things too far. In the end I went around with a bamboo staff with a head like a giraffe with which someone had presented me, it was also useful to measure things. In practice, as an adjunct to military-like occasions, it did not matter very much. In Rigl el Fula there was no guard to turn out anyway.

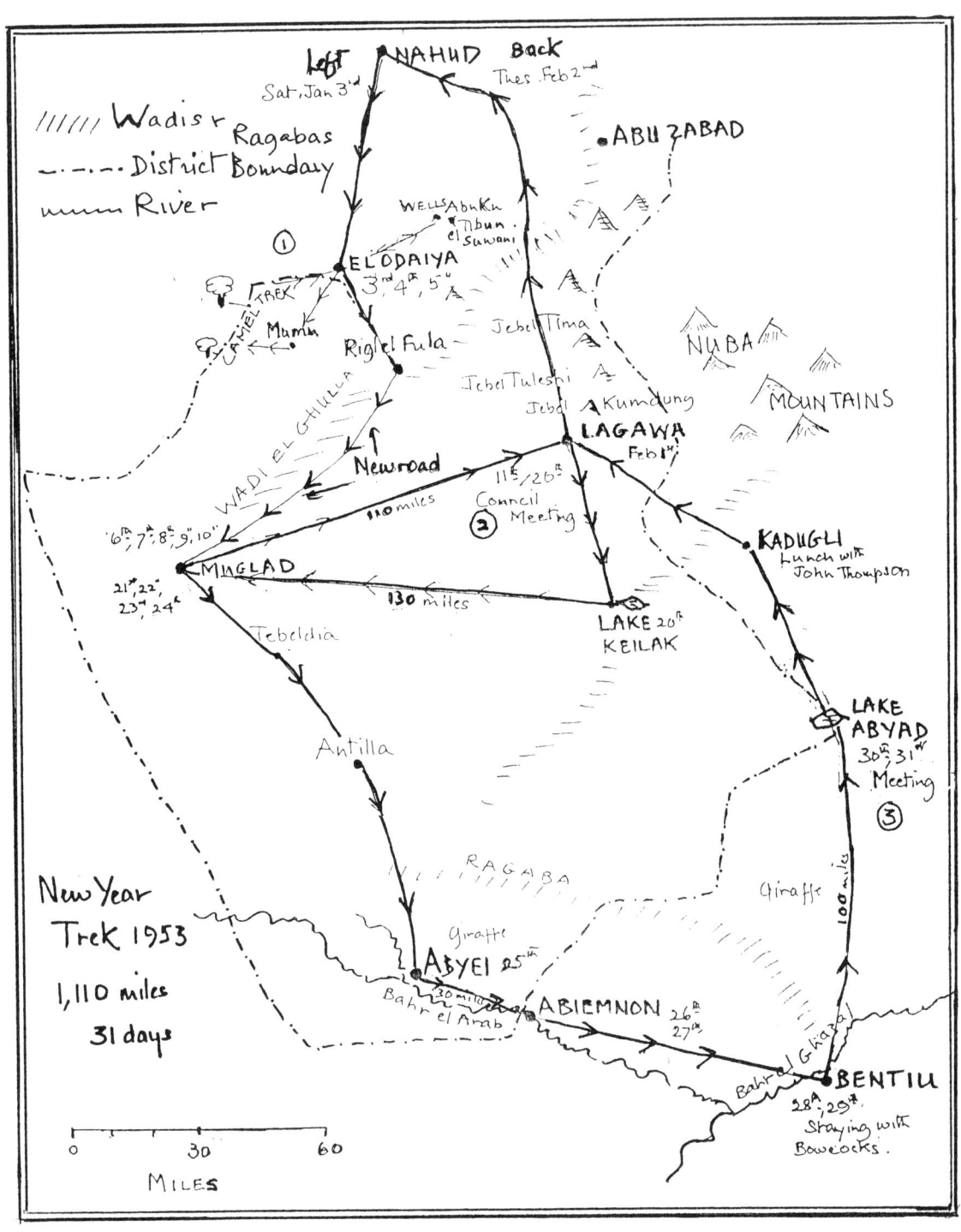

New Year Trek. In distance this was like driving over rough Tracks in a hot lorry, from London to Inverness and back

It included ① Camel trek to settle boundary dispute.
② Council Meeting in Lagawa
③ Inter Provincial Meeting at Abyad.

11. NEW YEAR TREK.

The beginning of January 1953 saw us off on our travels again.

Saturday, 3rd January.

We drove sixty miles south to El Odaiya for another animal trek, but this time for a different experience, on camels. There is a dispute between the Hamar and the Humr about a boundary between them. It is important because of the ownership of the gum trees. After lunch we drove about 14 miles to a tree which marks part of the boundary between the Hamr and the Humr, about a dozen Omdas and Sheikhs came with us. The question was, where is other end of the boundary line? Everyone talked at once and no one agreed. However, it was decided that we would try and ride along it to determine the matter. Back at the rest house, the discussion continued over tea.

Sunday, 4th January.

Had an early breakfast then drove along the Abu Zabad road to Abu Ku'. There was rhubarb going on as they do not have any decent wells and want more. The geologists say there is no point in digging them as they know there is no water there. The people say that may be true, but when a decent well has been dug and it is proved that there is no water there, then they will believe it, but not before. As we came into the village we stopped to look down a well they were building themselves, they had got as far as they could, no sign of water so they had come out to pray for water to fill it. In the meantime, we are digging two wells five miles away at Tibun el Suwani where there is water. However, we shall have to see what happens at the next Council meeting when the Omda asks for more money.

There are more complications than meet the eye, because the Omda of Abu Ku' is Sheikh Hammad Mohamed Humeida who also runs the market. If the wells were dug at Tibun el Suwani, and water was plentiful, there would be an irresistible case for the market to move too, but into the homeland of Sheikh Mulah who is the Court President!

We sat on the verandah of a grass shop while this discussion went on, making our way through orange, coffee, tea, biscuits and sweets until we felt somewhat over full and a bit sickly. Then we drove the five miles to Suwani accompanied by Sheikh Hammad, Sheikh Mulah and all the parties. We churned through dull dry scrub, then suddenly there was a great hollow with enormous great trees, wells and cattle watering. A grass house (and a loo) had been built for us on the assumption we were going to stay the night. There were lots of cattle and people using the existing wells, these are not properly lined.

The new wells are being built on steel yokes (a round circle). The lining of stone and cement is built on top to a height of about four feet, then the yoke is let down by digging underneath. This is repeated until it all gradually sinks down to the water table. The work is going well.

There was one group of six camels with two babies round a wooden trough being filled up by the owner from a water skin which he let down. Three of the camels took it easy and lay down to enjoy their drink, all their noses went in at once when the water was brought.

While I was looking at well construcion, Anne was taking it easy sitting on the bough of a tree with Sheikh Mulah. He was worried that we have been married for over a year but as yet, there is no sign of a baby on the way. He had noticed that her eyelashes were curling. This greatly encouraged him, he said was a sure sign!

We had a picnic lunch (a sort of doughnut filled with mince, nothing like the pasty Anne had ordered from Beshir!), then a rest. After this yet another long discussion about water supply, wells and the forthcoming elections which had been delayed so that they could be supervised by an international commission.

Anne & 'Uncle' Mullah at Tibun el Suwani

Monday, 5th January.

We got up at 5.30 and went off in the lorry soon after 6 to Mumu 20 miles away, where we collected various Omdas and Sheikhs. Under the directions of a guide, we turned off the road and plunged into the undergrowth through which we bumped and wound our way round trees and brushed over bushes for about six miles. Eventually we came across the rest of the party with the camels in the middle of nowhere beside a humeid tree. We had breakfast and then our lorry with the servants returned to El Odaiya.

The object of the exercise was to decide the boundary between the Felleita and the Hamr from here to Um Selieb, another tree about 12 miles away. This was gum tree country and so of course tapping them was an import source of revenue.

Anne recorded the trek in a letter.

We mounted our camels. We were provided with the best and most superior ones, they had handsome saddles, trappings and a huge white sheepskin rug each for us to sit on.

"Which direction do we start off in?"

The Messeria point northwest; the Hamr point due east. Eventually we split the difference and M led off on his camel steering NNE by N. I followed, closely escorted by a mounted policeman who luckily did his job very well, or I might still be suspended in a prickly tree. Every time I was absent mindedly sailing into the branches of a tree, the camel forgetting that I was sitting on top of him several feet higher than his head, there would be terrific clucking noises and a camel's nose would appear rapidly alongside and head me off in the opposite direction. Camels are most amusing creatures and like their owners, the Arabs, specialise in indigestible noises. I never knew if the gurglings and gurkings were from the camel or the policeman. We rode along following Mike's compass just straight through the bush or whatever you like to call it, mostly smallish trees and bushes, dry grass with big trees every now and again. All getting pretty dry at this time of the year, except for the evergreens.

When we started at 9.00. there was quite a nippy wind and we wore sweaters for an hour. It got quite hot towards mid day although there was still a breeze. We both got nice and sunburnt, though having put masses of calamine on beforehand , we did not get sore.

There were sixteen camels in the party, two donkeys and two runners who rushed along with axes blazing the trees as we went. Every now and then we stopped and everyone argued as to whether we were going in the

Camel Trek
Defining the boundary between two trees.

right direction or not. They all waved in different directions so Mike steered a middle course and hoped for the best. We came across one Arab with his house and cultivation, but otherwise, not a soul. We thought it would only take two hours but it was over four by the time we arrived eventually at our destination, The Tree. Here we found our lorry and lunch awaiting us. A very welcome sight as we were beginning to wonder how we would ever find one tree in the middle of nowhere. We arrived with a flourish at a springing trot, very comfortable. We had lunch, then M went over and wrote down on paper what had been done, with all the Nazirs and sheikhs. Strange to say, they all agreed for once. This was a terrific relief, M was so afraid that we might have to do it all over again!

We then came back to the rest house, had a cold sponge, cool drink and lay on our beds reading our post which had been left by the Hunters as they passed through.

Michael continues.

In a letter home written the next day, I said how relieved I was that Anne had survived the camel ride, but I might just as well have tried to leave my foot behind. Riding a camel is quite different to a horse, there is no bit, and you just guide him by a rope on a head collar. A camel moves its right legs together and then its left ones, so there is a continuous rolling motion. Anne took to it at once. She is also so good with the old men and talks away to them all; it is very good for them to see how we do everything together, they never do, their wives are kept well out of the way. They also like asking her when I am going to marry some more wives as they like seeing her indignation!

Tuesday, 6th January.

.....being the day after the camel ride. We left El Odaiya and drove the 25 miles to Rigl el Fula where we walked round to see how the building was going on; had lunch and off again to Muglad. The Council's road team had just opened up a new track down the Wadi el Ghulla and we used it for the first time. A lovely drive, green trees most of the way and at times we were going down leafy tunnels; some of the trees were like mimosa, covered in little yellow balls which scented the air. At times we would actually cross the Khor, on each side there would be enormous trees swinging with monkeys. Everywhere there had been water, the ground was covered with empty snail shells. We stopped for tea and to save boiling a kettle used the picnic hamper Anne's parents had sent us for Christmas, really most useful, Anne says that the Hunters are very envious of it! There was a thick undergrowth with every sort of bird flying around. We would have loved to have stayed the night watching for animals as we know there are a lot of lions around, but sadly had to press on. Every now and then there were pools surrounded by huge shadowy trees, cattle drinking underneath, women were filling their water pots and a little foal having a good paddle beside its mama. We went through a great herd of camels, unusual, but at this time of the year they wander south for grazing and for the mothers to give birth. There were four baby camels, just born, one white fluffy haired one, very sweet with a sophisticated and old/wise expression.

Arrived in Muglad to find the Hunters in the rest house. We settled into the other room and shared the meat safe in the middle. We had five days in Muglad, John tried cases while I did Council business and looked through the various police, prison and Native Court registers.

Amongst my Court duties, I had to hear appeals from the Nazir's courts. One of the more interesting was the following:-

A man married a wife who became pregnant, this was certain because she had a bulge in the right place. However, no baby appeared although the bulge remained. The husband lost patience with his wife for failing to produce the baby and divorced her. She then married a second husband. After being married for twelve months, she did have a baby and the bulge disappeared. Husband No 1. then claimed the baby, on the grounds that he had put it there two years before. Husband No 2. was adamant that the baby was his. Babu had found for the defendant. Fortunately, I was able to call Anne as an expert witness, and confirmed the judgement!

While the men worked, the girls chatted their heads off and caught up with darning and dressmaking. On one evening we went duck shooting with Foster, a young vet who turned up, he had supper with us in the evening. Another evening we went for a walk on our own as the Hunters went to call on the Medical Assistant. Friday is supposed to be our day off, but on trek it hardly makes any difference, however we did all take our tea to a fula (pond) about five miles away, lots of water and all covered in a mass of white water lilies.

The great event of the stay occurred on Saturday when we were bidden to tea with Babu. This took its usual form, but afterwards Anne and Mary were informed that Babu's wife would like to see them.

Anne wrote.

Babu led us into the house, first through a room empty of furniture, all the chairs being outside for the tea party, but the walls were covered with ancestral portraits in heavy gold frames. In the next room was Mrs Babu seated on a huge gilded bed in the middle of the room. She rose to greet us. Babu introduced us in Arabic and explained that his wife could only speak about twenty words of English. We soon discovered she was quite fluent, the only Sudanese lady I have met who could speak any English at all. We sat on chairs while she reclined on the bed, attractive and quite beautiful. She had yards of diaphanous pale blue organza floating about her and under her tob we caught a glimpse of a flowered silk dress. Her hair was swept back and then the usual hundreds of little plaits began and hung all round her shoulders. Two huge engraved gold discs dangled from her ears and round her neck was a deep collar of pearls and diamonds.

Babu's magnificent bed.

The bed was most spectacular, more at home in an oriental palace rather than Muglad! All heavy gilt with enormous ornamental ends. Behind the pillows in the bed head was a mirror and above that a red velvet lined recess, in which, protected by a glass door, were pictures of Him and Her. The bed was covered with a spotless white damask bedspread and a rug folded at the foot. Mary and I admired the golden construction, but she dismissed it as 'old fashioned'.

I asked if we could see Louet, her son of five months, so we were led out through another little room in which was a sunken bath a brocade bath wrap lying beside it, across the garden to the 'nursery'. This was a large round mud walled room with a grass roof lined inside with a striped awning. All round the room were iron bedsteads and on one of these was Louet. A huge dark head covered in curls and two dark feet were all that was visible of him in his dress, white with embroidery, v. sweet and most English! A nanny was asleep on the end of his bed, but they both woke up and Luoet was bounced up and down. The other children were then brought in and introduced one by one; all rather tubby with large heads and black curly hair, just like Papa to look at. They have been married for nine years and have four sons (one of whom is Asim, now a Member of the Royal College of Physicians) and one daughter.

Babu also has the children of his other marriages; he had to divorce his four wives before Sayed Abdel Rahman would allow him to marry his grand daughter.

Monday, 12th January. Anne's letter from Lagawa.

Left Muglad yesterday morning early and stopped for breakfast by a beautiful fula covered in yellow water lilies, a birds' paradise included some lovely cranes. Mike shot some duck to help the larder. We stopped again for lunch and a sleep and eventually arrived here at about 4.30 (110 miles). Geoffrey McComas is arriving on Wednesday for the Council meeting. We will probably be here for a week

We are staying in the D.C.'s rest house which has a central grass roofed room where I'm sitting now, then there are four separate other rooms for sleeping.

Lagawa,
Friday. 16th January.

On Monday evening we walked down to the suq and called on Mekki Amin, the dear old merchant who has a shop and gave me a leopard skin. We drank orangeade and then got up to leave but that was not allowed until the coffee being made in his house some way away had arrived and we had drunk it; so we stayed twice as long as we meant to. We then went over to see Nicola, the Cypriot merchant and drank fizzy 'banana', so called, but it certainly did not taste like it!

Tuesday.

M deep in the budget all day in preparation for the Council meeting. In the morning he held the finance committee here in the rest house and in the evening he went on doing it by himself and would not even stop to go for a walk and have tea with me!. Just before supper Sheikh Hammad turned up so he had to stop and be polite for an hour or so..

The canvas of my camp bed went and so Mekki is seeing to it being redone in skin. We did not think it would be possible for it to be done in a day, so we wondered what Mekki would do, knowing that he would not hear of Sata Sit being bedless for even one night. Sure enough after tea we saw a peculiar procession coming up the road, which turned out to be a large white enamelled iron bed borne aloft by two prisoners! So, I have a beautifully sprung bed for the next few nights.

Wednesday.

M again had the Finance Committee in the morning. I took my red and white check dress down to the suq to be machined at Mekki's shop. Nearly all the shops have a large treadle machine outside where the tailors run things up all the time. Before I had even time to explain what I wanted done, it was seized out of my hands and BRRRRRRR.......RR went the machine and a seam was done! It of course caused great interest to all the passers by and soon quite a crowd had gathered to watch Sata Sit's dress in progress. The tailor himself was most impressed by all the darts etc giving it shape in the bodice and said how narrow it was. As you know, you'd hardly call my figure narrow so you can imagine how voluminous and shapeless they make dresses for Sudanese ladies, who I suppose do not wear foundation garments and so do not like their figures defined too clearly! The tailor took several mental notes and measurements with his hands and said that now he knew how to make a 'French dress'. I would like to see the result. I refused the kind offer of having a sewing machine brought to the rest house whenever I should require it; I shuddered at the thought of the commotion there would be, a lorry, twenty prisoners to unload it, the crowd of onlookers all just for a seam or two!

That evening we drove out to the fruit garden at the foot of the hills and then walked back, rather nice, there are some very pleasant walks about; Such a change from Nahud where on any path or road you take one step forward and go back two in deep sand and there aren't any nice places to go to outside the town

Thursday. Michael continues...

Geoffrey McComas arrived for breakfast, the first time that he had visited us in his new capacity as Inspector of Local Government for Kordofan. The Council meeting lasted all the morning.

At the Council Meeting in Lagawa

Nazir Izza Din Humeida of the Zurug
Always an entertainer with his wonderful expressions and gesticulations.

Mekki Amin
Leading merchant in Lagawa
Most hospitable and generous with his toffees

Sheikh Mullah
Court President Daggage
Anne's 'Uncle'.

This was an important meeting. It was the first attended by the Ngok Dinka, led by Deng Majok; there was the budget; then there was an important announcement to be made at the end.

Until now, the Ngok Dinka had been outside the Messeria Council. A lot of patient negotiations had gone on over the last two years to convince them that if they decided to come in, they would not be swamped by the Arab majority. The Arabs had to be persuaded that the Dinka should be treated as equal citizens. The budget was always quite a headache, more so this time because we had not got a council accountant. I had had to prepare the whole budget myself, although it would not operate until the end of June when the financial year started. Having got it through the Council it then had to go to the Governor and from him to the Department of Local Government in Khartoum.

We had the meeting in the school hall. All went well, we welcomed the eight new Council members from Abyie and got the budget through. The hero of the meeting was Deng Majok who insisted on raising his taxes. One Member got up and said that the members did not get enough pay, the Council was no good and the Dinka should go home where they belonged. He was quickly squashed from the chair before he said too much; but then Deng Majok got up and torpedoed him by saying that he ought to be glad to come and help his country for nothing.

At the end of the business, Geoffrey McComas made a special announcement .He read a letter from the Governor. Western Kordofan was to become two independent Districts, each with its own District Commissioner. Peter Hogg was being promoted and a new D.C would be appointed to Nahud. I would become D.C.Messeria, with a Merkaz (District Headquarters) in Rigl el Fula. John Hunter would be Resident Magistrate for both the two new Districts, continuing to live in Nahud. They were all taken by surprise and there was general delight except for an outburst from Babu who said that Abu Zabad should be in the Messeria and not Hamar District. At much about the same time a press statement was issued in Khartoum and there was an announcement on the wireless Radio Omdurman. We of course had known what to expect, as it all stemmed from a visit Geoffrey Hawkesworth had paid to Nahud in September.

As Geoffrey and I, exhausted (at least I was), walked back to lunch, we were accosted by the Member who had wanted more pay; he told us how much he had enjoyed the meeting and that the Council was great!

Anne records that

Mike returned for lunch yesterday decidedly hoarse, having been speaking on and off for six hours, 9oc to 3 oc!. It was the last day of the meeting yesterday (Friday) and today all the members return to their respective homes and we hope to have some peace. Nazir Deng Majok has 'dropped in' five times during the last two days for a 'little chat', usually at least three quarters of an hour just before a meal. The subject was first his eldest son getting a job and then his 40th wife, whom someone else says is his wife and not Deng's at all!

On Thursday evening we went to the schoolboys' entertainment which was remarkably good, a historical play with amusing topical acts in between each scene. Some wonderful 'bull' dancing by Nuba boys from Kamdung dressed in grass skirts and with horns on their heads

Friday.

Mike at the Council meeting again from 9am until 3pm

In the afternoon we went to a very nice tea party at the headmaster's, my special friend, a dear old gentleman. It was rather like a school treat, we all sat up at a long table, fourteen of us altogether, me at one end and the host at the other. We had the usual tea, orangeade. then tea to drink and cake, biscuits and toffees to eat. Then the host disappeared and came back with some delicious Mars bars, straight out of his parafin 'fridge so they were all cold. The first I've ever seen out here, he had bought them in Khartoum. He then disappeared again and brought some guavas and then a whole bowl of oranges. I rather wondered how to eat mine in an elegant fashion without a knife or spoon but I need not have worried as there was soon a most inelegant sucking noise all round as everyone tackled their orange very heartily, covering themselves and their surrounding with juice and just throwing the skins over their shoulder. I was lent someone's dagger to cut mine and so did eat it in a slightly more dignified manner, though everyone else had finished by the time I had started.

We leave here on Monday and go to Keilak on our way to Muglad, then we go down to Abyei, on to Bentiu and then Abyad for the inter Province meeting on the 31st. Back to Nahud about the Feb 3rd when we hope to find the house clear of builders. (We had persuaded the PWD to make our small dining and sitting rooms into one by putting an arch in the wall). We are giving our letters to Ian Gillespie, the Chief Veterinary Inspector who is staying here too and goes to El Obeid to day. He is being packed up now, so I must stop.

Anne's next letter is dated Muglad, 22nd January 1953.
We arrived here last night and found a huge heap of mail awaiting us. Then she goes on to comment on all the home news, her mother's wisdom teeth, the new cupboard in the dressing room 'I am glad our card arrived on the right day, the red blobs are bourganvillias by the way, not roses, Nahud does not produce them!! We like your description of Mike sitting in a collapsed deck chair; that is our very smart canvas trek bath! She also comments on Christmas presents which have arrived a month late.

Then follows a discussion about when we might come on leave. We were to have gone April - June but we had been warned that as Peter Hogg was leaving Nahud I would have to hold the fort there until Peter's Sudanese relief arrived in July. The Governor General was due to visit the District fairly soon, this had to be fitted in, but was now postponed. We had hoped to be home for the Coronation but that now seemed unlikely. (In the event we did convince the Governor that there was no point in me staying to look after Nahud so we did see the Coronation procession).

Then she continues: -
We left Lagawa last Tuesday (20th January) having had nine days there, a very busy time for Mike what with the Council etc. We went to Keilak for the night, lots of water in the lake with a lovely view from the rest house of the long blue strip of water with the rocky blue mountains in the distance. Thousands of duck. We tried to increase our larder but in spite of all the millions we did not get a single one. The lake is so vast they all stayed in the middle and never came within range.

Nazir Sereir's son, Nur el Din, who is the Court President here came with us, having got back, rather muddy at 7 oc, he informed us he was expecting us to tea! So, after a quick bath and change we went out to tea, just he and his father; a pleasant change from all the crowd that were in Lagawa who all came in for 'cosy chats' continuously, each to complain about the other.

M...
Nur el Din was a bit of a problem. He was well educated, had been through Secondary school and spoke English. His older brother Abu Gabber Hag Agba was the Assistant Executive Officer in Muglad. Nur el Din had become his father's 'successor in waiting', but was only in his 20's while his father was still relatively young. He was very isolated and lonely on his own in Keilak, I thought he ought to go and get experience somewhere else for a time, such as the army or as an Local Government officer outside the Messeria. However on this visit Nur el Din told me he was going to stand for parliament.

We left Keilak yesterday morning and drove here 130 miles, stopping for lunch and a snooze en route and tea at that lovely place Kundukr with its enormous tebelgi tree full of monkeys.

Anne, Muglad, Friday 23rd January.
I have persuaded Mike not to go to the office today being Friday, as it is time he had a day off. Even so, Ahmed Abu Gasim (the Executive Officer) has been talking for the last two hours about various things. This afternoon we are going to take our tea out for a picnic by ourselves so we won't be disturbed,.

Our new cook Beshir, has settled down well with the others. He is very willing but his puddings drive me to despair sometimes! Soufflés, which have gone flop and rice pudding which is solid. We have been very spoilt by Mohamed and we realise what a good cook he was. Still, I must persevere with Beshir until he is a good cook too, I don't mind teaching him things. He is very economical which is a good thing, Mohamed was very extravagant at times.

Abyei, Tuesday, 27th January.
On Friday evening we went off in the lorry for a picnic by ourselves. We intended to go to one of the lakes near Muglad, but having wandered round and round among the trees and without finding it. We just sat down under a nice tree instead. Just as good really but no water to look at.
On Saturday Mike went to the office as usual and did not return for lunch till nearly 3 oc. He can never get away in Muglad, dozens of people always turn up at the last moment. We went for a brisk walk in the evening.

On Sunday (25th January) we left before breakfast and had a very pleasant drive down here taking our time en route. We stopped for breakfast at Tebeldia and found the rest house caretaker had 'gone for a holiday' leaving his young son in charge so at least he did not have any complaints this time!. We looked at the garden and picked a bunch of bananas, not ripe yet, but they should be so in a week if we keep them in the dark.

Having thought summer had come as it had got so hot, it suddenly became very cold, driving along before breakfast the wind was very nippy indeed. We even kept the windows shut most of the way but the servants on the back in their sweaters and overcoats looked very chilly poor things. Sulum, the policeman who came on horse trek, was travelling with us. Being on leave he wasn't in uniform. Mike said he looked like an Oxford rowing coach, with a striped scarf yards long round his neck, overcoat and long thick trousers, completed by white rimmed sunglasses!

We passed a large ferik on the move; dozens of bulls all loaded up and horses, donkeys, dogs and herds of cattle, scattered along the road for miles. We were lucky in seeing the principal lady and her entourage. We stopped and took photographs as it was an impressive sight. The grand lady was perched upon her bull with a sweet puppy in her lap. All the pots and pans in their leatherwork trimmings, tassels of leather thongs hung down like curtains on either side. The bull's head was decorated with leather thongs so that he could hardly see his way, also bells and ornaments dangling here and there. Behind her came another lady, her bull adorned, but more moderately as the second wife. Escorting them was a mounted outrider with a long spear over his shoulder.

We stopped for lunch at Antilla, a place with a lot of huge trees. By the time we had a snooze we spent about two and a half hours there. Ahmed abu Gasim was travelling with us in his lorry so he came and had coffee before lunch and chatted. He is an absolute poppet and has been in the government service for years.

We passed Foster's camp beside the road, he is Pastoral Research, so we stopped to see how he was getting on. He is finding places where reservoirs can be made for cattle. We had tea with him and arrived here about 7.

We stopped lots of times on the road for guinea fowl, there were just dozens of them. We also tried to stalk what we hoped was another kudu, it had small horns but we think it must have been a hartebeest. This is another kind of antelope the size of a small horse of which there are lots. The kudu is rare, the female one does not have horns while the male has tall twisting ones like on the Province badge. Anyway, it was great fun trying to get near, especially as she had a wee baby trotting by her side. Too adorable it was. We watched them for about ten minutes but every time we moved a little they moved too keeping about 75 yds between us. The baby did not appear at all worried and gambolled around in circles by itself, trotting back to ma every now and then.

We also saw six gazelle springing away in their graceful way when they saw the lorry. We then followed an ostrich down the road for over 100 yds. It was quite the funniest sight imaginable. We wanted to get close and take its photograph and thought we would have a better chance of doing so from the lorry, but the faster we went, the faster it went zigzagging along the road at about 40 mph wondering where to turn off. She took the most enormous strides, and her body wobbled from side to side. A very funny sight, exactly like one of those enormously fat women in vulgar postcards clad in a black bathing suit and running off into the sea having burnt the backs of her pink legs!

Yesterday, Monday, Mike went in to the office. I went with him and then walked back to the rest house, about two miles. Everyone was quite amazed at Sata Sit wanting to walk all that way and thought I would collapse with fatigue as the result. They can't imagine that I should ever want to take any exercise, and there being no tennis or anything, walking is the only means of doing it. As much as I would have liked to I refrained from running in sight of anyone as that really would make the rumour go round that Sata Sit was mad. It was very pleasant walking and I did the same again this morning, one feels most energetic. I do wish I could speak Dinka as then I would drop in on one of the houses I pass and have a chat. At the moment I can only say "Chubak" and hold out my hand with the fingers spread out in their form of greeting. If I continue in Arabic, occasionally they can understand a few words and reply. Most of them think it is a huge joke and guffaw with laughter (not meaning to be impolite) and gabble Dinka at me!!

I did have a long conversation with a Dinka lady this morning, though neither of us understood very much, she was not wearing any clothes to speak of and was carrying a huge hamper of grain on her head and puffing away at a large pipe.

The country just outside Abyei is very flat. In the rains it is mostly swamp, now it is short grass and rather dry. The expanse of plain is broken by trees here and there, singly or in clumps. The Dinka dwellings, which are scattered around about a quarter of a mile apart, look like thatched farms on the downs in England, that is, in the distance. Close to you see that they are a group of grey thatched round mud buildings, a large centre one and four or five little ones which are grain stores on legs.

Beside the road from the rest house to Abyei itself, winds a branch of the river which is edged by craggy old trees. The river here is almost dry but there is still a lot of water amongst the grass growing in it where masses of birds of all descriptions paddle and wade about. these include lovely golden crested cranes, huge black and white birds with golden crests on their heads.

Last night Mike had to go on with his case in court so I asked Ian Cunninson, the anthropologist who is working here, to come and see the river where there is deep water and a ferry, about eight miles away. He had not seen it before and was quite impressed. We sat in the back of the lorry while Segeir drove. We saw a lovely water buck quite close. The ghaffir of the ferry had a poisoned foot so we brought him back and took him to the dispensary and then waited for Mike outside court.

It is now 3 pm and we are just off to Bentiu, this is in Upper Nile Province and in the Nuer District, but it is the shortest way for us to get to Abyad rather than going all the way back via Muglad, Lagawa and Keilak. We are only driving 30 miles and staying the night at Abeiemnon, then going on tomorrow. We hope to see giraffe which will be fun. The lorry is ready, so am giving this to Ahmed Abu Gasim to post in Muglad.

PS. The rest house ghaffir, a Dinka, has just come with his last minute orders; an increase of pay, a pair of shoes size 9 and a flit gun.

 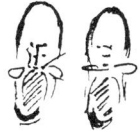 

Abiemnon. En route to Bentiu. Tuesday, 27th January.

It is so lovely here, I must write and describe it. We arrived at about 5 o'clock having driven about 40 miles from Abyei. Our great excitement on the way was seeing giraffe for the first time, about 200 yds away amongst the trees and long grass beside the road. We stood up on top of the lorry and watched as they poked their heads out along the branches of the trees and watched  us with as much curiosity as we watched them. One long neck after another appeared and then one would move over and stand beside another as though to compare notes. There must have been about twenty of them altogether. I wanted to go near to take a photograph but as the grass itself was about 10 foot high, Mike said it was impossible so I had to be content watching from the cab of the lorry. We saw one baby with its mama. When we eventually drove on again several of the nearer ones started ambling away with a slow motion gait, just like rocking horses.

We were given some tea to drink in the suq. This consists of a small circle of four or five mud shops with little thatched verandas. The top of one roof was adorned by a crocodile's jaws. There are a lot just down the river from here. There are some West Africans who catch them by shining a lamp at night and spear them when they come up, thinking the light is something good to eat. Sometimes they catch as many as 20 a night. The suq was primitive but picturesque with its inhabitants strolling around in their birthday suits, their black bodies gleaming with oil and adorned with brightly coloured rows of beads round their necks, waist and ankles. Some wear a leopard skin cut in tassels round their behinds. The policmen of course wear uniform – a silver plaque with the Province badge on their left arm.

Our bed by the river at Abiemnon

The rest house is right on the river and very grand. It has about a dozen little thatched houses in a big enclosure; a tall fence of sticks round three sides, the river (Bahr el Arab) being the fourth. In the middle are two huge spreading trees and the little houses are scattered round them. Some are round like a cottage loaf with a small thatched verandah in front.

We are sitting outside with our lamp. The moon is full and I can see a lovely stretch of silvery river with the banks full of deep dark shadows. Every now and then there is a plop as a fish leaps out of the water and makes a circle of ripples. In one direction there is a line of fires on the bank making flickering reflections in the dark water. Two long canoes are moored nearby rocking gently from side to side. Lovely and peaceful, only the sound of a drum beating in the distance and occasional voices as someone comes down to the river to fill their water pots.. Then a frog starts up croaking and is answered by the chirping of a cricket. The only unpleasant thing is the buzz of a mosquito but we are well covered with mosquito boots and long sleeved sweaters.

Lots of bats are flitting around the roofs making their high pitched squeak. So many flew out of the loo when I went towards it, I refused to go in. We are sleeping outside tucked up in our nets and are leaving tomorrow morning about 6.

Bentiu. Thursday. 29th January 1953

We left Abiemnon at 6.30 yesterday. Just before we left there was great excitement as two canoes came paddling down the river, one almost filled by a huge crocodile which had been caught by the West Africans. They brought it onto the bank and we had a close view. A

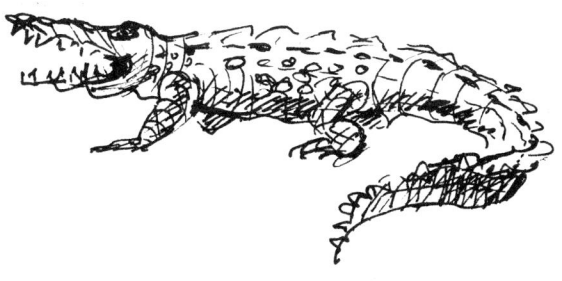

most fearsome looking beast about 12 feet long, its huge jaws tied up with a bit of rope, a good thing as it was still very much alive. The villagers were very excited as it will keep them in shermut (strips of meat dried in the sun) for a long time. I must say, however inviting the water looked I'd never venture in with a chance of meeting one of them. They lie in wait where you can't see them and suddenly 'Snap', and that's your leg off, or even the whole of you swallowed . All the rivers here are full of them. The only place one might have bathed was Lake Abyad, but would you believe it? Donald Rae (our predecessor) decided that there were far too many fish in the lake, so he carefully brought some crocs' eggs and put them in to hatch out. Now of course there are crocs there too!

We had a good drive here about 180 miles. We stopped for breakfast at another rest house on the river where there was a ferry, just a raft. We sat on it in mid stream sunbathing while the eggs were frying, lovely.

Later on, we had to cross over on one of these ferries which was rather hairy. We watched Sageir drive the lorry on but he got it crooked, the whole raft wobbled and we were afraid it would capsize. Luckily it didn't, but Mike insisted on everything being unloaded to make it less heavy before it went over. We took a photo of it in midstream being pulled over by the Nuer ferryman. It came back again for the luggage and us. We sat dabbling our toes in the water while we were waiting. How we longed to go right in. The water was as clear as anything, but there were water lilies and papyrus grass nearby which might have been the hide out for a croc. There are hippos here too.

The ferry

Lake Abyad, Saturday 31st January 1953.

We had a lovely time at Bentiu. It is a really most attractive place right on the river. We had to cross over on another ferry and were met by Philip Bowcock who is ADC here and was with Mike at MECAS in Lebanon. We stayed with them, though we actually slept in the rest house as they have not got a spare room.

Philip has just married Brenda who is three years older than he is. She is 28 and was nursing out here, a most attractive girl. I wish we could have gone to their wedding in Malakal, but we saw all the photographs. John

Longe gave her away and the reception was in their garden on the banks of the Nile. Jane Longe was a bridesmaid and looked sweet in a long white frock with a frill round the bottom Afterwards they sailed away in a steamer to themselves to honeymoon with the hippos on Lake No.

John Longe was the Governor of the Upper Nile Province which had its headquarters at Malakal. His wife, Mary was a childhood friend of Vi, Anne's mother. One of Anne's childhood treasures was a picture of Mary's camel when John was D.C. Eastern Kordofan in Um Ruwaba. The presents were on display at their wedding, except for one, but a note explained "Bridegroom to Bride: One riding camel". Little did Anne think that she would ever be in the Sudan herself!

The Bowcock's wedding was just after Christmas which seems to have been as much fun as ours in El Obeid, in fact it sounded most hilarious. At a fancy dress dance Mary Longe appeared as 'Mary, Mary quite contrary' with her watering can. John was a nurse looking perfectly priceless, with golden curls of goat's hair coming out from under his cap, black hairy arms, thick lisle stockings and large black shoes. The only things he forgot were his bosoms, otherwise he would have won the prize. He drove down to the nurses' mess to borrow the uniform, tried it on and then drove back in it through Malakal. The Bowcocks had a photograph in which John, Mary and the Deputy Governor were reclining on a sofa at the dance and looking quite ridiculous. Under it was written 'The Governor and Deputy Governor discuss the political situation'

When we arrived we had lunch with Pat Garland, the D.C. an immaculate bachelor aged 35. We were most impressed with his house, spotless white furniture and white rugs on a shining polished black floor. His Nuer servant stood behind his chair very carefully rolling the bitters round the glass before adding ice and then the gin.

The Bowcock's house is a gem, quite the most attractive we have seen, just like an English thatched cottage with a pretty garden and lots of flowers, including roses, with a lawn running down to the water's edge. They trek a lot by steamer. They have their own which we went over, most luxurious with lovely big cabins with fitted cupboards, drawers and hot and cold water. They have a whole suite including Philip's office. On the upper deck there are mosquito wired balconies for sitting and sleeping. More steps lead up to the sunroof where they can have tea in the evening. Below, or on a barge alongside, go all their servants, Philip's office staff, a cow, chickens, the servants' animals and their lorry; so they are quite complete. It must be great fun, we are going to try and go for a trip with them though what excuse we will have we can't imagine.

Having arrived on Wednesday we decided to spend Thursday there and have a nice peaceful day, which we did and enjoyed very much. The Bowcocks were rushing round in circles getting ready for going on trek on the following day. Brenda not yet being used to the procedure, was in rather a whirl as to what to take. I assured her one got used to it and then it would take no time at all; it is quite automatic with us now. We had a super relaxed evening with them, enlivened by the arrival of a motor boat full of R.C. priests from the Mission further down the river. They were Mill Hill fathers, they are allowed home leave after five years, but then spend the rest of their lives here until they are too old and have to go back to England. Once they had gone we had dinner and danced to the wind up gramophone.

Mike and I walked along the river in the moonlight hoping to see some hippos of which there are lots. Although we saw several dark shadows and heard lots of splashing it was difficult to see them clearly. They often keep the Bowcocks awake with their splashing and grunting.

Lake Abyad. Saturday 31st Januuary 1953.

We left Bentiu on Friday (30th January) morning and had a good journey here (100 miles). We had great fun seeing giraffe, at least 150 altogether, sometimes they were very close, They galloped along beside the lorry, easily keeping up with it at 40 mph. Their long legs hardly looked as though they were moving. There were some tiny little baby ones. For about twenty miles we saw more and more, sometimes amongst the

trees and sometimes on the open savannah.. Apart from some big fat baboons and other monkeys we did not see anything else.

We had lunch with Pat Garland who was already here. No-one else turned up until 6.30 when Jack Hunter, (D.C.Jebels) and Robin Crole (A.D.C) arrived from Dilling and Bill Monteith (D.C.Tegali) from Talodi. So, we were six for dinner which we provided. The Longes arrived for breakfast this morning. John, Mary and Jane a sweet little girl aged 7 also John's cousin Vera Longe. This morning the men had their meeting and the ladies chatted and had cool drinks under a tree. Our camp consists of a large grass house, one for the servants (and a convenience each) and then a central mess; all in a wood about three miles from the lake.

Lake Abyad. Sunday 1st February.

After lunch yesterday everyone went off to the lake. John, Pat and Mike tried to get some duck. Mike got a goose but that was all. Mary, Vera, Jane and I watched for a little while, then left the men to their wading. They didn't get back until dark. The lake is vast, miles of it though one can't get near to the real stretch of water as it is completely surrounded by green marsh. There were thousands of golden crested crane, it was amusing to see them dancing, they really might have been doing an eightsome reel. They did all sorts of steps with their feet and jumped up and down with their wings spread out, a lovely sight.

Jane is now keeping up a running conversation with me as I write so it may be a bit disjointed. We are getting packed up, as we are leaving after breakfast. The Longes sent you all their love and hope they will see you again before long. They leave for good in April as you know and are most grateful to you Daddy for seeing about their passage home by sea. They will be moving into their house in Suffolk, an old Rectory. They will be at the Abiemnom meeting in March, so we will see them again before they go. Mary cut my hair yesterday morning before we left. I could not bear it as it was, right on my shoulders, I was going to do it myself, or get Joanna to, but neither of us have any experience and Mary has cut the childrens' hair for years. The perm has been chopped off now so it is more or less straight though it does not look too bad really. I think I shall try Joanna's Toni for the ends. My hair seems to grow feet out here it is so hot.

New Year Trek 1953

M   A   Brenda   Philip Bentin. Staying with the Bowcocks

M   A   Mary & John Longe Pat Garland
Jane (Vera)

at the Abyad Meeting

Lagawa, Monday, 2nd February.

We drove from Abyad yesterday through the Nuba Mountains where we had lunch with Robin Young. Mike was quite ill on the way, we arrived at 5pm and went to bed early and had a good long night. He is much better this morning.

What a nice thought to see our house, syce, animals and of course the Hoggs and Hunters. Although the time has flown and we have thoroughly enjoyed the trek, it seems ages since we left. This is all such fun, we would not change for anything (unless we have to). We enjoy being out on trek and yet it is so nice to get in and see everything again, one appreciates it all so much more than if one stays put all the time. Our friends who settle down to just house keeping in England don't know what they are missing.

Nahud, Tuesday, 3rd February.

Arrived today 4 pm

We have been out for 31 days and have driven about 1.100 miles.

The house is much improved. While we have been away the P.W.D. has been in, the wall between the sitting room and dining room has been taken down and a big arch made instead. Abdel Rahman the syce has cleaned it all up himself.

The Nuba

A Kasha lady

A Kasha brave

Sultan Hami Suleiman of Kasha   Sultan Dangali Ali of Shifr

12.   THE NUBA

Most of the Nuba in Kordofan live in the Jebels (Mountain) and Tegali Districts. However we had outcrops of rock along our eastern border. So, as the Arabs had come in from the west, the Nuba had retreated into the hills and there they are, still in our District, somewhat detached from their brothers to the east. Out of an endless plain of dry scrub there rise these isolated rocky hills of huge boulders full of nooks and crannies, valleys and ravines, deep caves and craggy peaks. Gnarled old trees, cactuses and poison trees, with their brilliant pink flowers grow out of the rock. Perched precariously on the rocks or nestling snugly into the hill side are the Nubas' circular mud houses and grain stores with neatly thatched roofs; the entrances being through a round hole half way up the side.

The Nuba are African in origin and are dark skinned. The men are strong and stocky while the young girls have figures of which modern models would be glad. They adorn themselves with coloured beads and bangles, sometimes their bodies are painted with patterns, or more often intricate tattooing or cysting. These patterns are made by pricking the skin with a thorn and rubbing in ash. Hairstyles are of great variety. Many of the men have coxcombs, and spend hours grooming each other's hair. The girl's hair is woven into hundreds of tiny plaits, or sometimes just a mudpack or oiled fuzz. The girls wear rings in their noses, and in some hills, glass spikes through their chins and sometimes extend their nostrils with gold coins. Their fascination in us was as great as our interest in them. Often Anne was the first white woman they had seen.

Each inhabited hill has its own language and customs. They keep chickens, sheep, goats, cattle and pigs. (On the whole they do not share Islamic aversion to pigs; I have seen a lady suckling her baby on one breast and a piglet on the other.) During the day the animals graze on the surrounding plain below, then as dusk falls the drums beat to call them back to the hill. Deep wells amongst the boulders provide water which the ladies carry gracefully in earthenware pots on their heads. They grow their crops either on the hill or below on the plain. At harvest time the women carry the dura up in bundles to a special rock where they winnow it with a wooden batten. The grain is stored and the stalks used for fodder or thatching.

In the Jebels District next door the Nuba Chiefs are known as Meks, but ours are entitled Sultans. They are appointed by the Government, but are allowed to follow their own traditional processes of election; normally their choice is endorsed but with the proviso that if the successful candidate cannot control his people, he will be removed. We had six Nuba Sultans, who ranked with the Arab Omdas, and were subject to the authority of the Nazir of the Zurug, Iz el Din Humeida. This was quite different from the position of the Ngok Dinka at the other side of the District in Abyie. Their Chief was not subject to the Nazir Umum, Babu Nimr, he ranked as a Nazir in his own right.

KASHA AND SHIFR

Anne...

We enjoyed our visits here, especially as something unusual always seemed to happen. We were able pay a visit to Kasha during the rains in August 1952, thanks to the road which Donald Rae had made. The hill was lovelier than ever, everything green and lush, with

Jebel Kasha

the view of the other mountains, shades of purple in the blue distance. We arrived early and settled into the rest house tucked away at the top of the winding rocky track. This was not improved by three large mounds in the middle of the road. Three graves, with everything the person underneath might want, a stick, a gourd, a water jar and a flapping white rag to keep the evil spirits away. M suggested that next time they should choose a place that did not obstruct the traffic.

From Kasha we went to Shifr about five miles away, to inspect progress on a new well being built. As we came back the drums started beating to bring the animals in, sheep with tiny wee lambs, goats and cows appeared from all directions.

We came back to an amusing scene between a nude Nuba lady and AR. He had evidently asked for water to be brought for our bath and she had returned with only a small bowl. He was trying to tell her he wanted a lot of water, she was doubtful if he could drink or even wash with more than she had brought. All the other servants were chuckling in the background and AR was getting quite embarrassed.

The object of our visit was to ensure that the Sultans of both hills came to an inter District meeting to take place at Wali. As we were about to leave we had to render some first aid. Sultan Mahdi of Shifr had not wanted to come to the meeting as he was busy with a sibr (celebration) of his own. However, when the lorry arrived to fetch him, he was persuaded and got in. On the way back to Kasha two of the passengers started an argument, with the result that one hit the other on the head with an axe.

We arrived to see a large throng and pushed through to find the victim lying on the ground. We had to get our policeman to clear a space as about two hundred people were crowding in to feel his head to see if his brains were coming out. Anyway, we sent for our medicine box and I cleaned him up and bandaged his head. Later on when the lorry comes back, it will take the disinfected Kashy in to the hospital in Abu Zabad. Having dealt with the patient, I thought I should check my treatment in the First Aid book. I found I should first treat for shock. 'Look for pallor round the lips', he was jet black (pallor difficult to perceive); 'Loosen all tight clothing', but he was stark naked; 'Keep the patient warm with hot water bottles', but the temperature was over 100 in the shade!

All this delayed us and after Mike had issued dire warnings to Sultan Mumi of what would happen if the Kashas decided to go and attack the Shifrs we continued our journey. Wali was further than we thought and we did not arrive until after dark at about 7oc. It was lovely driving along as there was a full moon and the Jebels looked ghostly grey rocky shapes rising up against the stark sky.

Jack Hunter, DC Jebels, was our host at Wali. The grass rest house roof kept rustling as lizards slid about in it and showered us with old ants' nests so we slept outside, quite well until 7oc. After an early breakfast, Jack and Mike went down to the meeting.; a great assembly under some big trees a little way from the rest house. The object of the meeting was a boundary case.

The Nuba (Jack's people) said that the land up to a jebel called Abu Domu had always been theirs and that they had sibrs (or initiations) on top of it; that it was the focal point of their initiation rites, the boys had to run there crossing Khor Shalengo, up to the top and back; that their cultivations had always been where they were and that they did not know they were on the wrong side of the boundary and in any case they did not know there was a boundary in the first place. Our Nuba said they also had parties on the top of Abu Domu while the Messeria said that the boundary had been fixed for 40 years, but they did not mind the Nuba cultivating over the boundary as long as they paid 30 piastres.

Having discussed all this for an hour or two, I joined them and we all drove off in a convoy of lorries including two suq lorries with about 40 people in the back of each. The object of this was to see exactly where people said the boundary was, all different of course. After a hairy crossing of the deep gully which was Khor Shalengo, we eventually arrived at Abu Domu. Jack Hunter being a very hearty Scotsman said 'Lets go up'; something only he would suggest at 12 o'clock on a very hot day. The jebel was like a round cone made entirely of slabs of rock, on some sides just sheer smooth expanses, but on one side it was possible to climb it. The Nuba were swarming up it like ants, quite incredible, even on flat smooth almost perpendicular rock, they just seemed to stick to it as though they were walking upstairs.

Abu Domo

I kept up with Mike till we were just about half way, then I'm afraid I gave up, in spite of having been lent some gym shoes several sizes too big for me by a kind policeman as my shoes had no rubbers on them. If it had not been in the mid-day sun and very hot I might have gone on, but I decided not and very reluctantly descended with at least three-quarters of the visiting party who thought the same. As Jack Hunter had shot up to the top, Mike felt he had to too, but wondered how he was ever going to get down again. Actually he got one of the Nuba to walk in front of him and did what he did, the trick was to walk sideways, crab-like. It was at least an hour before they eventually arrived at the bottom, all decidedly hot and dripping.

By the time we got back for lunch it was 3.30. Mike and Jack could not stop drinking gallons of water for the rest of the day. I was thirsty enough without so much exercise. I might have mentioned before, that Jack has really prize legs; I don't think I have ever seen anything like their size, carved grand piano legs aren't in it. We think he must have climbed every mountain in Scotland. A.R was furious with Mike and said he should never have done such a stupid thing, Mr Hunter was tough and quite different!

The sequel to the assault at Kasha was that the assailant was tried by the local court. The President was a Nuba who was a retired officer in the Sudan Defence Force, Rizagalla effendi Zaki MBE, an upright and charming gentleman. The accused was found guilty and sentenced to one year in prison, it was also made clear to him that six months was for the assault and the other six months for causing the District Commissioner's wife so much trouble! (This part of the judgement had to be revised).

At harvest time Kasha really excelled itself. When nearly everyone else was talking about elections they had their harvest home. They drank merissa (locally brewed beer) for two days, they then threw rocks and fought amongst each other for three hours until bad light stopped play. The score was one dead, 29 injured, 110 accused and the remainder were witnesses. Of course no one knows who did it (the killing), as everyone was in their house. Some heard the noise and came out but before they could see who was there, they got hit on the head with a rock and 'felt tired", so went back in again until the police and the medical assistant arrived to take them to prison or hospital or both. Kasha is going to love independence.

TIMA

Tima is quite different to Kasha. One has to wind in and out before reaching a cul de sac in the mountains. Rocky walls go straight up round a little green valley. One has to return the same way to get out as one comes in. Usually the rest house is a little apart from the local houses, but here we felt really part of the family as the Sultan's grass houses were only a few yards away.

The heat built up during the day and even at night it was unbearably hot and stuffy so we had to sleep outside. Our mosquito nets provided some privacy from the inquisitive eyes of the Sultan's relatives who peered through cracks in

Tima Rest House
Built of rocks with a thatched roof

Sultan's Compound

Ostrich egg on roof for fertility

their grass walls. Every nearby cough, child's cry and dog's whimper echoed round the tiny valley. The Sultan, Khamis Gellab, was a good host and spent most of his time with us while we were there. He was notable for his record making noises of appreciation, his belches started in his toes and rumbled all the way up until the final explosion. There were some good wells further up the valley and he had a delightful little garden with bananas and guavas.

TULLESHI

Michael...

Tulleshi, the largest of our Nuba hills had a turbulent history.

It has 24 square miles of mountainous territory. The tribesmen were quite safe and self sufficient in the mountains which formed a natural fortress. From there they were able to carry out raids on the Messeria, rustle their cattle and had few qualms about killing any who tried to prevent them. There were 3,000 inhabitants divided into the "male" and "female" sections. The traditional Chief was one Kia Ora, he was also the Kujur (wizard), but the female half also had its own Sultan or Wakil, Tia Kafi who was also the grain priest. In 1928, the then Sultan Barkelli was deposed, and Tia Kafi was appointed as the 'Government' Sultan as well as being the 'Peoples' Sultan, he was then in his late 40's. Even so, he did not find his people easy to control.

Each half had their own distinctive tribal names. The "male" names were Kaka, Kafi, Tia, Tutu, Kakwa, Kaki, Tiso, Kame. "Female" ones were Kaka, Kito, Kia, Kiki plus the last four males ones ,Kakwa, Kaki, Tiso, Kame. Each adult also got a further name at puberty, Effendi, Onbashi, Coriat (Percy Coriat was a DC in Kordofan from 1934-42), Mohamed etc. Female names had a local origin Kanboro, Koto, Washe, Doro.

In 1926, one of the settlements, Karalanya had sheltered a murderer so the village was burnt and the Government imposed a fine of cattle and their rifles were impounded. The inhabitants were also forced down the hill, but then with a reversal of policy, let up again. In 1945 things had got so bad that the mountain was evacuated entirely. The houses on the top burnt by the army and a demonstration of firepower held as a warning. New settlements were made at the bottom of the mountain where the Tulleshis could be more easily supervised and controlled. The Male villages of Lantan, Tigafa and Karalanya on the top were descended to Shagowa, Slina and Lato, while the female village Tutu went to Lumbo and those of Law and Turdi to Ras el Fil.

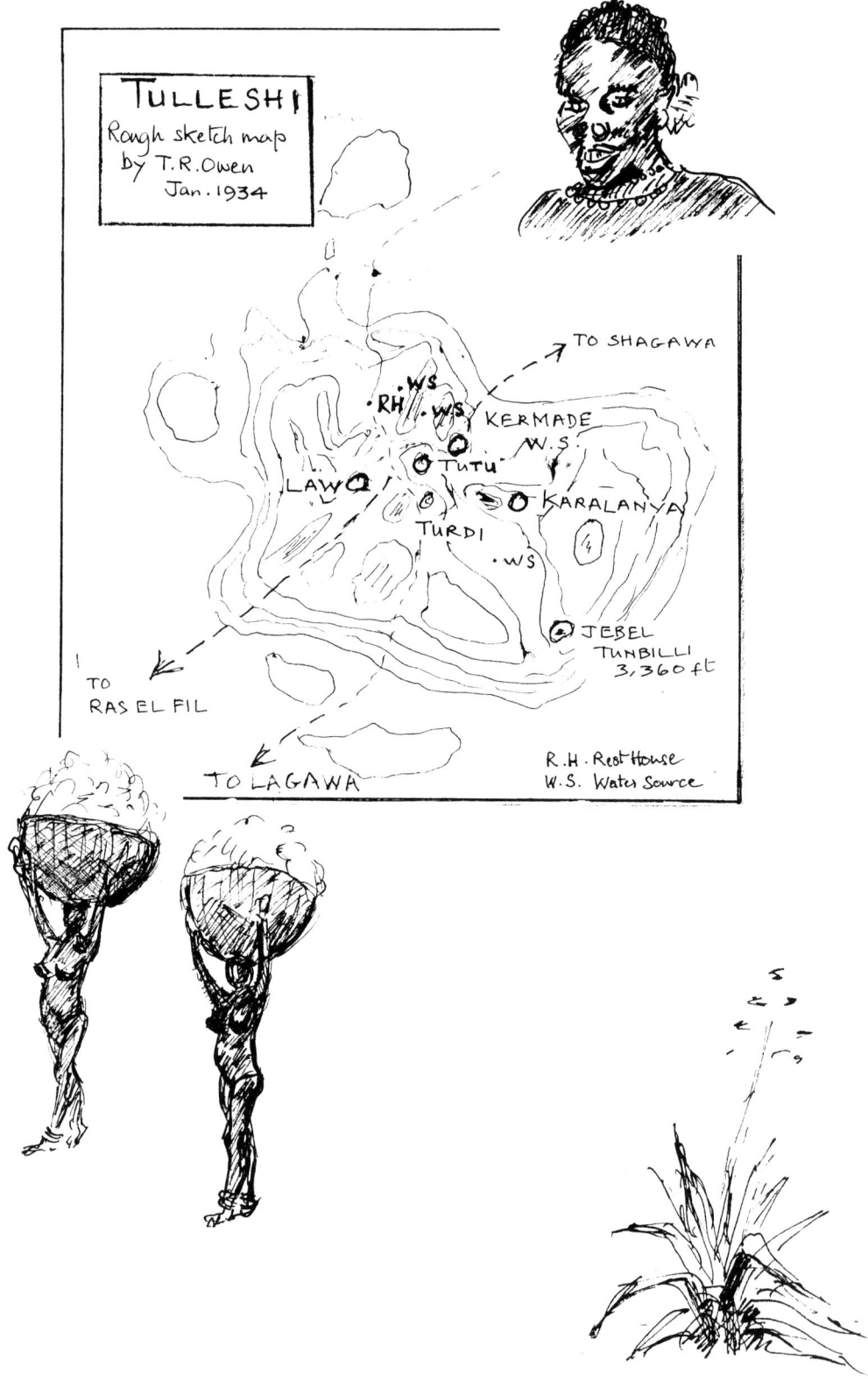

In our Merkaz files I found two interesting accounts of visits to Tulleshi by former DCs:-

J K K Morrison. Sept/40. "On breasting the brow we were confronted by a confused mass of armed and battling Tulleshi. Late comers informed us after hurried but warm greeting that the Tutu and Karalanya were fighting over the rain. We managed to separate the combatants who were still on the stick stage before the spears came into action. A number of the combatants were sent down to carry up our baggage.

"It transpired that the Tutu had cornered the rain and with their chief's approval the Karalanya had come to 'look for' the rain. The Tutu saw the Karalanya marching on the cultivations and feared that the Karalanya were going to cut down their grain and beat up any livestock as this is the best way of finding rain in someone else's cultivation.

"Later in a general meeting it was proved to everyone's' satisfaction that the Tutu had cornered the rain for the simple reason that their cultivations had had more rain than anyone else's. The Tutu were called to sacrifice a fowl with the proviso that if this did not produce rain for Karalanya in two days they would be required to sacrifice some pigs. The domestic fowl proved inadequate, but I presume enough pigs were sacrificed after our departure, as I spent the night in extreme dampness."

T R H Owen '43. "Three murderers still not given up. The retainers (tribal police) sent to arrest them returned saying that the murderers would kill anyone who tried to arrest them. They would surrender to no one except the DC. I went to house of no.1. Gone.

Then to house of no. 2. Found him sitting at the top of his alley with three spears, two fish spears a claymore and a knife across his knees. The retainers and Omda discretely retired. He allowed me to come up and disarm him. Then he asked if he could put his spears in his house. We let him. He then went in and said he would not come out. When I'd winkled him out the second time, he came quietly, but his brother rolled up and said he would kill any one who took accused off. He relented after an interval."

When we came to the District in 1952, things were quiet and the Tulleshi had found other occupations. They still had their cattle and their cultivations but they were now growing cotton, taking advantage of the ginnery in Lagawa. Tia Kafe had died in March 1950. Following the traditional pattern three king makers had been found from alternate families, the sacred ring of chieftainship, Tugan, had passed to Basha Kireisha. Probably a source of satisfaction to him. He used to attend as a member of the court at Ras el Fil until Tia Kafi told him to sit on the ground while he sat on a stool.

The Tulleshi still enjoyed their traditional dress. The men wore little but decorated themselves by fixing ivory discs to the outsides of their noses, putting feathers in their ears and adorning themselves with beads. The women wore a small skirt with a grass tail at the back, they were also fond of pushing a piece of polished glass though their bottom lip.

Kia (or Kurki) Ora and Tia Kafi, were still mentioned with awe. Although they lived on the same mountain, they had never met. It seemed that the combination of spiritual and temporal powers would have been disastrous and the whole mountain would have gone up in flames. Richard Owen described it thus:-

"When Kurki meets Tia and Tia meets Kurki
It's wahid fil mia, when Kurki meets Tia
They'll last through the ye-ar, the outlook is murky
When Kurki meets Tia and Tia meets Kurki".
(wahid fil mia - means a hundred to one)

One of the DCs described him as "a delightful little wizard and much appreciated as the High Priest". Another of his attributes was that he could only move clockwise. He only once left the hill and went to El Obeid, but he had to go via Abu Zabad and come back through Dilling (ie a clockwise journey. It must have been a bit inhibiting).

I found that there was a Nuba in the Police in Nahud, so quickly got him transferred to Rigl el Fula, where he started talking to me in English. It transpired that he was Tia Kafi's son, Mekki, he had been to school in the CMS Mission at Katcha. Mekki Amin, our merchant friend in Lagawa told me that Mekki Tia was named after him, he had helped to bring Mekki up and more or less adopted him.

Once again, we were indebted to Donald for a new rest house on the north side of Tulleshi. On one inspection we found it full of cattle droppings. We were told that it was normally occupied by a bull, he very much objected to being asked to move and they were unable to do anything about it! They had to be told very firmly that the entrance to the hosh (enclosure) must be stopped up and if it was not clean next time some firm action would be taken. In the meantime the bull was fined £1.

It was under Mekki Tia's guidance that I was able to climb to the top of Tulleshi early one morning. One of the strange things was that we were accompanied by the cattle. There was not enough water for them at the settlement near the rest house at the bottom of the hill, but there was plenty at the top. On a little sheltered plateau with a view of the Jebels stretching as far as the eye could see was Tia Kafi's round mud house and grain stores surrounded by a mud wall. He lay buried in the middle of the little compound, his grave marked with a stick and earthenware pot. Allowed to lie there in death, but not in life.

Tia Kafi's grave

KAMDANG

Anne...

Kamdang was only five miles from Lagawa, so we never actually stayed there. In August 1952, thanks to Donald's all weather road we were able to pay a visit to Lagawa during the rains. The Sultan of Kamdang's house was actually on the road, so we promised him a special visit as we returned. We left Lagawa at 9, everyone turned out to see us go, it was the first time a sit (English lady) had been in Lagawa during the rains.

An assembly was awaiting us at Kamdang. Having shaken many hands we were ushered to our seats on an angareeb draped with a gaudy embroidered bedspread under a grass roofed shelter. The best stones had been found for the elders to sit on in a big circle around us. In the background was the Sultan's house protected by a grass screen; through every nook and cranny and over the top peered the goggling eyes, full of curiosity, of his wives and relatives. Dozens of naked children also appeared from every direction. They were not so shy, in fact one rushed into the middle of the circle and yelled loudly when he was removed.

The Sultan's name was Faragalla Tobago, a delightful old boy, passionately loyal to the Hakuma (the Sudan Government) and a very good influence on his fellow Sultans. Mike discussed business, mostly with the Sultan who sat on our right but others also joined in with their views on the subject. Presently a table was carried along and placed in front of us, followed by orangeade and hot sweet tea in small glasses. There were only four of these, so when we had finished, ours were filled up and given to someone else, complete with our dregs. Slight commotion was caused in the middle when a hen was carried by, squawking loudly in protest and was given to our servants in the lorry. No sooner had she been deposited than she escaped and rushed squawking into the midst, nearly knocking over the table and finally disappearing into the tall sweetcorn growing all round with several little black bodies in pursuit.

the hen ran squawking....

ABU GENOUK

This was the most remarkable of our jebels as it was so isolated. It stood on its own about fifty miles away from the chain of hills along our eastern border. Anne described our first visit...

We arrived here at 4.30 and found the grass rest house in a very dilapidated condition. It was built on a mound at the foot of several hills which rose up behind with the most beautiful panoramic view in front. There was complete silence, not a soul or any sign of life to be seen. We had tea enjoying the peace and waited. Not for long, as very soon Sultan Ismain Ali appeared. He presented us with a sheep and joined us for tea. Gradually more inhabitants from the hidden village above appeared and as darkness fell they squatted round us in the light of the lamp while M listened to what they had to say.

We slept well outside with plenty of blankets; it had suddenly turned much cooler. At 7am wearing sweaters and accompanied by the Sultan we set off up a long winding path between two hills, the higher we went, so the view over the plain behind us grew; greeny blue turning to such a deep blue on the horizon that it might have been the sea.

We reached the top and there suddenly, down below us in a complete hollow with rocky peaks all round was the hidden village.

The Sultan led us down and invited us to drink coffee in his house, a rabbit warren of little thatched houses with grass screens between them. We were ushered into one of these little courtyards and sat on an angareeb covered with a rush mat. The Sultan disappeared into the nearest mud house which we guessed was the kitchen. Much activity went on inside sounds of chopping, grinding and stirring, smoke billowed out and a tray, teapot and glasses were taken in along with some goats, they soon scampered out, presumably having filled the milk jug.

Meanwhile all the members of the family came to meet us. Tiny babies in mothers' arms, one adorable toddler with a mass of curly hair was being held by mother while aunt went through its curls picking out any signs of life she could catch. As a contrast a very old great, great (?) grandmother toddled along. She shook us both warmly by the hand and to our amazement kissed our feet. She told us how grateful they had been to us when we, the British administration had brought them back again to their jebel after the dreadful Mahdia in 1888. Only she and one old man are still living there to remember it all. She told us that the Mahdi's army arrived at the top of their hill and killed everyone with spears, not even sparing the babies. Only she and one or two others escaped and later on the Hakuma (Sudan Government) collected them and brought them back to Abu Ganouk in 1901 and now they are all happy. (It is hardly surprising that they are not going to vote for the Umma party, they fear the same thing may happen again). Old Grandfather also came and saw us and several very mischievous little boys, sons of the Sultan. He also had a teenaged daughter who had a very pretty hairstyle; little gold coins threaded amongst hundreds of plaits, the ends of which were decorated with fluffy bits of white cotton in its raw state, like cotton wool. It really looked most effective. Eventually the Sultan emerged with some marvellous 'coffee', very sweet and milky but quite good. We chatted as we drank several glasses before saying our good byes and descending to the rest house.

TUBUK

Our lorry was all packed up ready to go on to Jebel Tubuk, one we had not visited before, thirty five miles on. It was a delightful place, we sat under an enormous tebelgi tree chatting to the Sultan and some old men who were busy making spears and choppers, a blacksmith in fact. The Sultan, a nice old boy, was smoking his home made pipe. This had an earthenware bowl, nicely patterned, on a bamboo stem, to which was attached by a bit of string, a pair of tongs. With these the Sultan picked red-hot ash from the smithy's fire and lit the peculiar looking tobacco (dung?). When his little smouldering fire burnt well he let the tongs dangle down and puffed away contentedly. We were told it would take an hour to climb up to the village and sadly we did not have time.

Sultan's pipe & tongs

ON THE WAY TO TORRAGI

One day we were in the Jebels District beyond Kadugli winding in and out of the hills to a meeting at a place called Torragi. We passed a wonderful wrestling match in progress. We stopped to watch and a way was cleared for us to the front row of the spectators. It was obviously an important event in the league table. Everyone around us was dressed up to the nines in safety pins, combs, bangles, beads, skins and sunglasses. The general appearance was a mass of well oiled dark bodies gleaming in the sun.

In the ring, two or three couples were wrestling at once. They were ghost like figures covered in grey ashes so they could get a good grip. In between each round, a troupe of seconds dressed up with grass tails and bangles came leaping into the ring carrying skin shields in one hand and waving rattle like objects in the

other. These turned out to be carefully grown gourds with spouts. They were filled with more ash dust to shake over the competitors. The wrestlers, by now black with sweat from their exertions, would once again become ghost like as they were enveloped in clouds of dust. Meanwhile they were also able to mop their faces with the grass tails of their seconds, rather like a boxer with his towel.

The next rounds then began. The umpires, who were distinguished by wearing Bombay bowlers, leapt around conducting the proceedings with spears or sticks or if they were lucky, a whistle, which they blew continuously, regardless as to whether it was to stop the round or not! When a wrestler, much to the joy of his supporters, had finally succeeded in throwing his opponent to the ground, the troupe would leap in and carry the victor off on their shoulders amidst shouts and cheers. It was great fun to watch, more so than our meeting!

13.   THE DAGU

The Dagu are reputed to be of West African origin. They claim to have been the ruling race in Darfur during the 15th Century. When the Arabs came in from the west they came east into what is now Messeria territory, then in about 1800 the Arabs followed them here. Any further migration to the east was blocked by the Nuba Mountains, so they had to retreat up some low hills to the west of Lagawa. On the whole they have adopted Arab dress but they have retained their own customs.

We now have three Dagu settlements, Dar el Kebir, Warina and Selodi. The largest is Dar el Kebir (the big place) which is an attractive valley surrounded by low rocky reddish hills. Each village is in the charge of a Sultan, who ranks as one of the Arab Omdas, however, he is monitored by the tribe's spiritual leader, the Jindi. Each have their own extended family who are responsible for electing their own leader when there is a vacancy. Traditionally Ahal el Jindi (people of the Jindi) were plebeians but were much richer than Ahal el Sultan (the people of the Sultan). The Jindi acts as a sort of brake on the Sultan and in the early days of Warina, the Sultan was actually exiled for a year by the Jindi. Things are rather complicated as we use the names of the hills in which they now live, while they sometimes call themselves by the names of the places in which they used to live either in West Africa or Darfur.

The Dagu Sultans are now under the Nazir of the Zurug, Izz el Din Humeida and they came into the District Council in 1951. They grow their crops, have animals and, like the Zurug and Nuba, they now grow cotton for the ginnery in Lagawa. Unlike the Messeria and the Nuba, they are not a warlike people which probably accounts for their decline since they ruled Darfur. Their cultural activity is music, they specialise in long wooden horns, not unlike Swiss alpine horns, producing long low notes.

Dagu Orchestra

I could not find very much about them from the District files, though there were some notes written by Travers Blackley, a previous DC in 1923. He recorded that in one of the hills Jebel Tamanyig (which I think must be Warina), The Sultan asked to be called the Jindi. This was quite a departure from the general tradition. The reason given was that when the Dagu lived in Darfur they were ruled over by a Sultan who was a Tamanyigy. One day his courtiers said that such a great man should only ride on a horse as all other big men did. This flattered the Sultan, so he ordered a tetel (hartebeest) to be saddled. He got on it and the tetel bucked and ran away and he was never seen again. After that the ruler of Tamanyig was always called a Jindi as if he was called a Sultan the mad tetel might come back and carry him off!

On one occasion, one Kaka Hamadan from Selodi complained that his father had been a Jindi. When he died Ahal el Sultan (the people of the Sultan) appointed someone else in his place when Kaka was not present. On investigation it appeared that Kaka's father Jindi Hamadan had asked to be buried away from the hill. This was a Sultan's privilege. If a Sultan is buried in the hill, the Dagu fear that his ghost would return and instruct the new Sultan in the art of oppression. Kaka had either to disobey his father or local custom. He chose the latter and therefore lost the jindiship

Blackley said that while he was in the Gezira in the Blue Nile province he had helped to solve a mystery. When the cotton irrigation scheme started off, some of the Dagu went there to work. Everyone wondered why it was that all the big nuts from machines of the Sudan

Railways and the Irrigation Department went missing. Blackley realised that the Dagu's favourite weapon of defence was a club, known as a dedomaria. Sure enough, it was discovered that it was the Dagu who had taken the nuts and put them on the end of their sticks to make good clubs.

Anne and I set off from Lagawa one day at the end of January 1994 to supervise the election of a new Sultan for Dar el Kebir at the settlement called Marengo. I knew that this was not going to be an easy task as passions were running high. However, one problem that was not going to present was a favourite trick perpetrated when a Sultan died. This was that a gang would bury the nahas, the copper drum and symbol of chieftianship. If the drums were not present, a new Sultan could not be properly appointed. In practice it was a bit of blackmail as the drums were usually returned in exchange for a bull. In this case the Sultan had not died, he was in prison having 'eaten' some of the tribute instead of paying it into the Council office.

We found Ahal el Sultan and Ahel el Jindi all assembled and lined up opposite each other. We settled ourselves in our trek chairs under a small tree in the middle. Everyone talked at once, but the most vocal was the old Jindi. He explained at great length why it was necessary on this occasion for an Ahel el Jindy and not an Ahel el Sultan to be elected Sultan. This view was, of course hotly opposed by Ahl el Sultan.

The sun beat down, the rocks got hotter, the atmosphere got dustier and the talks went on as they led absolutely nowhere. At the end of three hours I decided that democracy had run its course, so I stood up and demanded silence. I said that having heard all they had to say, I could see no reason for not following the traditional procedure for the election of a Sultan. Ahel el Sultan had a good candidate and I was not convinced that there was any need to make an appointment from Ahel el Jindy. I then appointed Abdel Rahim Sobahi of the Ahel el Sultan to be the new Sultan for a trial period of six months, if he was not a success they could have another try.

As we left, half the population were shrieking and leaping for joy and the other half were muttering darkly. The most miserable of all was the old Jindi; he was concerned because if he had co-operated in electing someone from Ahel el Sultan as tradition demanded, he would also have received six cows from the new Sultan, but as he opposed him, he won't!

14. THE NGOK DINKA.

Our visits to the Ngok Dinka in Abyie had to be confined to the six month period between November and April when the road from Muglad was open. We always enjoyed our visits, apart from anything else, Abyie and its problems were quite different to the rest of the District.

Anne, in one of her letters sets the scene:-
Abyie.

We left Muglad early yesterday and stopped for breakfast in Tebeldia. There is no village, just the rest house, its caretaker and several wells as it is the only watering place for miles around during the summer. The rest house ghaffir (keeper) was full of complaints that every night a leopard slept up the tree overhanging his yard from where it sprang down onto his cattle. He had already put up a very strong fence of wooden poles all round to keep the lions and hyenas out, but what could he do about the leopard up the tree?.

Breakfast over, we drove straight on down to Abyie, the road very good and amazingly dry all the way. We saw several gazelle and one kudu, the animal on the Province badge, a large deer with long twisted horns. He was standing beside the road, we got very close to him before he crashed away into the undergrowth. He was about the size of a horse. I had not realised they were so big. Gradually the scrub gave way to wide flat savannah-like country with just a few spreading trees and little settlements. We arrived here at 2 o'clock having been able to shoot some duck and guinea fowl on the way, 125 miles.

Kudu

View from Rest House Abyie.

We are staying in the new rest house a mile out of the village. It was put here by Donald Rae on a little mound with a creek at the back. We have a lovely view of one of the Dinka settlements with its luak and grain stores, so I am able to watch Dinka life from my chair. It is not quite so hot as right in Abyie itself. Also it has the advantage that as much as we love the friendly Dinka, they are rather inclined to want to keep us company all the time, Mike must have some peace to write up his reports. Nothing of course deters Deng Majok who is likely to appear anywhere, anywhen. The rest house is not quite finished, it lacks some doors and shutters. One important door is lacking so that a magnificent wooden throne is in full view at the end of the verandah. It is very unusual not the have the little house away in the garden. During our first lunch we were deafened by terrific scraping and banging noises. We discovered that the rest house caretaker, a tall Dinka, had crawled in through the hole at the back for the bucket under the seat in order to replace a tin full of sand he had forgotten to put in. He had not liked to carry it past us during lunch. How he twisted himself through, we can't think. I now feel a bit precarious when I am enthroned in case he comes in again.

Michael continues...

The Ngok are southerners, but living in a northern District. They are Nilotics very slim and tall with remarkably long legs. They are not nomads

A Dinka home

the grain stores

A luak

Under construction.
The different types of grass make patterns on the domed roof

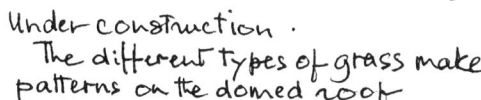

Inside. A dung fire smoulders under the platform where the family sleep. The cattle each have their own peg

A Dinka settlement
Watercolour sketch

Dressed up for the party

The dance in full swing

like the Messeria, but pasturalists. They were, so legend has it were led to their present country by one Aiwel de Jok. They came to a river and could not get across, so Jok pushed his daughter Acai into the river and the water spirit took her and in return parted the waters. So, they settled in Abyie and the surrounding country just north of the Bahr el Arab that flows eastwards and joins the White Nile at Malakal. Their Chief (or Nazir) is Deng Majok Kwal, under him there are eight Omdas who look after the various sections of the tribe.

The open countryside is scattered with settlements consisting of a large thatched, round mud based house and several small ones on legs. The larger ones known as luaks are for sleeping and also act as cattle byres, the smaller are the grain stores. The luaks are unique in Africa, being double storied.

Anne describes one:-

This was the first time we had been inside one and it was quite fascinating. A delicious smoky smell wafts out of the small round hole which is the entrance. Inside it is very dark and cool; above there is a huge lofty domed roof with the thatch supported by a framework of rafters all draped with wispy cobwebs. In the middle, supported by upright wooden poles is a platform covered with mats, this is where the younger men sleep. Underneath burns a smoky fire of cow dung, round this the animals are tied, each one to its own peg. When we went in, the cattle and sheep were out grazing except for the baby ones that were still inside. When the flies are bad a continuos smoke fire bus so the whole place is full of smoke. Can you imagine the atmosphere?

Their cows and bulls are almost treated as their children, Dinka sing lovely soothing songs to them and all their products are used, not just milk to drink but shampoos, hair packs, face lotions and skin tonics are all from their cattle.

M continues: -

The Ngok hold a cocktail of religions, by and large they are officially described as 'pagans', although this by no means should suggest that they had no religion at all, they believe in a complicated kind of ancestor worship. Some, who have been to school or worked in the north have become Moslems. The various Christian missions were allowed to maintain missions and run schools in the south, but have 'spheres of influence' so that they did not compete. The Verona White Fathers were licensed to work in Bahr el Ghazal Province and at some time they were authorised to include the Abyie in their area; so some of the Ngok were Roman Catholics.

Chief (or Nazir to give the Arab title) Deng Majok or Deng Majok Kwak Arop, to give him his full name, was a complex character, As one of his sons put it "he was neurotic about wives, of whom he had over a hundred". Deng Majok's position was never quite as secure as he would have liked owing to his half brother, Deng Abot. He was an ever-present shadow and would not have been above plotting Deng Majok's down fall if he ever had the chance. The reason for this is somewhat complicated.

Their grandfather was Arop who had two sons, Kojamam and Kwal. The elder, Kojamam died soon after birth. Although Kwal was the younger boy, when he grew up he had to marry a wife to Kojamam, buying her with the cattle that would have been Kojamam's inheritance. Kwal therefore married Nyanaghar. She then refused to live with him so all the cattle were returned to her father except for one. Kwal then married Abiong Malek with the same cattle. The next drama was that Nyanaghar then changed her mind and Kwal remarried her with his own cattle. This raised the question of whose wife she now was? Kwal's or bearing in mind that one cow of the first marriage had not been returned, had she remarried Kojamam?

To try and resolve the question a ritual 'tot' was performed with the slaughter of a white sheep. It was agreed that Nyanaghar was Kwal's wife and the senior, while Abiong Malek was Kojama's wife. Both women were conceived by Kwal. Before giving birth the sacred fighting spear was placed against Abiang's hut in anticipation of a girl child and the fish spear was put against Nyanaghar's hut in anticipation of a boy. So it was that Abiang duly

Deng Majok

bore a girl and Nyanaghar, a boy who was Deng Majok. Later on Abiong bore Deng Abot. Although Kwal was progenitor and guardian of Deng Abot he was not his legal father because this was Koijamam. Although Deng Majok's mother was the senior wife, it is possible to claim, and Deng Abot certainly did, that he, as the eldest son of the eldest son had the prior claim to succeed Kwal.

Kwal had been a very fine man and a strong chief, but as he grew older he lost his grip. Deng Majok, from his early life had not only shown great qualities of leadership, also natural authority which made him a friend of Babu Nimr, the Nazir Umum of the Messeria and acceptable to the District Commissioners. He was appointed to succeed Kwal while he was still alive although it was agreed that the symbols of Chieftainship, the Sacred Spears should remain with the old man. On Kwal's death, two years later, part of the tribe attempted a coup to declare Deng Abot as Chief, but it so happened that the DC was near Abyie at the time. With the support of the majority of the tribe, the Sacred Spears were give to Deng Majok to confirm not only his chieftainship, but also his priestly authority.

Deng Majok had a commanding presence emphasised by his height, well over six foot, and his elegance. He was always beautifully dressed in a long robe, scarf and turban. There was no doubting his authority over the Ngok in general and the eight sub-chiefs or Omdas in charge of the tribal sections. When we first came to the Messeria, the Ngok were not part of the relatively new District Council. The Arabs had not wanted the Dinka to be part of "their" Council and the Ngok did not want to be an obvious minority amongst the Arabs. Lengthy negotiations had gone on, and largely through the friendship and understanding between Nazir Babu and Deng Majok, the Ngok were admitted and attended their first Council meeting at the beginning of 1953. This was an enormous act of faith that confirmed that the future of the Ngok lay with the north rather than the south.

Despite his undoubted authority, Deng Majok had two major problems. The first was the feeling that his brother was looking over his shoulder and watching for any slip which could be used against him; the second was his obsession with collecting wives which meant that he was nearly always in debt. Wives were expensive owing to the necessity of 'paying' for them in cattle. The Dinka reckon their wealth in cattle, not money, their cows are their first love; they will spend hours washing, grooming and singing to their favourite cattle and especially their oxen, so to part with any of them for a wife is a serious business.

The custom of bride cattle is really a contract to enforce reciprocal obligations. It demonstrates the stability of the union, involves ancestral spirits in the union as cattle represent continuity, acts as a legal indemnity for the loss of the woman's services to her own family and as compensation for her upbringing. Also, in an exogamous patrilinial society a woman cannot bear children to her own kinsmen, so her bride wealth provides them with means to marry a woman outside their own group.

I was still responsible for the administration of the local court of which Deng Majok was President. This, so said Richard Owen, a previous and distinguished District Commissioner of Western Kordofan, now Governor of Bahr el Ghazal, was the worst in the Sudan. By this he did not meant that Deng Majok was unjust or exceeded his authority, but that the records were pretty chaotic. Despite this, Fadl, the Court Clerk held on to his job, mainly because there was no obvious successor. One of his best efforts was to tell Paul Howell when he was ADC Messeria that some missing tins of petrol had been eaten by white ants!

Anne continues:-

I am sitting beside Mike who is now doing the Abyie prison inspection. This consists of sitting at a table and going through a large book 'List of Convicted Prisoners and their Particulars' in front of him. The Sergeant of Police beside him calls up each prisoner in turn from where they sit in a large semicircle a few yards away. Nearly all completely nude with the black slender bodies of the Nilotics. They are immensely tall and long legged. I feel rather important writing away as they probably think I am writing a report. It is about 5.30 in the evening and beginning to get dark.

Prison inspection over. Then Chief Deng Majok caught us and has ushered Mike behind a tree to have yet another confidential whispering session, no doubt his matrimonial muddles again. These are unending and most complicated, perhaps because he has so many wives, 35 at the moment I think. Whenever we meet him he always has something confidential to say and Mike has to disappear with him. In the evening we went down to the suq (market) and chatted. There are only a very few shops as yet and most of them are not open as stores have not started to come through since the rains.

The next morning before breakfast we visited the dispensary and the school. The Dinka are very clever, here they learn English during their first year at school. 'Good morning Sir' was the greeting we got from all the little boys except one who could not remember it all so he just said 'Sir' with a great grin as we were leaving. Unfortunately none of the school stores have arrived yet so the boys were doing their sums in the sand but Lino Wau the headmaster is quite exceptional and would not allow a little thing like that to impede progress. He did have a blackboard on which Peter Hogg's and Mike's names were written up; it was explained that this was part of a civics lesson.

(This visit took place before the Ngok joined the District Council. Once this happened, the school was financed by the council and the supply position improved, but Lino Wor was far too able to be allowed to stay in Abyie. When he was promoted and transferred to another school he was succeeded by a Nuba. A few headaches were caused when a southern Roman Catholic Dinka was replaced by an arabised Moslem Nuba!)

In the evening we drove down to the Bahr el Arab, the river where the ferry is. It looked lovely and blue and we were very tempted to strip and dive in with everyone else. We refrained, partly for prestige and partly through fear of crocodiles. The iron ferry (once a tank landing craft) was propelled over to take us to the other side and back.

We stopped on the way back at a bend in the river where we saw some fishing going on. First of all a barrier of sticks is built in a shallow part to stop the fish swimming down stream, in front of this they make several islands of mud, sticks and rushes. At night a fire is lit on each one to keep lions away. The fishermen then sit having stuck long bamboo sticks in the water all around them. They wait until they see a stick move then quick as lightening they thrust in their long spears and bingo, they have a fish!

Dinka fishing at night.

On the way back we saw lots of brown monkeys, we tried to take photographs but they would not let us near them. At 6 o'clock we were invited to tea by one of the merchants. We sat outside in the village square lit by two lamps under which lots of frogs hopped about catching the bugs that were attracted by the light.

.. The next morning, Mike was due to conduct an auction of cattle which had been paid as fines, the Dinka do not have money, so if they misbehave and have to be fined, they are fined in cattle. We arrived promptly at 7 am and found not a soul. However, within half an hour we were joined by a lot of people. Then sixty head of cattle were driven along and grazed round about until it was their turn to come into the circle. In the circle there were five long pegs to which they were tied while they were auctioned. As well as the five tied to pegs there were usually five more just keeping them company. Some of the bulls insisted on keeping a eye on their wives while others would come and make eyes at their girl friends. Mike and I sat at a table, Mike thought he would be doing the shouting, but someone suddenly started off so he didn't have to, but he did have to ring a bell when each bargain was made and make sure that the prices were not too low. They were low, only about £5 for a bull and £8 for a cow and a calf. (In Nahud one has to pay £20 for a cow and a calf). So, instead of auctioning 60, he would only allow 30, leaving the rest for a time when prices were better.

It was all very orderly, the bidders and audience sat in a circle all round and the cattle were shooed in and out by tall naked prisoners. Occasionally a bull needed a little persuading and the odd cow broke its rope but most were very quiet and docile and quite oblivious of any thing around them. The money was handed over straight away . Mike counted it and put it in the cash box. £195 altogether for 30 cattle. We were very late for breakfast - 10 o'clock. Guess what? We had fish, the first we have had since we were at home.

Yesterday we had a good drive back to Muglad, stopping for lunch and siesta and then tea.

15. THE PROVINCE JUDGE VISITS ABYEI.

A bumpy journey.

One of our special treks started on March 3rd 1953. We went off from Nahud in company with the Hunters. Their lorry had a hole in the cylinder block and the only vehicle they could get was a dreadful boneshaker suq lorry. They started off in advance but we had only gone a few miles before we found them sitting in the road. We got to El Odaiya at noon but they did not roll up until 1.30 having had another six stops. After lunch we volunteered to try the rattletrap, so Mary could rest as one of her migraines had started.

It was the first time we had been in a suq lorry and it was quite an amusing experience for the first hour or so, much more energetic than bouncing up and down on a fresh horse; the vibration and noise was quite terrific. Our average speed was no more than 15mph but we occasionally got up to 20 on the very flat stretches. Every time we came to some sand, the engine screamed into third, we charged into it, then the pace got slower and slower, the engine ground and groaned, the driver changed down through the gears until we were hardly moving except for violent jerks like St Vitus's dance. After a few minutes the engine would give out, there would be a terrific roaring and bubbling, clouds of steam and a fountain playing out of the radiator. There would then be an interval for it to cool off and be filled up again. Then, diggings in the sand, planks put under the wheels to enable it to get out again which it did with much pushings from behind. At last, off until the next sandy bit

So it went on until a final boiling when we decided to have tea. There the Hunters in our lorry caught us up, much refreshed by a snooze. We went on the Muglad in our own lorry and got in at 8pm, 162 miles.

Educational problems in Abyei.
Michael...

The next morning we went straight on and had breakfast in Tebeldia where the rest house ghaffir Azzozo had, as usual, a great list of complaints and wants. These included the deepening of the two wells, digging another one, cartridges for his rifle, a shotgun, some clothes and a Council badge. We had lunch at Antilla and got to Abyei at 6pm, 123 miles. The road was good, we stopped at intervals to shoot guinea fowl and to wait for the Hunters to catch up. We saw pa and ma ostrich with their family of five chicks, some deer and monkeys but nothing else of interest. Two RC fathers were waiting for us with a letter from the Bishop asking permission to build a church. They used to have a grass one, which has now fallen down, and they propose to build it in brick.

In the morning I went with the Fathers to the site and finally agreed they had better build a temporary church in brick, but at the same time I would try and get them a lease for a permanent one. They were a pleasant pair, especially the brother, Bro Bertoni who is the builder; they claim to have 150 adherents in Abyei, though I rather doubt it. I went on to the school to discuss its future with the Education Officer from Wau, a chap called Cox, who was at St. Peter's Hall (my College), before the war. Abyei is of course on the border between North and South, so at the moment the wretched boys speak Dinka, then they learn Arabic and English. They do arithmetic in Arabic for their first two years and in English for their last two years. They end up knowing a little of everything, but are not up to the standard of exams in either the North or the South.

Meanwhile Mary and Anne had a walk along the ragaba (creek) and saw all sorts of lovely birds wading around amongst the drinking cattle. They then got down to housekeeping gossip and compared notes. Our sugar consumption has gone down considerably since old Mohammed left. They were interrupted in their calculations by the arrival of Kevin Hayes, the Province Judge and Geoffrey McComas, Inspector of Local Government, from El Obeid.

Dinka Dancing.
Anne…

In the evening we all went to watch an exhibition of Dinka dancing, especially laid on in honour of the Judge's visit. It took place on the flat ground just outside the village. We were ushered to seats of honour and given drinks. At first it was difficult to see anything except a cloud of dust, but gradually one's eyes got used to it and we could see two or three hundred Dinka already dancing. The mens' party clothing consisted of a coiffure of cow dung, giving them a reddish coloured wig of rather thick tufts, beads and ivory bangles round their right arms and feet. Their only clothing was a small cheetah skin round their behinds. Many had covered themselves with grey ash dust or red brick dust, using the combination of the two colours and that of their black bodies to make wonderful all over patterns. One looked as if he wore rust coloured socks and shorts with a grey shirt. As they got hotter and hotter their war paint dissolved in rivers of sweat and they were left just with their own black skin. In their right hands they brandished a spear, usually a barbed fish spear, and in their left a bunch of spare spears. The ladies wore a strip of gaily coloured material around their hips and some were decked with beads round their necks, arms and ankles.

During the first part of the dancing, all the ladies jumped up and down in the middle while the men danced round them in a huge circle, leaping in the air doing intricate steps with their feet and antics with their bodies, usually landing in a dramatic crouch position. They thrust at each other in turns, one would thrust and the other slide back or jump up so that the spear just missed. It seemed quite effortless, but it also looked as though someone would be arrested for causing 'death by a rash or negligent act' before we were finished. All the time a continuous chanting, singing chorus went on, in perfect time to the beating of the drums.

In the next stage, the ladies joined the men in the circle and all moved round together at quite a slow pace until the rhythm quickened. Then each girl turned to face her man with her arms stretched right over her head; she did terrific bounds backwards like a reversed kangaroo while her man leapt forward pursuing her. The girls' spring backwards was an amazing movement as not only did she cover a lot of ground each time, but twisted her body so that it might have been cut in halves, flicking up her behind and then her bosoms, all in mid air. This continued for some time, then the girls retired into the background while the men too moved back in a long black mass, leaving a great open space in front of us.

The entertainment ended with what Kevin described as an 'N.C.O's TEWT (Tactical exercise without troops)'. The men came into the arena in pairs, one behind the other, doing a series of girations and spearing in perfect unison. They came bounding up to us, did a terrific leap ending in a crouching position at our feet, bowed their heads down and drove their spears into the ground as near to our toes as possible. They remained like that for a few seconds before bounding away. The timing was most impressive, it was explained that this is the way they approach each other in battle. The leaps had much the same effect on the enemies' spears as a violent zigzag would put off a torpedo attack. Also, the one in front protected the one behind.

We all enjoyed it very much. One would have to go a long way to find such perfect physique combined with natural grace. As a finale the warriors all stood together with their arms stretched above their heads, making themselves look even taller than they are already; they bounced into the air to a terrific height with no effort at all. Geoffrey and M went and joined them, much to everybodys' amusement but they will have to have a lot of practice before they can jump a quarter as far off the ground. We gave them five bulls with which to celebrate.

The Judge hears a case of spear throwing.
Michael...

On Friday morning, the Judge of the High Court heard a case in Abyie for the first time. It was also the first time that a judge had been seen in robes in the Messeria. There was some doubt if the Dinka were as impressed as they should have been. 'Turks' clothes were much the same to them. I asked what they thought of the judge's wig and they just said that their own were made out of cow dung. (In Nahud, the comment was 'His Honour the Judge has got frightfully old').

The Judge and Geoffrey McComas (court member) arrived in style in the judge's saloon, to be joined by Deng Majok who was to be the third member of the Major Court.

The case concerned a Dinka who had flung a spear at what he thought was a monkey sitting in a cultivation amongst the stalks of grin, afterwards he found it was a woman. The spear had gone right through her and she died. The Judge had, of course read the proceedings of the Magisterial Enquiry and very much doubted if the accused could possibly have thrown a spear the distance he claimed. So, before the case started, the Judge wanted a demonstration of spear throwing.

We lined up three prisoners with spears and a sack of grain 50 yards away. No 1 prisoner got up to 40 yards, so we brought the sack back to 40 yards for No 2. He threw two overs, but at the third shot his spear went right through the sack of grain and out the other side. It was hard to believe that a spear at that distance would have such penetrating power, it almost stopped at the height of its trajectory and then came whistling down. We then put the sack back to 50 yards and asked No. 3 to throw as far as he could; he got up to 62 yards. These were random chaps and not experts. I wished I could remember what the record javelin throw was? (87.33 yards in 1988).

While the trial went on I had to spend the morning going over accounts and looking at our brick kilns which had not got on as fast as they should have. What time the trial was proceeding; then came the time for the Court to consider its verdict. The court had to be cleared, for there were no chambers available in the grass hut that served as the Chief's office and court. The heat, so Geoffrey said had been stifling, most of the population of Abyie had crammed themselves in to listen to this unique entertainment. Most of the evidence was given in Dinka which then had to be translated into English and/or Arabic, so the proceedings had not been all that quick. The flies had a variety of heads on which to settle or buzz, but once the courtroom was cleared the choice was limited but obvious, they all settled on the Judge's wig. The spear throwing demonstration had proved the accused's point; he was acquitted of culpable homicide but sentenced to two years for causing death by negligence.

Inter Province Meeting at Abiemnon.

In the evening we all went on to Abiemnon, a pleasant drive, the road weaving along the north bank of the Bahr el Arab. We saw baboons and several sorts of gazelle on the way. We found John and Mary Longe, Governor of Upper Nile Province from Malakal, Pat Garland with Philip and Brenda Bowcock from Bentiu, and Ranald Boyle, A.D.C.Gogrial, already installed. Ranald is a nephew of my honorary aunt, Eileen Bailward, he is the same age as me and a submariner. He is so angry about the South being deserted that he has resigned without waiting for any compensation. We all dined together at one long table, a wonderful dinner; roast duck and orange sauce. This and an excellent breakfast the next day of grapefruit, porridge, kedgeree, eggs and sausages, toast and marmalade and coffee, were all produced by our Upper Nile hosts. Our picturesque surroundings right on the river we have of course, described before.

In addition to all the cottage loaf thatched houses, several grass houses had been put up, we were in one of these. During the day we all sat in groups under the spreading trees. At night everyone slept outside and being full moon we could see everyone climbing into bed under their mosquito nests; luckily these did make one a little private inside, but not sound proof. Several complained about a roaring snoring in the night. We suspected that was His Honour the Judge. We had our bed put under a tree right on the river and it was lovely to hear the fish plopping in the water.

The most important business of the meeting before breakfast was a duck shoot. We split up on both sides of the river and walked for miles. On the way we passed a completely starkers gentleman covered in ashes standing in a pond. We politely said 'Chubak' (hallo in Dinka), to be countered with 'Good morning Sir, Going shooting? I am afraid there are not many duck around this morning'. We did get some whistlers, the bag was about ten, some had fallen in the river. Philip had to swim to get his. John Hunter and Geoffrey McComas found that the reeds on the bank were deeper than they thought and arrived back covered in mud wearing just their vests and pants.

After breakfast we went over to where the Dinka and Nuer were thrashing out their problems. Our Executive Officers, Ahmed Abu Gasim and Abu Gabr came over for an orange squash later in the morning to report progress. Then there were more arrivals; Richard Owen, Governor Bahr el Ghazal from Wau and his wife, A.C.Beaton the Deputy Civil Secretary, and James Robertson, son of the Civil Secretary, Sir James Robertson. They drove to the far bank, then had to cross over in a canoe. Last year they did the same thing and the canoe capsized as they were making a formal entry. this time all was well. Peter Hogg had also caught up with us. Including the Kordofan contingent, there were eighteen of the Sudan Political Service families present.

After lunch, Nazir Babu and followers came to tea to discuss the possibility of a new Court at Subu, the new cotton growing area which was opening up south east of Muglad. After an hour and a half of talk, we got back to where we started and still no decision. Then more duck shooting and I wasted a lot of cartridges. Both Governors plunged in to get their birds, we expected that at any minute they would get eaten by crocodiles or be seized by the water snake which the Dinka say lives on the bottom of the river and stretches all the thirty miles from Abiemnon to Abyie.

In the evening we had a meeting with Anthony Beaton who was really touring the Southern Provinces to find out what people were thinking and to raise the moral of the Political Service. He did not tell us very much that we did not know already and could only give the vaguest forecast for the future. It seems that short of having another war in the Canal Zone or the prospect of the Sudanese political parties boycotting the elections, H.M.G. could not do much more than it had. If one has not got the strength to enforce the policy that one knows is right I suppose the best thing to do is to go. It is very difficult though, to explain to the Southern Sudanese that they are to be sacrificed and they had better make the best of it. I am glad that most of my parishioners are Arabs who are used to bend with the wind anyway. The southern D.C.s are having a very difficult time.

The drive home to Nahud

We left after breakfast on Sunday for Abyie, had two hours there. Then on to Tebeldia for the night with Kevin and Geoffrey. Muglad on Monday where I spent the morning laying out nine new shops with a cricket tape, two spears and some pegs. In the afternoon we drove thirty miles out to a place called Tibun. All their water had dried up and they have to buy it from Muglad at 7 piastres for a four gallon tin, about 5d (now about 10p) a gallon. Some of them were loud in their protests that the government had left them there to die of thirst, until I found that those who shouted loudest had only just got there and did not even come from Kordofan!

We left Muglad the following morning, stayed the night in Rigl el Fula and back to Nahud the next day. We found everyone rather the worse for wear. John and Mary exhausted by the suq lorry journey, they had had to sack their safragi and the house was upside down as the P.W.D (Public Works Department) were doing some alterations for them and builders were all over it. Peter had arrived home to find Joanna and the children were not well and their seconda was ill too. In spite of this they have to go off to a northern meeting today. We on the other hand are full of beans having been able to take the journey in easy stages. It is Friday and blowing a gale outside, so we are sitting inside with the doors shut reading and listening to the wireless. It really might be one of those muggy wet days in England except instead of rain, its dust.

(We have just had a letter to say we have two official Sudan Government seats for the Coronation Procession, either in the Mall or Hyde Park but at the moment it seems we may have to hold the fort here).

16, ANNE'S TWENTY FIRST BIRTHDAY AND THE MOVE TO RIG EL FULA.

In the end we did go on leave in May so we were able to see the Coronation procession from seats in Hyde Park. One of the other highlights of our leave was that Babu came and stayed with us at Bunchfield, the home of Anne's parents. The Sudan Government invited a party of Sudanese notables to take part in the celebrations. Babu represented Kordofan, so we asked the Sudan Agent in London if we might invite Babu for a night.

We drove over to Horsham where the Sudan party was visiting the National Stud and took Babu back to Lynchmere afterwards. In an interview with Francis Madeng Deng, (son of Deng Majok), Babu is recorded as saying
"…we travelled and we travelled until we eventually arrived. What did we find? Their house was on the top of a mountain. That was the house of his wife's father. His own father was a clergyman. He was ill, we went to greet him. We spent the night at the home of his wife's family, they made a dinner party for us. His sister with her husband were coming, it was in our honour. Then we went the next day to visit his father. His father had a palacious house. It was said to belong to the church, not their own. The father of his wife owned their house. At that time, they were on vacation, they had not yet left the Sudan".

Anne's mother was rather apprehensive about the visit, especially as she predicted that he would be very cold and that he would not bring any luggage. Against the first eventuality, a log fire was lit in Babu's bedroom. As regards the second, when we asked Babu if we could get his luggage, he said he had it with him, a large Brigg's umbrella! So Anne's mother was right. Despite this, he was offered and accepted a bath, which he said he enjoyed. He talked about the fire in his bedroom on the first floor forever afterwards. His dignified presence, his emma (turban) and flowing robes made a great impression on all our family and friends, despite the language difficulty.

We were able to show Babu a little of the place in which we lived before putting him on a train at Haslemere for Waterloo, where Peter Hogg retrieved him. The Sudanese party stayed at the Strand Palace Hotel. If no other engagement had been arranged, Babu said that he enjoyed listening to the band and watching the dancing. He was a wonderful mimic and his imitations of the expressions on the faces of the people dancing and the beat of the music were wonderful. He arrived back in Muglad full of stories and with a magnificent silver plated tea set and a silver bowl with the special Coronation mark of the Queen's head.

Nazir Babu at Bunchfield. Coronation 1953

We wrote home on the 8th August 1953 to say we had arrived in Nahud safely after returning from leave. The horses were well, one of Buttercup's twins had died, so we were left with only Dandelion. Rachel the duck was very pleased with herself as she had four turkey chicks to look after, she had taken them on when their mother deserted. Augustus the ram was huge. We gave the servants Coronation mugs and they were delighted. Abdel Rahman gave me some 'damoria' cloth from Shendi, his home town, which was very hard wearing. (I had it made into bush jackets and shorts. Christopher wore them when he went to the Sudan 30 years later, he met Abu Gabr Hag Agbar, by now promoted as Governor of the Nuba Mountains Province who greeted him by saying, "You've got your father's jacket on").

The Hunters were on leave and when they returned, John would be the Resident Magistrate and an A.D.C. no longer. The Hoggs had moved to Khartoum where Peter was now Deputy Director of Local Government. Peter had always been very supportive and had a fatherly concern for our welfare, especially Anne's. He was a gentle giant with great charm, very tall and with his twinkling blue eyes peering out of rather bushy eyebrows he seemed to take a lofty view of the world. He had been an Oxford rowing blue, was probably the best Arabist in the Political Service, having passed the Advanced Arabic examination with distinction. He was a noted ornithologist and knew every bird we saw. So, our happy corner of Nahud seemed very empty.

Our main concern was to move to Rigl el Fula as soon as possible. The new Sudanese D.C. in Nahud was upset when I moved my office furniture and tried to retain our Sub-Mamur so I wanted to be out of the way before he had any other ideas. We went down to Rigl el Fula with two lorry loads of the office furniture, files and some of our belongings, then back to Nahud for a final clear up.

It was Anne's twenty first birthday on the 23rd, she recorded the celebrations and final move on the next day:-

Rae Roost (our name for the rest house).
Rigl el Fula 25th August 1953.

We decided to have a special 21st birthday picnic on our last day in Nahud, so off we went at 5pm. The servants waved us good bye, obviously thinking we were rather mad. It had been raining very hard, and we found the track to Jebel Nahud two and a half miles out very difficult to find and we had to bump through the undergrowth sometimes. About half way out the track became the deep and sandy bed of a river which brought the rainwater off the hill and we were soon stuck. After half an hour we managed to dig ourselves out and decided to go off the road where there was grass and it might be less sandy. Of course we stuck again but a kind man on a donkey helped us.

By this time it was getting darker and darker with black clouds gathering. The going got worse and worse and there were brilliant flashes of lightening so we decided to turn back and just managed to turn the lorry round. The rain then poured down, the windscreen was hinged up and we could not get it down so we had to peer underneath it. We ground along what became a fast moving river with water up to the doors. However, we made it back, just, very wet and everyone was amused at the whole outing. We still had a nice picnic though. The house was quite bare, so we cooked our sausages and mushrooms out in the mosquito wired part of the verandah and drank the hock which Geoffrey and Mary Hawkesworth had kindly sent us.

Yesterday morning, 24th August

Our own lorry and two hired ones were finally loaded up. Our furniture had been put on the day before, so only the servants' belongings remained . It was really amusing, each wanted his trunk or bedroll, pots and pans or bundles not to be squashed by the others, and his own angareeb (bed) to be put on last of all. AR won, by not producing his best angareeb until everything was loaded and tied on! Eventually the two big hired lorries with AR, Zeinab and their little niece sitting in front of one and Ahmed and his wife in the other, set off. Mike, meanwhile was saying goodbye in the office and I was trying to see that delicate belongings of ours such as the long mirror, lampshades and frangi-pani tree were not put where our numerous passengers would sit on them. Needless to say when we did set off, we found the others ten miles out parked in the middle of the road while they 'changed the oil'. It had to be done every three hundred miles, of course they could not possibly change it before they started as they had only done 290 miles. They caught us up in El Odaiya, where we had a sandwich lunch.

The road was not very good; all the time threatening black clouds ahead of us got nearer and nearer. About half way we got bogged in a really muddy place. Mike who was driving steered to one side but the lorry slithered in the opposite direction and there we were surrounded by water and mud in a deep rut. Everyone rushed round digging and cutting branches, all issuing orders about the best place to dig, but everyone continued in their own way. Whenever I put my head out of the window to see how things were going I got splattered with large blobs of black mud which were showering up from everyone's diggings. Ibrahim, the driver's assistant was made to undress completely and wallow in mud under the lorry. He was rather embarrassed at first, but they all said "Go on, we are all men and Sa'ata sit can't see out of the window". Once there, he rather enjoyed it.

Meanwhile the black clouds arrived overhead, there was thunder, lightening and torrential rain so that everyone except myself inside and Mike in his mac was soaked as well as covered in mud. Our precious lampshades gradually disintegrated in their cardboard carton and our month's supply of flour became a sticky dough as the water dripped through the lid of its tin. Everyone's bed rolls became sodden and only the frangi-pangi tree enjoyed its refreshing drink. After many attempts and much pushing, we at last backed out. Then, getting a good running start we roared along the way prepared with branches, floundering and leaping in all directions as the wheels slipped in and out of ruts under the black water. Quite a commando act, inside I did not know which way up I was!. We almost got over, then stuck in the last few yards but not for long. Then the other lorries arrived and we all stood and watched them. The first got stuck in the first few yards. After waiting for some time, we decided to move on before the next downpour. By this time the rain had stopped but the road was a river. Every now and then we had to stop and pick our passengers and chairs, pails and things which got shot off. However, everyone was happy and cheerful inspite of their wet muddy state.

About five miles from Rigl el Fula we came to a khor which is normally dry. The banks had been washed away and the water was three feet deep. We had the choice of spending the night getting eaten by mosquitoes and rained and thundered on, or walking, we decided to walk.

Beshir (cook), Hassan (messenger), Ali (our kitchen prisoner), Ahmed Deng (accountant and one of Deng Majok's sons) and two other Dinka passengers, decided to come with us, but the six others on our lorry decided to wait for the two other lorries to catch up with them. So, at 5.45, armed with a torch, our raincoats and sticks to keep our balance and shoo away any hyenas, we set off. Muffetish (M) strode into the water, guided out of potholes by one of the long legged Dinka. Sa'ata sit followed, holding up her skirt as discreetly as possible, not for long though, her foot slipped and to save herself going headlong she put out her arms for balance and her skirt billowed out from the waist. Luckily the water was not very clear or transparent or all the onlookers might have seen her pink panties. My arms were grasped by two sturdy supporters and I made a good crossing without being swept away by the current. Needless to say I was weak at the knees through laughing.

We walked for a hour and a quarter through mud and water, most of the way having great difficulty in keeping our feet or our shoes on. Several of the party went flat in the mud. It was very dark towards the end and I did hope to see at least one hyena; at one point I thought I did, but it turned out to be Ahmed Deng the accountant who had walked on ahead. We had to cross another khor about one and a half miles from the first one, waist deep in water. Walking in wet clothes is not very comfortable and we were glad to see the lights of Fula ahead of us.

Everyone was most surprised when we suddenly arrived out of the night. We went to Mohamed Ibrahim Abdel Hafiz, the Sub-Mamur's house and he gave us tea. Meanwhile Beshir lit a fire, so when we got to the rest house we were able to have a nice hot bath. We borrowed two spoons (no forks available) and two plates to have our supper out of tins. (Luckily we had already brought our stores down here). A policeman went off in a small boxcar with some prisoners to push it when it got stuck. They got to the first khor, the one nearest here, then walked on to the lorries to see if any of the ladies would like to come back. They were all settled down for the night so did not feel inclined to get wet wading through the khors. AR sent our washing things, tooth brushes and shaving gear along. He tried to unearth our cutlery but could not find it.

We were very glad to be warm and snug in our beds in the rest house and glad we had walked, it was an enjoyable experience and good exercise. Luckily for the campers, although there was thunder and lightening it did not rain again until 6.30 the next morning, just as we were setting off to see how they were getting on.

It was only a shower, so off we went in the small boxcar, laden with prisoners with spades. We got to the first khor and found the water had subsided so the prisoners dug away the bank and put down gravel from the river to make it a less slippery slope. While we were doing that the three lorries turned up on the other side. They had dug out the banks of the other khor and got over. We watched them coming down and up. I expected the lorry with our furniture to topple over any moment it came down at such an angle, but all was well and we drove back in convoy.

All our belongings, including silver and glass have survived the journey very well. We spent all day unloading, unpacking and fitting everything into our new, but we hope temporary home in the rest house. On Saturday we are going down to Muglad for a few days.

Our furniture makes a perilous crossing

17. LIFE IN RIGL EL FULA

The District Diary for August 1953 reported that "The District Commissioner and Mrs Tibbs returned from leave at the beginning of the month and have now taken up residence in Rigl el Fula no.1 rest house".

It was bliss being settled in Fula at last and being able to relax from the continual trekking. By this time the Council building was progressing well and although not quite finished I was able to have my office in it. Ahmed Abu Gasim, Mohamed Ibraham Abdel Hafiz, the Sub Mamur and the other Council staff had moved up from Muglad, so at last we were all together. Apart from the convenience, we were now able to get to know them all better, especially Ahmed Abu Gasim and his family. He was a Mamur with a long record of government service and was nearing retirement. His original home was in the Blue Nile Province where he still had a small farm looked after by his first wife. His second wife and five children, Mohamed, Omer, Fatma, Omeima and Sadik came with him to Rigl el Fula. We got to know them all very well and we became very great friends. We also learnt that Ahmed was descended from the Prophet and so was entitled the 'Sherif', (Honourable), so this is what we usually called him.

It was fun planning what we hoped was to be the new rail head in the Western Sudan, so we had to look at things as we hoped they would be ten years hence, so I laid out sites for a mosque, schools and hospital. Fortunately I was very friendly with the Province Prison Officer in El Obeid, so shortly after we got to Fula, some fifty prisoners arrived under the charge of an excellent sergeant and five other warders. They, of course had to build their own prison, but with a plentiful supply of stone, this did not take long and they were then free to help with the next phase of building work. Another advantage of the move was our communication system. In Nahud we were on the telegraph system, but in Fula we had nothing. So, it was decided that we should have a radio telephone, locally known as the "Over". This was under the charge of a large and cheerful Nuba, Mohamed Kafi. His duties were to make sure we were on the air with the Governor's office in El Obeid twice a day, once in the morning and again in the

Life in Rural Fula

The Rest House — Rae Roost.

We had an excellent bath water system. The water arrived by donkey each morning. A fire was lit under the hot water barrel and by bath time, the water was piping hot.

The cannas thrived outside in the bath water

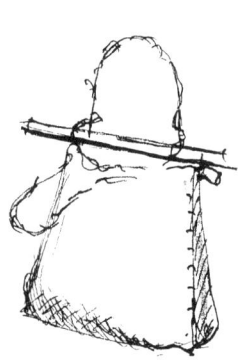

The canvas bag in which our drinking water hung from the lorry on trek.

Now we had good water here from the 'donkey' — not 60 miles away as in Nahud.

evening. The Over had to be switched on, warmed up for five minutes and then we were ready to go. One would hear Mohamed Kafi announcing "Anna (I) beamal (am making) standing by. OVER", and with luck one might be able to hear the other voice in El Obeid 150 miles away. The frequency was fixed and we were under very strict orders not to fiddle with it. The trouble was that it was the same frequency as Radio Monte Carlo, so more often than not our conversations were completely drowned by the latest Monaco pop song. The advantage was that if some unpopular instruction was coming over it was easy not to hear it at all. The disadvantage was that mail took an age to get to us via Nahud, though we were able to get a weekly service by lorry or donkey if the roads were bad. We used to get the occasional visitor but we hardly ever knew they were coming until they had arrived.

The rest house was a solid white painted stone building. It had two rooms and a verandah, at one end of which was a small store and at the other a bathroom. Outside the latter was a sort of buttress with fireplace and chimney, on the top was an old oil drum. This was filled every day by a donkey fitted with a thing like an enormous canvas life jacket full of water. At the bottom of each side was a tap from which petrol tins were filled and then passed up to fill the drum. As bath time approached, the fire was lit and there was our hot bath water. A similar buttress without a fire provided the cold water, just piped through the wall. One room became our bedroom and the other our dining/sitting room. With our animals in view, we put a wire fence round to give us a garden. This was dominated by a "Rae sized" white painted little house containing an unusually palatial wooden throne. The usual sanitary arrangements in Sudan towns was by a bucket system but we had decided we did not want the expense of running one in Fula, so one sat over an eight foot deep hole. In one corner of the enclosure were two stone built tukls with grass roofs for the servants, screened by grass fences. For some unaccountable reason the kitchen (another round hut) had been put in the middle of the road outside

During September we were visited by the Governor, Geoffrey Hawkesworth and Geoffrey McComas, the Inspector of Local Government, who wanted to see what we were up to and to discuss finance and buildings. Ahmed Abu Gasim had gone to Khartoum to buy stores and see his second wife in Omdurman, the Sub Mamur was on trek and we had no accountant, so I was doing all his work and doing the cash and keeping the accounts. Every Friday, the builders queued up and I had to pay them all, a sticky business with very gummy Egyptian notes. It reminded me of coming back from patrol in a submarine when I had to pay all the crew in cash with some strange currency, fortunately neither they nor I knew if I gave them the right money, sometimes I was up and sometimes down. However, the builders knew exactly what was owed, so I had to be careful.

We also wanted money for a primary school, a Merkaz (District HQ), some police houses and not least our own house. We had been having great fun with the plans for this and rather unusually were proposing to build it ourselves rather than getting the PWD (Public Works Department) involved. Geoffrey Hawkesworth quite liked the plans but said the Province Board of Public Health should approve them.

Outside the Rest House Fula
Geoffrey McComas A   Geoffrey Hawkesworth M

This was a body which included the Province Medical Officer, the Chief of Works, the Commandant of Police and the C.O. of the Camel Corps; I had taken its minutes while I was in El Obeid, but never quite discovered what its function was, (its approval for our house eventually arrived over a year later, the day we left for ever and nine months after the house was finished). We had a cushy ride up to Nahud with the two Geoffreys in the Governor's saloon and saw them off in the Sudan Airways Dove, before doing a short horse trek with Nazir Izz el Din.

We also had two visits from John and Mary Hunter. The first time they arrived very late. We expected them at teatime. By 8.15pm we started supper but heard an engine at 8.30. They arrived in a brand new lorry with a high roof and fitted with gadgets, it had only arrived that morning. They were late because of the new arrival which was being run in. They got down and started dinner while their servants were to go to the rest house in the water yard and settle them in. In a few minutes, their driver, Onbashi (Corporal) Sulieman appeared with a face as long as a boot. He had hit a tree stump in Rigl El Fula 'High Street' and the front axle was bent like a tuning fork. So, poor Sulieman had to beg a lift back to Nahud and eventually returned with spare axle and a gang from the Depot in Nahud who mended it. So John and Mary stayed three nights rather than the planned two.

All was well with our bath water system until the Hunters stayed and their tent was in the direct path of the irrigation.

The second time they came, we had our own guesthouse in the 'garden'. This was a superior trekking tent that Ahmed Abu Gasim had bought in Khartoum for the Council, we were allowed to borrow it. The Hunters were our first guests. They insisted that we had our baths first, so we bathed as quickly as possible. When we pulled out the plug, there were great shrieks from the tent as we had forgotten that the bath water would run straight into it. However, they mopped up, had their baths and pulled out the plug!

When they had recovered for the second time we had a drink and started dinner, to be interrupted by Abdel Rahman, the scyce holding a four foot long snake he had just found and killed by our little house. This was all rather too much for Mary who insisted that they kept a pressure lamp alight in the tent all night. Whenever John started to go to sleep, 'John, the lamp!' so he wearily had to lean out of bed and pump it up again.

We did have a little more snake trouble, the monthly diary reported that 'one of the builders was bitten but fortunately the tumergi (male nurse) was able to give immediate first aid and the patient is recovering'. One three footer was killed by a marassla (messenger boy) in the D.C's office, it was believed to have come for a gun licence". The most dangerous of all were the little vipers about 9 inches long that loved living in grass roofs.

Some other incidents of local news were also reported:-

"District Commissioner Jebels is shortly delivering some Um Borroro to the Police at Abu Zabad for escorting to Southern Darfur. Police in Abu Zabad have been asked to provide an escort".

The Um Borroro were West Africans who came into the Sudan with their distinctive very long horned cattle. They were a menace as they paid no taxes, their cattle were not inoculated, and they took the Messerias' grazing. Occasionally they had to be rounded up and escorted home. Sadly, the Abu Zabad police were not successful. The Onbashi (Corporal) and two Nafars (Constables) took the group over but the Onbashi reported that the Um Borroro, who were wizards, caused a great mist to descend. When it cleared, they were nowhere to be seen. The hard hearted authorities took a poor view and the Onbashi was reduced to the ranks.

"There has been a case of small pox in Muglad, Gummar Ali el Gullah, Uncle of Nazir Babu Nimr died from it. Medical Inspector, Nahud has sent a Medical Assistant and four mumarideen (male nurses) to set up quarantine".

An Um Borroro bull.

We had been fairly lucky in not having an epidemic for the last two years. Before that, there had been an extensive outbreak of cerebrospinal meningitis throughout the southern part of Kordofan and quarantine zones had to be set up. Through quick action, the small pox was confined to Muglad, but unfortunately the local butcher got it and concealed it, so it got passed on to his customers. He and all his family died. I had to spend quite a long time in Muglad assuring people that the quarantine zone was necessary and that vaccinations were not a sinister government plot. I ended up by being vaccinated in public, every day for a week

During one of our visits to Muglad we drove out with Nazir Ali to visit a ferik where an election for a new Omda had to be held. About forty elders were assembled in a circle. There were two young candidates, Mohamed and Osman, both about 23, and close relatives of the former Omda who had died. Both promised to be good if the other was chosen; for some reason it was known that Babu wanted Osman, who did not seem to be a popular choice. The discussion lasted over two hours and everyone had his or her say. Eventually, even Ali had to agree that Mohamed was the best choice, so I was able to stand up and appoint him. There was great cheering, branches were torn down from the trees and waved over Mohamed's head, though he did not appreciate the enthusiasm with which one old man hit him on the head with a branch of thorns.

A short story recorded from an exchange of telegrams:-

DISCOM FULA FROM DISCOM NAHUD (SENT BY LORRY) FOLLOWING FROM PRESSOFF KHARTOUM QUOTE MERCHANT ABU KU WIRED RADIO ABOUT FIRE DAMAGING 24 SHOPS ABU KU LE10,000 STOP CONFIRM UNQUOTE.

DISCOM NAHUD RPT GOVERNOR ELOBEID FROM DISCOM FULA VIA RADIO LINK NO NEWS OF THIS IN RIGL EL FULA WILL VISIT ABU KU TODAY TO FIND OUT.

PRESSOFF KHARTOUM RPT GOVERNOR EL OBEID DISCOM NAHUD FROM DISCOM RIGL EL FULA STOP MESSERIA INTEL 4 5/11/53 STOP PLACE ABU KU STOP OCCURANCE FIRE IN SUQ DAMAGED 24 SHOPS BURNT DOWN ALL GRASS EXCEPT ONE MUD GRASS ROOF STOP 7 GRASS HOSHES AND CONTENTS DESTROYED NO HURT ANYONE STOP DAMAGE POSSIBLY LE10,000 STOP LOCAL COMMITTEE FORMED ASSESS DAMAGE AND PROVIDE RELIEF STOP TO GOVERNOR EL OBEID REQUEST PERMISSION LOCAL COMMITTEE ABU KU ASK CONTRIBUTIONS FOR RELIEF FUND CHMN SH MULAH MOHD FEGIR COURT PRESIDENT STOP PLEASE REPLY DISCOM MESSERIA ABU ZABAD ENDS.

Ahmed Abu Gasim came back from Khartoum full of joy. As well as the tent, he had bought two cement block-making machines, some barbed wire and tennis net. He had also arranged a supply line from Port Sudan with one of the merchants there. We had absolutely nothing, if we ran out of nails, that was it. If we bought them in El Obeid, there was the transport 150 miles to us, as well as the 200 mile rail ride from Khartoum, so it was much cheaper for us to have our own supply line right back to Port Sudan with delivery to El Obeid where we could pick them up. Ahmed A G came to tea with Omer, his 5 year old son, to tell us all about it.

The elections were approaching, but before them we were due another Council meeting which was for the first time to be in Rigl el Fula at the end of October. The Council chamber was ready, but all the Members had to be accommodated which meant building dozens of grass houses for them to stay in. The commissariat side also had to be arranged with a good supply of sheep and bulls to feed them on. As the Council Members began to arrive, they were shown progress in the buildings and most of them dropped in for a chat about their own local affairs, either in the office or at home. They included Nur el Din, Deng Majok and Babu. As an elder statesman Babu has already been appointed to the Senate so is not standing for election to the House of Representatives; however he has persuaded his father in law Sayed Fadal to stand instead.

We had been worried about Deng as we had an alarming report from Abyie. He had been attacked by a dissatisfied defendant in a marriage case who stabbed Deng five times in his back and left side, but fortunately not seriously. Both had to attend hospital, the defendant through injuries received from the other court members and spectators. Then the Nazir's tribal section and the defendant's section had to be separated from each other three times by the police who fired over their heads. No one was injured, though extra police had been sent down from Muglad as a precaution. Anyway Deng was very cheerful but said his Dinka Council Members were fed up as they had to talk in the Council all day and then in their house all night as Babu was getting at them on behalf of his father in law, the Parliamentary Candidate Sayed Fadal. As soon as he left, Nur el Din, the other parliamentary candidate arrived!

Babu had talked to Deng about all being one family, Deng agreed and said in that case he would like one of Babu's daughters for his son, Ahmed. Babu said he would think about it when the election was over, but Deng insisted on having the wedding bells first. Babu then said that his daughters were booked for his uncle Mekki's sons. So, Deng asked Mekki who had said it was quite OK, Deng could certainly have one of them for Ahmed. What? everyone is asking, will Babu do now? First round to Deng!

Our guests were Geoffrey McComas and the Soil Conservation Engineer called Symons. The technical people like him and the Agricultural Inspectors were very much inclined to wizz round the District without one's knowledge and then send in a report on what they thought should be done. If I had known they were coming, we could have shown them where their particular wares were needed, after all it was our Council which had to pay for the wells or haffirs (small reservoirs) and we had to maintain them afterwards and provide a ghaffir (caretaker and collector of the money). So, I am asking them in turn to Council meetings as part of their education.

It was a great boon to be joined by Geoffrey on some of these occasions. He came to Kordofan to relieve David Evans as D.C. Obeid, but the administration had been completely handed over to the Town Council. As Inspector of Local Government he always provided a sympathetic ear when Council problems need unravelling and was able to support our budget proposals en route to Khartoum. We always welcomed his visits, apart from being able to discuss some of our problems, he was able to tell us what was happening in the wider world and some cantonment gossip! We felt rather guilty in taking him away from Pam and his children in El Obeid.

Our part of the entertainment was a large tea party for all the Members, guests, staff and anyone else who was there, about 80 in all.

This is Anne's description: -

Everyone in the world seems to have been here for the Council meeting. Eighty came to tea on Monday and it was a very successful party. Everyone sat on carpets in the garden in a long oblong in front of the rest house amongst the tubs of bourganvillia. All the cakes were down the middle where there was a gap for Abdel Rahman to move up and down to fill up the tea cups from our silver tea pot, he was helped by six other safragis. M and I circulated chatting to all the guests in turn.

Unusual to English tea parties, everyone here collects like a swarm of bees a little way up the road and they all descend en mass. We stood at the gate to shake hands as they came in. First of all, Babu and the Nazirs, then the Sheikhs and Omdas followed by the effendia in their best European clothes. Finally, we were towered over by all the tall long legged Dinka led by Nazir Deng. He was wearing a most magnificent green satin robe, under which, round his ankles showed white pyjamas, yellow socks and white shoes; he is the vogue for fashion if ever there was. Everyone had iced fresh lemonade to begin with, then tea and cakes, biscuits and meringues, finally sweets and toffees. Luscious sucking noises took the place of the tea hissssipping chorus.

AR was head butler and had organised all the crockery very well. Under his direction relays of runners had run round Fula collecting cups and saucers, teapots and plates from the residents an hour or so before the party began. By 5pm exactly, everything was ready.

The kitchen in the middle of the road

During the previous three days, Beshir and I had spent many pleasant hours in the kitchen in the middle of the road or outside it. Everyone in the village looked in to see how we were getting on. We turned out Swiss rolls, sponge cakes, fruitcakes, rock buns, biscuits etc. I measured all the ingredients and added them to Beshir's basin, while he stood as an almost mechanical beater, stopping only to put more wood into the stove or remove the last cake out of the oven. He really worked very hard and so did AR and Ahmed. Luckily there was plenty to eat and enough over for them to have a fill, I also sent some round to the Sherif's wife and took some over to Zeinab, she and AR had lent us quite a lot of crockery, including their best flowery tea pot.

The Council meeting lasted three days and finished yesterday, sitting from 7am until 2pm with a break for breakfast at 10am. So M, as Chairman and doing a lot of speaking felt pretty voice weary by the end. He finished off by telling them how their new government would work, illustrated by a great chart he had designed to show how the responsibilities go from the MPs and top officials to the bottom amongst the ordinary people. Geoffrey said it was an excellent speech and everyone was very pleased and gave M a big vote of thanks at the end. It was held for the first time in the new big Council chamber, the ceiling of which was finished the day before.

Now lorry loads of chaps are being packed up and sent home.

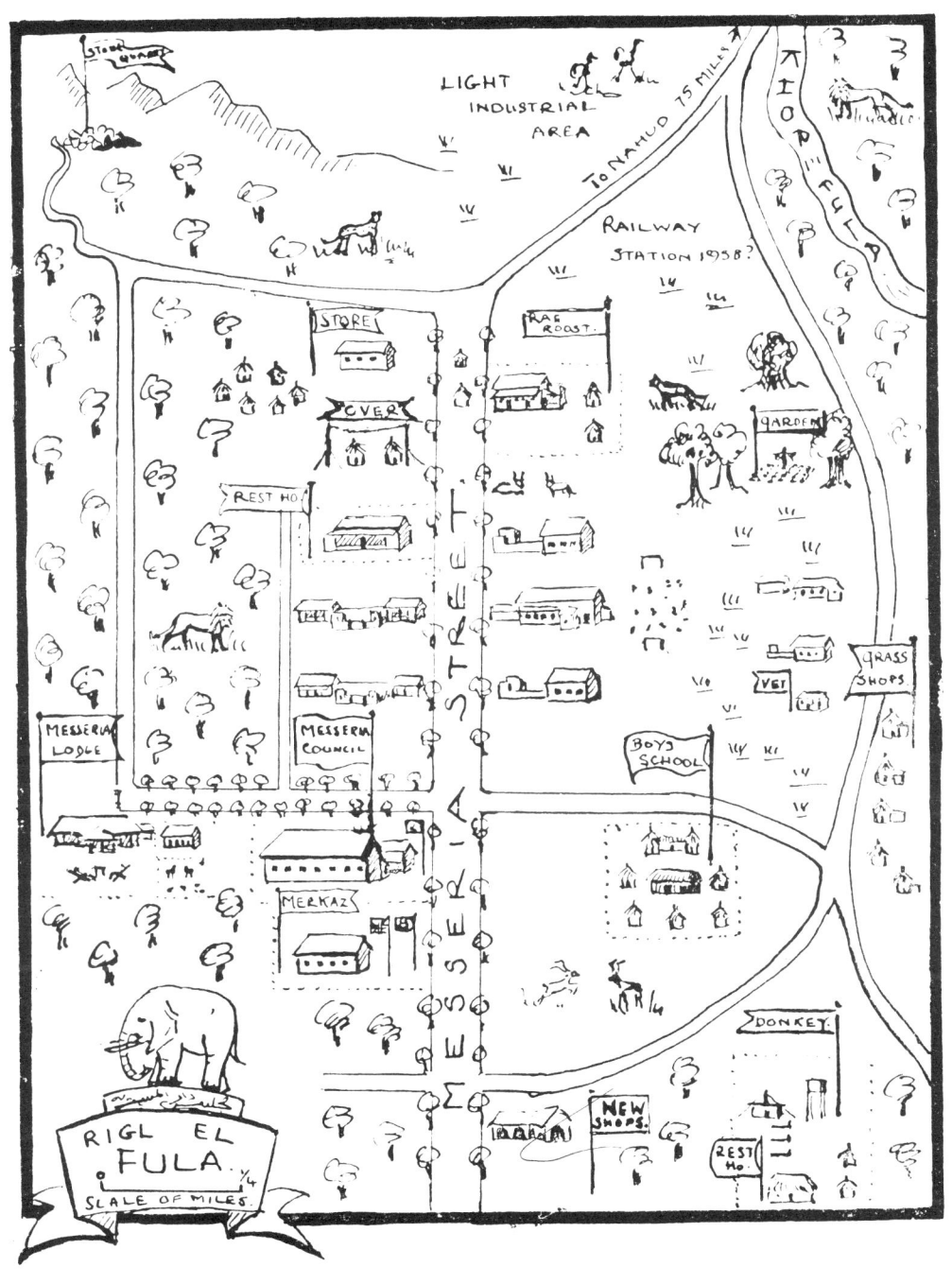

Our Christmas card 1953

Plan of new town of Rigl el Fula

18. ANNE IN RIGL EL FULA AND OUR HOUSE.

The rest house was a bit cramped and we were short of space for visitors; but It made all the difference to our lives to be settled in Rigl el Fula We badly wanted to get started on our own house and were determined to have something different from the normal standard public works plan. We had great fun drawing the plans and choosing the site. We decided on a patch about 150 yards south of the new Council Headquarters where there were some mature trees that would blend into the house and provide shade for the stable yard. We cleared a road up to it and planted neem trees on either side to make an avenue.

This account is from Anne's letters, the first one dated 9th September 1953: -

Great news, a message on the 'over' from the Governor to say the money for our house has been granted, though £E1,000 less than the £E4,500 we asked for. At last, we can really start off. The foundations cannot be dug for about a month as the workmen must finish the present batch of houses and also all the stone has to be hewn and carted from the jebel (hill) two miles away, but that will start at once. We went up there this evening but could not see much because of the tall grass everywhere. It was all fresh and green; the trees are covered in leaves. John Manton, an Agriculture Inspector arrived yesterday, two days late and stayed for two days. It was a change to see a white face for the first time since leaving El Obeid six weeks ago; although I can't say we miss it. We played quoits in the evenings and watched the effendia playing football on the open space beside us. John went off again early this morning.

We are all very flourishing except for Zeinab, who was sick before breakfast this morning, great hopes all round. She and the Seconda's wife came in the other morning and we had a great twitter together. I have also been to her house, which although it is just a round grass roofed tukl is quite immaculate and unbelievably neat inside. AR was busy doing all their cooking this morning, as she was not feeling well. The material which he gave M has now arrived made up in a bush jacket and two pairs of shorts, very nice indeed. The Sherif's wife and five children came round for elevenses the other morning, all in their best clothes, delightful children ranging from 13 to one years.

There are various holes around the veranda to drain it when it floods. They are used much more often by frogs, mice and caterpillars. Yesterday I opened my dressing table drawer and a large frog jumped out, the day before a six-inch long caterpillar crawled over the bed and today a long nosed shrew sat on the rug quite unafraid. This evening a large mouse scurried behind the cupboard and yet another toad joined us in the bath. So, we have decided to close the drain holes up, I am tired of catching creatures and putting them outside. I did half an hours vigorous digging before breakfast as the beginning of our vegetable plot. The spade belonging to our lorry is not made for a gardener digging deep spits as it is all curly to go under wheels stuck in sand?

The site for our house is now cleared, the grass and the avenue up to it all scythed down. We marked the trees, which have to be cut down in the middle of the road. Yesterday we had Babu and two other sheikhs to tea. Building has been held up as we ran out of cement owing to Babu bringing the lorry back from El Obeid full of his own belongings instead of our cement but we have now laid out the stable block and marked it all with pegs.

October 28th.
We marked out the house this morning before breakfast and the foundations are now being dug. There are at least forty builders and workmen swarming around the site and the walls of the stables are progressing rapidly. Lorry loads of sand from the nearby khor (dry river bed) are arriving and two 3'x6'x6' concrete tanks have been built in which to store the water for building, they will be useful for the animals and garden later. It is really such fun that it has started at last. We do not expect to move in much before January. Although the walls may be up quickly, the finishings like doors all have to be made by the carpenter..

November 3rd. Progress
Stables. Foundations finished and walls built including plastering inside. Time taken eight days.
House. Foundations marked out, dug out and filled in. Time taken, five days. We are going to have a bull slaughtered for the builders to celebrate.

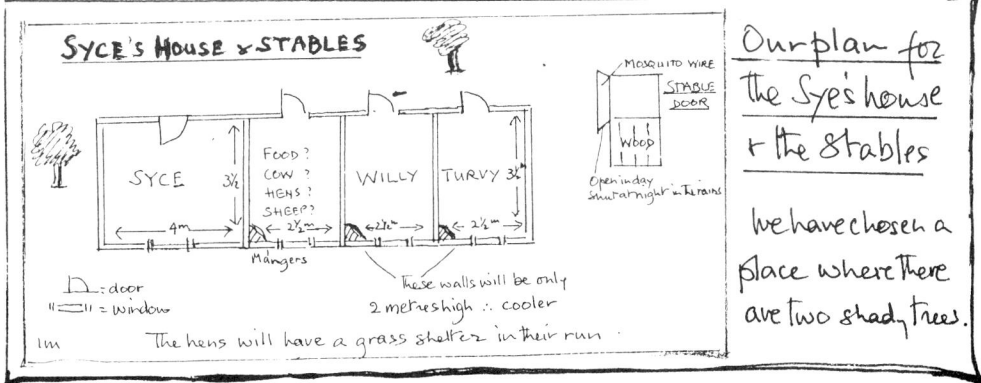

Progress of our house.

The foundations are dug.

M sitting by the front door. Headbuilder Ahmed behind.

Between the kitchen & the pantry

Did I tell you we now have a cow and calf given us by Omda Musa Shwein, the old chap who gave me the lion skin? The boy who drove them up gave us a message to say her name was Arnouk, a golden crested crane, so they too now share the rest house garden and have a little grass shelter. What with guests in the tent and the servants in their tukls we are a merry party, soon to be joined by our own livestock. The cow goes out to graze everyday; the calf is tethered in the garden. At first there were great bellowings and the mother rushed backwards and forwards every five minutes between mouthfuls to see if her calf was all right. Now she goes further afield and then returns to lie down under a tree nearby where she can keep an eye on her calf. At night she comes in too. We have not had much milk yet as the calf usually gets there first, he is big, more of a young bull really.

November 6th. Muglad.
We are here for two days if M can get through the work quick enough; we don't want to be too long, as we have to keep a sharp eye on the house. The house is now up to window level. Our bath, three sinks, a wash basin and our kitchen stove have arrived. The last has been installed temporarily in the rest house kitchen. The others clutter up our verandah. They were ordered in Khartoum by the Sherif and came to El Obeid by lorry. By way of unloading they were just thrown out so the bath and stove were broken. They have now been mended and the contractor was made to pay £E10 for his carelessness.

The other day during the night we heard our lorry arriving from Nahud with the syce's wife, sheep, turkeys, hens and duck. In the morning we found them all flourishing in the rest house hosh (enclosure) which is now fuller than ever. Rachel the duck came up in her own carriage with her four grown up turkey children and started bossing them around as soon as they were let out. We have left instructions with Ibrahim, the prison warder to have a wire run made for the poultry or we shall have no tomatoes left. The sheep roam loose to graze all day with the cow but they all come back to sleep at night, safe from the hyenas. The horses are on their way to Fula with the syce. We do not have goats, they are browsers rather than grasers and are so destructive that M has issued an order banning them from a radius of five miles around the town. Any stray goats are put in the pound and the owners pay a fine to get them out again.

Zeinab is feeling better and is taking iron and vitamin pills. I brought some white poplin and muslin material for her from El Obeid to make a nightgown and a smock for the new arrival. I got some patterns from Mary Hawkesworth, so now we have great dress making sessions. AR also bought her some very pretty dress material for herself which delighted her, but there is no one here to make it up. She does not know how, so I am going to help her. AR said he bought the material to make her very happy, as if the mother is happy, then the baby will be good and happy too. I am just making two new cummerbunds for AR and Ahmed and a pennant for our lorry which M is now entitled to fly as a DC. It is green with the Province badge on it 'embroidered' in white. We have been up to our house last night and again before breakfast this morning.

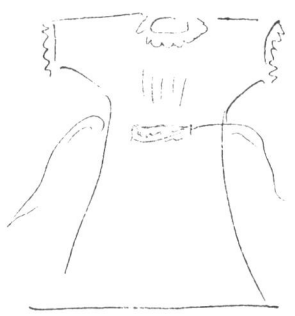

November 10th. Back at Fula.

We have just had tea in the garden after a lovely ride; the horses arrived three days ago. We rode before breakfast yesterday too. It is so different riding here; Nahud was just dull sand and scrubbly trees. We ride up and see the house, now at top of window level all round. We have had to have one or two places knocked down again, where they have not done the right measurements. Nothing too serious. Luckily we got back from Muglad in time to stop a disaster at the pantry end of the house. We wanted the inside wall between the pantry and store of cement blocks to save space but they built the outside wall in blocks as well.

Coming back from Muglad we saw a beautiful female leopard, it was dark and we suddenly had her in the headlights. We stopped and she just stood there very close indeed, then with a graceful leap, she bounded into the undergrowth. We also saw a civet cat with lovely tiger markings and a pair of foxes trotted along in front of us for quite a way.

Three days ago, M and I had been marking the places for windows in our house. On coming back to the rest house at 10.30am, we saw a lorry drive up. Out jumped Ian Cunninson on his way back from leave. No sooner had we directed him to our tent in the garden when another lorry arrived with another white and hefty arm waving from it. Out got 'Fretters', Miss Fretwell, a tough Inspector of Girls' schools. As our 'spare room' was now occupied we showed her to the donkey rest house, though of course she fed with us. She departed the day afterwards at crack of dawn, to inspire more fear into Sudanese school marms. Ian is still with us though is off to Muglad tomorrow to rejoin his ferik. He is living in every way, including food; with the Baggara for a year or two in order record their customs and habits. He is very entertaining and interesting and we look forward to reading his book. He is thirty, Scots, very nice and easy to have as a guest. He very kindly brought a slide projector from England for us. M thought it a good idea as then we can show people other parts of the District, which they will not have seen. We also hope to get other educational slides.

We had the first show last night in the Council Chamber. All the schoolboys, clerks, the Sherif and family, servants, police, carpenters, builders and notables of Fula were invited. The machine worked beautifully off our two car batteries. M got hoarser and hoarser trying to make himself heard above the far from quiet audience. Shrieks of delight, Oos and Aaahs. The first time M and I appeared there was thunderous clapping and cheering, this followed each time we reappeared. Sa'ata Sit (me) on a donkey got much laughter too. Eventually M persuaded them to keep quiet so they could hear what he was saying. Their nude Nuba neighbours got a good laugh and one or two of England caused quite a sensation, all that green grass and all those trees, now we understand why you want to build a house away amongst the trees.

Wednesday. November 11th

A very busy morning, both alarm clocks set to ring at different times for a. guava jelly and b. bottles of preserved lemon juice, both bubbling hard on the primus stove in the pantry while I was dress making. Needless to say the guava overflowed, a sticky mess all over the floor, just as the marmalade did yesterday. I made 8 quarter-pounds of lemon marmalade, enough to last us till next leave; fifty lemons bought in the suq (market) cost 1/- (5p), and seven pounds of sugar cost 7/-(35p) roughly a shilling 1/- (5p) per pound pot. If

Our shopping centre.

we had bought it in Khartoum, it would have cost 3/-(15p) a pound, so it's very economical. A sewing record for me, a dress in a day, but I might add it was for Ajegeha, AR and Zeinab's niece, aged 7. I made it like the ones I used to have as a child and she looks very sweet in it, white with green and red spots.

Zeinab also looks very elegant in her new creation. We had an amusing session this morning when she and the syces's wife came along for elevenses. Afterwards we went into the bedroom to try on the finished garments. They paraded in front of the long glass and were intrigued when I showed them how to see their own back view with a second mirror. Zeinab looked most attractive with her petite little figure and her mass of tiny black plaits hanging round her shoulders. In each ear dangled two huge gold coins, a present from AR, £E5 each, round her neck a necklace of small gold coins, also a present £E12 and of course, gold ring in her nose. They eventually went off in their new attire, well swathed in their tobs. The syce's wife remarked that the dresses were fit for a wedding. I hope I don't have to make her one now, her figure is somewhat splayed.

We are off to Lagawa tomorrow, a new direct road has been cut that we can use during the dry season. This means it should only take three hours rather than two whole days via the Jebels.

Now that the syce is back I can rather thankfully hand over my husbandry duties to him. I have been washing grain for the sheep, seeing that the cow's udders were washed with lifebouy soap, rounding up the hens and turkeys when they got out, holding Daisy's back legs so her lamb could have a good drink, 'Flitting' the calf for flies and directing the two new prisoners, more dopey than the last, to fetching hay, taking the sheep and cow out to graze, bringing them in to water at twelve and again at night..The performance at milking hours is quite a pantomime. Arnouk, the cow, rather fierce when near her calf had to be tied by the horns to a stake to stop her butting, then while the calf was getting the milk flowing, and drinking most of it, her back legs were tied together and then to another stake to stop her kicking. One of the prisoners was even more scared of the cow than Maimie (my aunt), so it all took some time. Each time the poor cow moves her toe he would make a rapid retreat and then make another attempt at lassoing the back legs. I, on the other hand am now quite scared of Augustus our ram, which he knows and takes advantage of, so I take refuge behind the water barrel so I can run round it if he charges.

Altogether, I have enjoyed it, though I am now glad to have time for other things in the evenings. The cool of the evening is short lived as darkness falls rapidly at 6 o'clock.

The Hunters have been staying for two nights. As soon as Mary appears she is besieged by ladies calling to see her, all with the same complaint. One has just come saying she has had a baby inside for eight years but it still has not come out. Mary gets fed up as there is so little she can do in most cases. Happily she has been able to confirm that Zeinab is now about three months pregnant

. Mary and I went off with Segeir (our driver) with two prisoners and a warder and found six more poison trees for our garden, from the nearby countryside. These are about 4 foot high with pink waxy flowers on the top, no leaves, growing out of thick tree like trunks, they have very few roots and transplant very easily. We also bought four more laying hens 12pt (12p) in the market, it being market day, one hen was extra as she actually laid an egg while travelling in from a village on a bull.

Our Dinka cow arrived today. At the Council meeting, Deng Majok had said he was sending us a cow for milking. We said that we would be very pleased to borrow it. As usual, it was one of those difficult decisions. A letter then arrived from Nazir Deng to say it was on its way. Two cows then arrived plus their calves; they had been escorted up from Abyie by two Dinka policemen. We said we could only have one and chose the pretty one, although she is twenty years old and may not give as much milk as the other one we fell in love with her at once. She has huge horns and black eye shadow. Her name is Aleak and the calf Dannielle. Deng Majok's son is here learning to be an accountant. He took me to see the cows this morning when they arrived. We were waiting for M to come, and as he was a long time Ahmed said "Won't you go inside Madam until the District Commissioner arrives?" He speaks quite good English, his father the Nazir knows no English, nor reads or writes in any language.

December 9th. House progress report.

The roof is now completely on, pointing of outside walls being done, nearly all windows in. Inside ceilings started, plastering inside done, and door posts being put in. Still to be done. Outside verandah, all floors, distempering doors and shutters to be made, mosquito wiring for doors and window, sinks and bath to be installed. We have been marking places for shelves. One servant's house finished, except for doors and windows, the other on its way up.

As usual, we are going to El Obeid for Christmas and invitations are already arriving by the donkey load!

Abyei,
26/11/53

Dear Mr. G. M. G. Tibbs

I hope you & your wife are well. Further to my conversation with Mrs. Tibbs at Fula about a milk-cow that I promised to send it to her; I shall today send the cow with a Dinka man to reach you earlier in Fula. I hope the cow will reach safely. Hence I would be grateful if you could inform Mrs. Tibbs about this. I am anxious to see you, both, in the near time.

Yours Sincerely

Chief Deling Majok

↑

This is the letter from Nazir Deng — The Dinka Chief. He can't write so he has dictated it to his son — N.B. The stamp is with his signet ring ↑ (The cow will have a 200 mile walk)

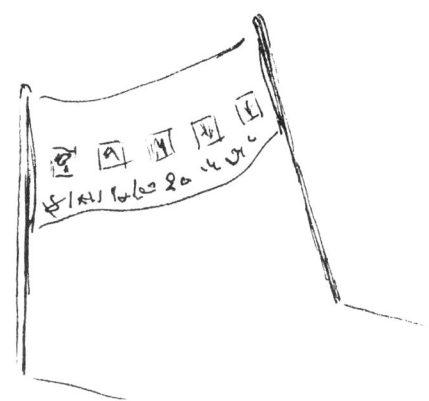

19. ELECTION FEVER.

While we had been busy worrying about the Council, building at Rigl el Fula, relationships between the tribes and the various day to day problems, great decisions were being taken about the future of us all. When I first got to Khartoum at the beginning of 1949, I had visited a session of the new Legislative Assembly. It had been the first time that Southerners had been included in such a body with representatives from the whole Sudan. However, political agitation for self-determination to include union with Egypt and/or independence continued. Matters were further bedevilled by demands from Cairo for Egyptian sovereignty over the Sudan to be recognised by H.M.G. In October, the Egyptian Prime Minister announced the unilateral abrogation of the 1936 Treaty and the 1899 Agreement concerning the Sudan and proclaimed King Farouk as King of the Sudan. There had been no consultation with the Sudanese, and even the pro Egyptian party, the Ashigga did not support this action. However, the race to independence had been speeded up. Then in Egypt, King Farouk was compelled to abdicate and General Neguib took over. It was he who wooed the Sudanese independents by agreeing that they should have independence from, rather than union with, Egypt if that was what they really wanted.

Talks between the Foreign Office and the Egyptians started off, then in January 1953, all the Sudanese parties signed an agreement with Egypt. The Sudan Government had been trying to include in any agreement, safeguards for the South and continuance of the administration of the country, but this cut the ground from under its feet.

We were in Rigl el Fula with Peter Hogg and the Buchanans (Director of Local Governemnt), when we heard on the wireless that an agreement was to be signed in Cairo that day, 14th February. We returned to Nahud where Peter found a telegram from the Governor saying that despite our personal misgivings, this was a great day in the life of the Sudan, It was to be a public holiday and a day of rejoicing. A large tea party was quickly arranged, tables were set out in front of the Hoggs' house. How invitations were sent out at no notice, I am not quite sure. I remember asking Peter what to wear; he consulted Lawrence Buchanan who advised that as this was an official occasion, we were on duty and should wear uniform office dress with decorations, so this is what we did.

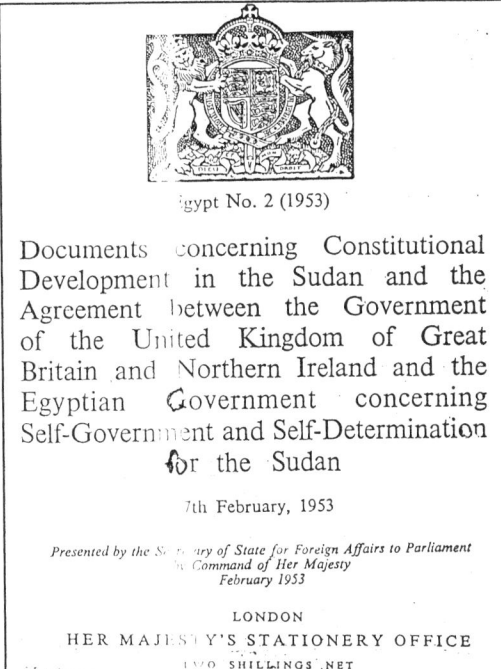

Egypt No. 2 (1953)

Documents concerning Constitutional Development in the Sudan and the Agreement between the Government of the United Kingdom of Great Britain and Northern Ireland and the Egyptian Government concerning Self-Government and Self-Determination for the Sudan

7th February, 1953

Presented by the Secretary of State for Foreign Affairs to Parliament by Command of Her Majesty February 1953

LONDON
HER MAJESTY'S STATIONERY OFFICE
TWO SHILLINGS NET

Cmd. 8767

When we realised what the agreement included, we were all horrified. The one between the Sudanese political parties and Neguib had included the appointment of a 'Commission' to work with the Governor General, another to supervise elections, with direct elections in the North. The Political Service, Sudan Defence Force and the Police were to be 'Sudanised' with self-determination in three years. We found that all these and more were included in the final agreement. On the bright side, the Egyptian insistence about 'Unity of the Nile Valley' had been dropped.

Next time we visited Lagawa, we learnt that some of the merchants and effendia organised a picnic to celebrate 'Freedom Day'. Nazir Izz el Din and Mekki Amin had a hard time. They said they had nothing to celebrate and shut themselves up in their houses all day. Now the riffraff are calling them traitors and going round to Mekki's shop and congratulating him, which infuriates him. He came round to the rest house and said he is going to drink molten solder on Independence Day, in front of the Sol of Police. There is nothing one can do to re-assure him. Although he is not a Messeria, his family originally came from Dongalla, he is accepted as one of themselves and they rely on his advice; so if there is a bust up, he will be on the right side. Faragalla, the Sultan of Kamdang also refused to celebrate and all his sons laughed at him.

I had a talk with Izz el Din and some of his Omdas, as they wanted to know more about this 'freedom'.

"Is there going to be any prison?"   "Yes".
"Are there going to be any taxes?"   "Yes".
"That's not freedom, that's nonsense"

Sheikh Sadig, the school master, was in favour of the agreement except for the three years limit before which we would have to go. In any case he said that the English had too high a sense of duty to walk out if the Sudanese wanted them. If they really had to go and there were not enough Sudanese to fill the D.C.s vacancies, they could be recruited from somewhere else. Asked how they could arrive, not knowing Arabic or anything about the Sudan and take over, he thought they could go on a course for six months and then look in the files to see how the English had done it.

Events moved swiftly. The Commissions were appointed. The Electoral Commission was under the Chairmanship of an Indian, Mr Sukamar Seen. A comprehensive 'House of Representatives Electoral Rules' was published in June. This covered such items as 'Manner of preparation of Electoral Rolls and Nomination of Candidates', down to 'Polling Station', 'Voting by Ballot Paper' and 'Voting by Token'

I wrote home on the 15th October from El Obeid where we had come for a few days to stay with the Hawkesworths. "Fortunately we had no appeals against the electoral rolls. John Hunter had 400 in Nahud from westerners who were whipped up by the 'Anti-Colonial Front'. We may have appeals in Lagawa and Rigl el Fula from candidates whose nominations have been turned down by the Returning Officer. I think that our Umma (anti-Egyptian) candidate will get in, but some unlikely places have gone over to the Egyptians, having been bought. One wonder why the Government cannot do more about this, but of course the responsibility is now that of the Electoral Commission. Geoffrey Hawkesworth is being fiercely attacked in the papers here and his removal demanded for 'trying to influence the course of the elections".

We left El Obeid for Lagawa, where I might have to hear some electoral appeals. We went down the new Dilling road that they have been making for the last four years. All very happy until 4.30 when the road became a quagmire. We were stuck in a hole for an hour, but a suq lorry pulled us out. It was dark, but we just kept moving. At last three miles from Dilling we came upon a torrent, some chaps were trying to walk across it but we decided it was not on' and camped. Fortunately Ahmed Abu Gasim had made us bring our tent so we were quite dry and comfortable. Although everything was six inches deep in mud, we slept well. Got up at 6am and found that the khor at which we had stopped had an Irish bridge about 8 feet deep, the water had spread about 50 yards on either side, so we were very glad we had stopped where we did.

Off at 7 and managed to get into Dilling for breakfast with the Jack Hunters (D.C.) and John Haggar (A.D.C.). We found Bukr, our Assistant Executive Officer from Lagawa waiting for us. He had Ahmed Abu Gasim's 15cwt boxcar and much lighter than our lorry.

We ground on until we found a long stretch of gravel covered in water about two feet deep.. Bukr did some scouting and said he had found a way round..We followed him crashing through trees. Suddenly the whole back of the lorry sank right up to the box. We dug, shunted and cut trees. Eventually we had lunch while Bukr went off to find some chaps to help pull us out. Five minutes later he came back to say his box car was right in. Twenty Nuba arrived in various stages of undress, they all heaved; suddenly the box car popped back and nearly hit Abdel Rahman which everyone except him thought very funny. Then they all came and pulled at ours, more heaving, more chaps. It was 7pm by the time we got her out, so we went back to the road and camped.

A night on the road.

At 7am the next morning the sheikh arrived to show us a good road. We came to a muddy patch, which the boxcar sailed over, but plumph, and there we were for the rest of the day. We did not get out until 5.30pm.

By this time, it was far too late to go on to Lagawa as I had to be back in Rigl el Fula by tomorrow (21st). We camped again and the next morning they showed us another way which did take us back to the hard road with chaps going ahead cutting down the trees that were in the way. We went back the way we had come, into Sallara, then on to Kasha where we had lunch. The Nuba there said they were all very tired as brothers of two of the candidates had been there and told them to vote for their man. They did not want to be rude, but could not vote for both of them and did not know what to do. I could not tell them, but they were very pleased with me as I had managed to get all those involved with the rock throwing contest out of jug and their sentences reduced from two years to six months. The offenders are now on leave to get their harvest in. They can then go out and work on the roads for a bit.

We went on to Abu Zabad for the night. Although it is only three days to polling day, some citizens are very confused about it. Some said they had not met this man called Election and wondered when he was going to come and see them. We eventually got back to Rigl el Fula at 5pm. Kind Ahmed Abu Gasim gave us cold lemonade and tea at his house and we had a good gossip.

The main talk in El Obeid had been, of course, the election. They think that we are lucky to be somewhat isolated from it. The Umma, Sayed Abdel Rahmans' party has five candidates standing for the Muglad constituency, though the official one is Sayed Fadal. He is Babu's father in law and quite unknown locally. Tomorrow I have to hear an appeal from another aspiring candidate; the Returning Officer has tuned him down as he cannot read. If I decide that he can, that will make six from the same party. They cannot understand the logic that if a party has only one candidate, he is more likely to get in. The Unity part has only one candidate.

By the middle of November, the election was going full swing. I reported in a letter that I did not think we would have any trouble; about 10% of the parishioners seemed to know what it was about.

The Electoral Rules were very comprehensive. District Commissioners were to take no part in the administration. So far as we were concerned, Ahmed Abu Gasim was the Returning Office for the Muglad constituency and Bukr Ali for the Lagawa one. There were very comprehensive rules. Rules for 'Polling stations and Polling', and 'Two ways of voting, by Ballot Paper or by Token'. As most of our electorate were

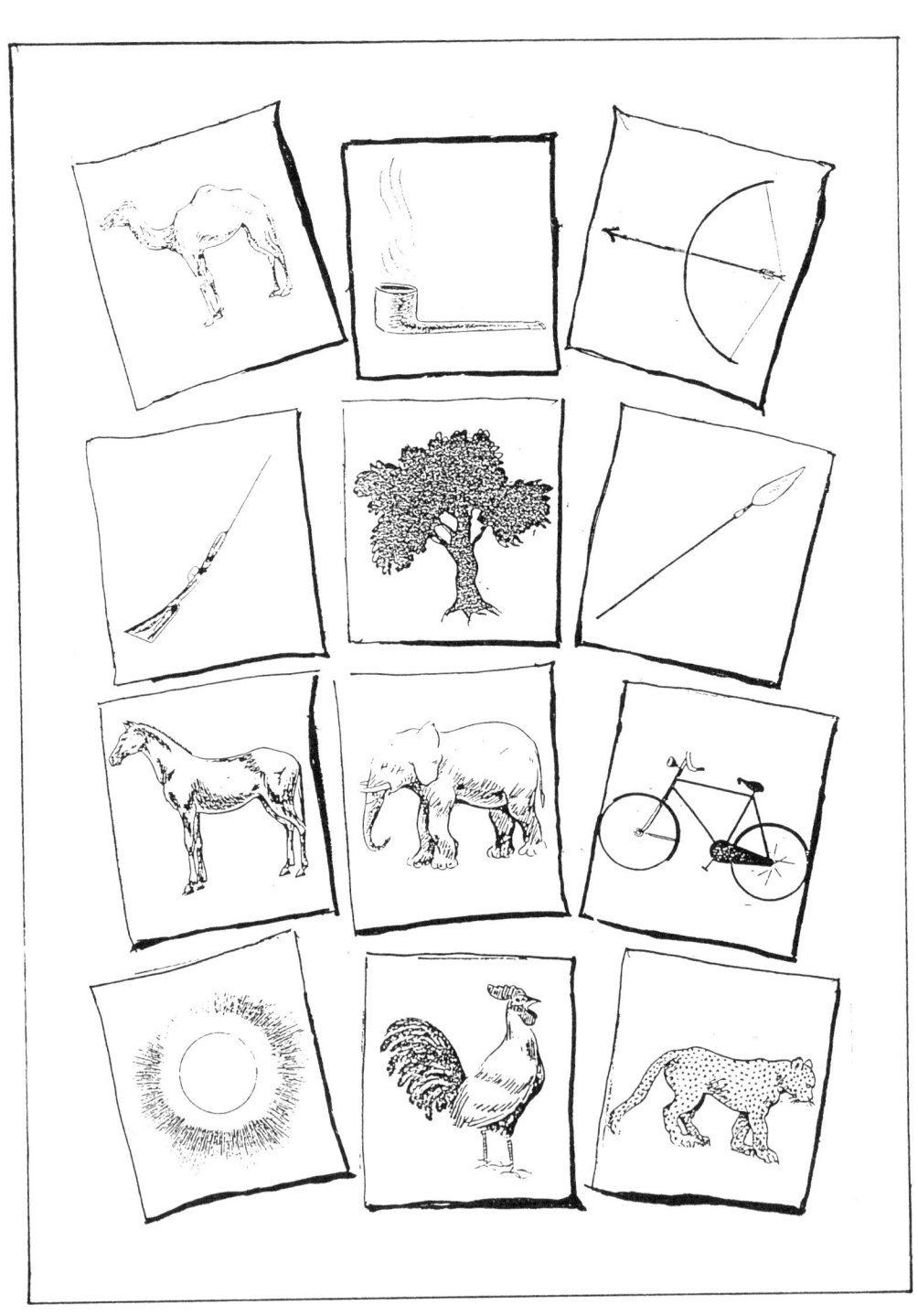

"Voting by token ------

.... the candidates being represented by symbols."

illiterate, it had been decided that they would vote by token. The Returning Officer and Committee had to explain the rules to the constituents, such as:-

15(1)...'each voter shall cast his vote by a voting token which shall not bear on it any of the colours of the candidates or their name. Voting Tokens shall be serially numbered and one token shall not be otherwise distinguishable from any other'.

15(6)-'the voter shall be given a voting token with which he will enter the room alone and cast his vote by dropping his token into the ballot box of the candidate in whose favour he wishes to vote'

-All summarised by number-

15(8)-'The provisions of sub rules (3), (9), (12), (13), and (15) to rule (19) of rule 14 shall apply to voting by token as far as they are applicable thereto, ballot papers being interpreted to mean a voting token and a ballot box to mean all ballot boxes at a polling station''.

At one place in Dinka land, they had a rehearsal. It was explained that they had to put a paper in one of the boxes. The 'Token System' was being used, the candidates being represented by symbols, a picture of a tree represented candidate A, a gazelle was the sign of B, etc. They said they all understood, so the rehearsal went on. When it was finished the room was covered in bits of paper, under the tables, under the boxes and some even stuck on the ceiling! In another place they started a primary election, (in the south it is being done in two stages). A large body of voters arrived, as ordered, without spears or clubs, but the other lot arrived complete with spears. This was of course too much for the first arrivals that departed at the rush to get their weapons. Voting was suspended for a week.

On our way to Lagawa, we called on Khamis Gelab the Sultan of Tima. He said he would vote for the axe as he thought it stronger than the tree or the hut, though he did not know whom it actually represented. I can't see the Dinka voting for anything other than the spear; (John Hunter says that in Nahud, the box of matches seems to be well in front). We then called on Faragalla, the Sultan of Kamdang. He is the father of the Unity (pro-Egyptian) candidate, but he is voting for Hammad Mohammed Dafaala, the official Umma candidate.

Voting started while we were in Lagawa and all was going smoothly. DC.s are not allowed anywhere near the booths in case we 'interfere'. In any case, I am busy with four Magisterial enquiries (commitments to a Major Court), seven other minor cases and I have to look at new shop sites, inspect the market, the prison, the police horses and mules and the hospital.

We came back via Abu Genouk, the large jebel (mountain) in the middle of the plain as I had to complete an enquiry there. In addition to the usual things on the lorry, we had two sheep bound with rope, two hens bound with string and a murderer bound with chains. The new rest house was not ready so we slept in the polling booth. The poor Sultan was almost in tears as he has agreed with three candidates to vote for them as he did not want to be rude. He really does not know which one he wants. I had to say I could not help, but dropped a few hints and hoped for the best. Our job is to be responsible for security, but we have now been ordered not even to explain what the election is about. We have to refer such matters to the local Electoral Committee. Fortunately I had a go at the Members after the last Council meeting and explained the implications. It is all so bizarre when one thinks that if there had been a pro-British party it would probably sweep the board.

We now have to go to Muglad on Saturday as there are complaints about illegal promises and bribery. I do not know if there is anything in it or not.

The scene now moves to –

Muglad, Declaration Day 28th November.

We arrived at 5pm last night to find a deathly hush, no complaints. I started to read Churchill vol. IV. Then the Police Sol (Sergeant Major) arrived and produced six cases against Sayed Fadal Mahmoud Abdel Karim, one of the Umma candidates and Babu's father in law. I start going through the police report with the investigator, Nafar (Constable) Ahmed Hag Agbar. Then Ahmed Abu Gasim arrives,, he is the Returning Officer. He had a letter from one of the Presiding Officers at Abyie and sent the Sol of Police straight down there; he had just arrived back with six, not one, cases. Ahmed Abu Gasim explained the complications.

The policeman, Ahmed Hag Agbar is the uncle of Nur el Din Serier Hag Agbar, one of the rival Umma candidates. So, the Fadal/Babu faction are saying it is all a frame up by the Nur el Din side. However, four of the informations are laid by Dinka. There are therefore all the ingredients of a first class fitna (i.e. a conspiracy into which everybody will drag everybody else if possible).

Action. Send my driver, Segeir to Nahud with Intel (news telegram) saying what had happened, but that in any case the Returning Officer would open the boxes to see who had won. The Police Officer should come down and check the investigation, inform the Resident Magistrate and ask him to come down if possible. Segeir departed at 9pm and arrived in Nahud at 2am.

29th November.

7am. Continued going through the police investigation and decided to carry on with two of the accusations as Magisterial Enquires to see if the accused should be committed for trial or not. Then Nazi Deng arrived and complained that Sayed Fadal removed an Omda and Dinka Sheikh from Abyie to Muglad; he demanded their instant dismissal as they both went without his (Deng's) permission and in any case they were both bailed to stay in Abyie

The informations against Sayed Fadal were:-
1. He gave £3 to Omda Akwa Deng and £2 to Sheikh Achwiel Mayot.
   (Informant, Abdel Rahman Ril, the Unity Party Agent).
2. He gave £5 to Omda Achweil Bulabek,
   (Informant, himself).
3. He gave £1 to Mulwal Buket, a Dinka serving in the Egyptian Armuy, but now on leave.
   (Informant, Ahmed Hag Agar).
4. He gave £3.25 to Omda Fagwat Deng.
   (Informant, himself).
5. He gave £1 to Omda Ngol Myot.
   (Informant, himself).
6. He gave lifts to voters to the polling station
   (Informant, Nur el Din Sereir – rival Umma candidate).
7. Complaint by those in no.1 above that their confession had been extorted by Policeman Ahmed Hag Agbar and denying the information they has laid against Sad Fadal

10am. Arrived at the Merkaz (government building) to find it surrounded by police with rifles. The votes were being counted in my office, so I had to start off the court in the Police office. In spite of all the guards round the place to keep the angry crowd waiting to hear the result at bay, there was no one in sight except for two chaps sitting under a tree. I found a nice old boy waiting for me. He was wearing a long galabia and guftan, spectalces and was about 48 years of age. This was the accused.

I opened the court and began. Proceedings were then delayed to find a Dinka interpreter. Found one. Another delay. Interpreter refused to swear on the Koran and said he could only swear on cow dung from Abyie. Find Nazir Deng Majok. He arrives, situation explained. Someone is dispatched to find his 'pillow' (half a gourd) which has some sand and two pieces of thorn on top of it. Interpreter and witnesses are content to swear on this, so the case can now proceed.

12 Noon   Case adjourned to hear the result of the poll.
    Fadal Mahmoud (Umma)   2,295.
    Nur el Din Serier (Umma)   1,790.
    Mussalim Ismail (Umma)   609.
    Ahmed Omer (Umma)   139.
    Abdel Salam Maboub (Unity) 114.

The Returning Officer decides not to make the declaration until the result of the case is known.

12.15 –1.30. Go on with the case.

3.30 – 6pm Start second case.

Then listen to English news from Omdurman Radio; a landslide for the Unity party.

8pm   Arrival of the Police Officer from Nahud with extra police to control the riot. No one in sight to make a riot anyway,

9pm   Arrival of the Resident Magistrate.

30th November.

Discussed pros and cons of the case all the morning with the Resident Magistrate and the Police Officer. Several statements have been taken from witnesses on oath. We decide that all the cases depend on no.7, but witnesses are required from Abyie. The Police Officer is despatched to get them

2nd December.

The Resident Magistrate finished a long drawn our case of an Omda who hunted giraffe without a licence and sentenced him to three months. I then formally dismiss him from his post as Omda. The Police Officer returns at last: His lorry's petrol pump had given trouble and he had taken 20 hours to get 120 miles.

I began taking statements at once before the new witnesses had time to get contaminated by other Dinka or anyone else! Arrived back at the rest house at 4.45. for lunch to find two very hungry wives.

3rd December. 10 am.
The Resident magistrate announces his decision.
1. Dropped, partly owing to no.7 and witnesses deny their first stories.
2. Magisterial enquiry to continue.
3. Stopped. Mulwal Buket had no vote so not covered by Corrupt Practices Ordinance
4. Magisterial enquiry to continue.
(In fact stopped through lack of evidence).
5, Stopped. No witnesses.
6. Closed, the law was not infringed.

10.30am. Continued with the Inquiry and examined the accused. Then took his statement after warning him that he need not say anything, or that he may wait for an advocate. He then gave a very long and irrelevant statement. Heard two witnesses who knew nothing. Finally, charged Sayed Fadal with giving Omda Achwel Bulabek £5 in an attempt to influence his vote and commited him for trial by a Major Court.

At 1pm, I made my way to the lorry outside and finally got into it at 1.30. In the meantime, the Police investigator was found guilty of intimidating a witness and fined £5.

In the other constituency everything went smoothly.
Hammas Mohamed Dafaala (Umma) 5,546
Beshir Mohamed Fegir (Umma) 852
Hassam Mohamed Nur (Unity) 911

The Major Court was convened in El Obeid. Sayed Fadal was represented by one of the best Khartoum advocates. The Court dismissed the case and Sayed Fadal was declared elected.

It transpired that most of the Dinka voted for Nur el Din. A lot of the Humr did not vote at all. They did not want Nur el Din as he was a Felleita (the other half of the tribe) and they did not want Fadal, so not wanting to offend Abu, they were content to leave it to the Almighty!"

Post Script
While we were in Muglad with the Hunters, they said that they were in a dilemma as they had both been offered jobs in Atbara, the large railway town in the Northern Province; he as Police Magistrate and she as lady doctor. They are trying to make up their minds. We will miss them if they do go as they are very great friends. Anne and Mary were brides together in Nahud and helped each other to learn the ropes. Mary has been particularly

kind in treating Anne's bad throats. Although now separated by 100 miles, we still meet them often and enjoy each other's company and hearing each other's news. If they go, we will be the only Inglise for 150 miles as the crow flies to Dilling and far more as the lorry goes in the rains. However, we are both well and cheerful and very happy with all our Sudanese friends.

(They did not go to Atbara in the end, but to El Obeid)

Polling booth - at Abu Genouk.

December 1953

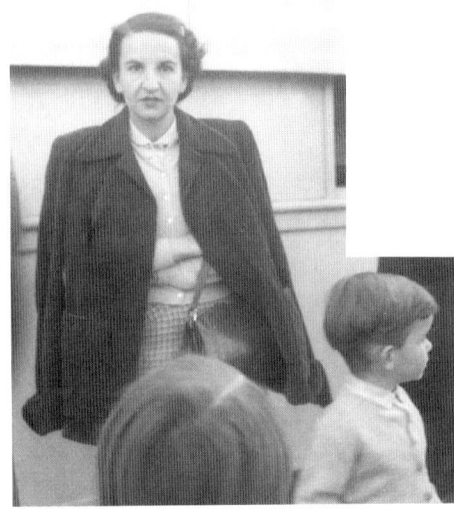

Mary Hawkesworth and Mark leaving Kordofan

The Sherif and his family

Our police force in Fula in their new uniforms.

M on Turvy Top.

20. 1953 DRAWS TO AN END, A BUSY DECEMBER, TO EL OBEID, ABYIE AND BACK AGAIN.

Early in December we did a quick dash into El Obeid to wave goodbye to the Hawkesworths who were leaving for good. They have been so kind to us both and to me before Anne came on the scene. Geoffrey has spent twenty-seven years in the Political Service, most of it in Kordofan and he knows and loves it all. The Unity party supporters have been conducting a vile press campaign which has been very wearying. They even tried to get people to boycott the auction of their furniture but fortunately people turned up just the same and they did not do too badly. Both of them were very tired after an endless round of farewell tea parties and dinner parties given by the British. The Inglese trying to out do each other, and countless Sudanese tea parties. In the end they were glad to go. There was a great crowd and an impressive ceremony at the station. Both the Camel Corps and the Police mounted Guards of Honour, which presented arms and had to be inspected. We cheered as the train slowly gathered speed bearing Geoffrey and his family away from Kordofan and most of his life's work.

Anne takes up the story....

Our lorry was already loaded up and as soon as the train pulled out we set off for home. When we got back, we had a slide party for the ladies. The Sherif's wife plus Fatna (10), Omer (7), and Mimi (4) arrived half an hour early, just as we were going to have our bath so we settled them with some Tatlers. The rest of the party arrived an hour late, Zeinab and Hajejah, AR's niece, Ahmed's wife, the Syce's wife and some relation of a police driver who lives here, also Anna Redman a nursing sister from El Obeid hospital who was staying over night. Orangeade and sweets, nuts and raisins followed the slides, and from the chatter and remarks we gathered they all enjoyed themselves.

We left Rigl el Fula on Saturday having waved Zeinab and Abdel Rahman off in the Council lorry. AR is taking Zeinab home to have her baby and will meet us in El Obeid when we go in for Christmas. We spent the night in Tebeldia. The next morning, with the Sherif in his lorry and a well digging team in four lorries, we had breakfast further down the road. We were looking for a well site, the beginning of an agricultural project, the area is very fertile and virtually untouched. The team is in charge of a delightful geologist, half Sudanese and half Syrian, George Kakarnis. Then on to Abyie where we arrived at 1pm.

No sooner had we arrived at the rest house when two Verona 'White' Fathers arrived on motor scooters, having ridden 100 miles from Wau with complaints from Bishop Masoon that their 'adherents', R.C boys, were being persecuted in the school for their faith. M explained that as the Messeria Council's remit now extended to the Ngok, this was for the school committee, the Nazir and the Executive Officer of the Council to discuss and he would arrange a meeting. We put them and their iron steeds in the back of the lorry and drove them back into the village where we were meeting Deng Majok and the Omdas. We all went and looked at the recently completed R.C. church and the boys' school's new boarding house. I also went with Ahmed to the Medical Assistant as A had a poisoned leg. He put spirit on it and said he would see it again in the morning. Back the two miles to the rest house, then the Sherif and George Karkanis came up for a drink until 8pm.

I made Ahmed put his leg up and we started to make up our beds, but what with Beshir (cook), Hassan (messenger) and Tilib (driver's assistant) all lending a hand, we had to sit down to get out of everyone's way. Musa, the policeman, said he has been a safragi and also tried to make our beds. He was corrected by Hassan who said that we folded our blankets differently - like that!

On Monday morning, the meeting for the Fathers' benefit was held in the rest house. M interpreted Arabic to the Italians who gabbled in Italian to each other, while Nazir Deng talked Dinka to his Dinka. The Fathers got rather squashed when they got down to the facts. They started off by making a series of wild complaints, which M had to nail down.

The main trouble was that the previous head master, Lino Wor, had been an ardent R.C. but the new one appointed by the Council is a Nuba and an ardent Moslem. M explained that the system now, is that at the beginning of the school year, boys and parents are interviewed by the School Committee. The parents say what religious education they want their boy to have in school, Christianity, Islam or none. Although the weekly holiday is now on Friday and not Sunday, the Christian boys are allowed time off to go to Mass. We showed the Fathers the list and asked them to say which boys they were unhappy about. They could not, but said that one boy had been expelled for going to church. The Headmaster said he had not been expelled, just beaten for being late back from church. When we checked the list we found he was registered as a Moslem and should not have been going to church anyway. In the end all the mountains became rather small molehills.

   In the evening I went down to the village with M and sat nearby while he inspected the prison and went through their cases. One chap, completely nude, was in prison for stealing some pants, perhaps he must have been cold, poor thing. Nazir Deng came to tea and entertained us as usual. He was glad to hear the cows that he had sent up to Rigl el Fula had arrived safely.

   The next morning I went down to the office with M and walked back. The sun was getting just warm enough to turn the cold wind into a nice fresh breeze. The river sparkled and in places was a mass of huge water lilies sprinkled with little ones, like yellow snapdragons, others were a convolvulus purple. There were all sorts of birds, clouds of tiny coloured ones and water ones, cranes, including golden crested ones, with their brilliant gold crests, also some storks. All the Dinka I met were as friendly and bare as ever, how I envied their tall slender black bodies. We had long conversations but as they understand as little Arabic as I know Dinka, it was all rather incomprehensible. One or two were going down to their fish traps in the river, others carrying corn in baskets on their heads. One gentleman had a very attractive bitch trotting at his heels, six suitors followed her, all fighting to be first in the queue while her master seemed quite oblivious of the commotion. As I passed the houses everyone came out to look and wave, their white teeth gleaming from ear to ear as they smiled.

   M finished his case earlier than expected, so we decided to leave that afternoon in hopes that by travelling in the dark we might see a lion, there being a lot on the road, so everyone informed us. We went with the Sherif taking Nazi Deng as well, as he is a witness in the Sayad Fadal case which is to be heard in El Obeid. A few miles out of Abyie we stopped at Na'am, Deng's favourite country seat, a collection of round thatched houses on a mound beside the river. All his wives, or at least twenty of them and multitudinous children came out to greet him. We were introduced, shaking hands with them all in turn, as they did with their husband. We then looked into the luaks and then the smaller houses, which were the ladies' bedrooms. The doors were small round holes,,Inside there were

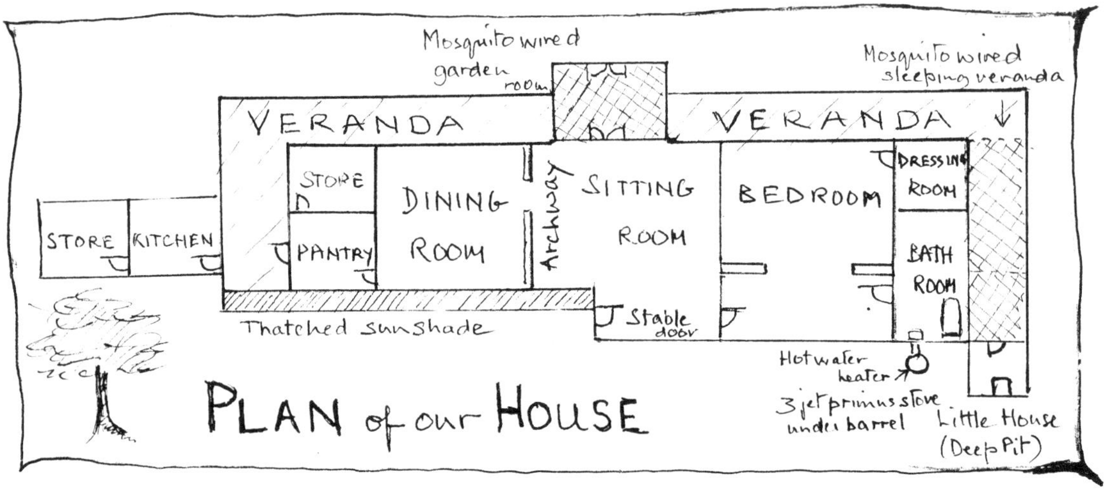

PLAN of our HOUSE

(Plan labels: STORE, KITCHEN, VERANDA, STORE, DINING ROOM, PANTRY, Archway, SITTING ROOM, BEDROOM, VERANDA, DRESSING ROOM, BATH ROOM; Mosquito wired garden room; Mosquito wired sleeping veranda; Thatched sunshade; Stable door; Hot water heater; 3 jet primus stove under barrel; Little House (Deep Pit))

The cooker arrives.

Tea is served.

How do you explain how to make a fireplace to someone who has never seen one?

This was the result.

Looking through the archway into the dining room.

The main part of the bedroom.

scrupulously clean mud-plastered floors, light grey in colour. Huge beds were made of rush mats on a framework of wood. Some were about a foot from the ground but some had second storeys, probably for the young children. We have not yet gathered if Deng has his own bedroom and invites his wives in, or whether he visits them, or has eight in bed at a time?

Having paid our respects to the Deng ladies we continued, shooting some duck en route. There is still a lot of water about and there were hundreds of them. We stopped at six o'clock on one of the ramps built across a river, usually dry, but it was still flowing. This one had lovely water lilies. As we wanted some to put in the pond in front of the new Council chamber, lots of passengers from the Sherif's and our lorry waded in and dug some up. It was dusk and as we stood watching, there was the piercing cry of a hyena, so close I thought someone was trying to tease me. The Sherif assured me it was real and then it called again, an eyrie sound in the silence of the night. It must have been coming down to drink. Despite their reputation they are timid creatures and will not come if anyone is near. We had tea and then went on for a picnic supper with the well diggers at their camp; hot soup, meat pate', home made potato crisps, tomatoes, cheese and apple. With the light of the moon and the campfires we could see without a lamp. We arrived at Tebeldia at 10, but sadly have seen no lion, only monkeys, some gazelle and a frog.

We had breakfast before we left the next morning. Then two hours in Muglad in the Merkaz (office) courtyard while M chatted. He refused to go into the office as once he gets there he never gets out again. On to Rigl el Fula; the Sherif had lunch with us en route. We went straight up to the house to see how it was getting on, ceiling nearly finished.

We spent the next morning making a mock fireplace with sticks and stones, then tried to explain to Ahmed the builder exactly what we wanted. How do you explain a fireplace and chimney to someone who had never seen one? In the evening, we had the Sherif and Mohmed Ibrahim Abdel Hafiz, the Sub Mamur, to a Christmas dinner. Afterwards we played Happy Families, having first translated the names into Arabic; they enjoyed it very much and the Sherif says he will bring his wife next time. They both came in smart suits and ties; the Sherif still has to wear his little wooley cap with a tassel and his black galoshes. I wish you could meet him, he is such a poppet.

We did have the Sherif and his wife to dinner later on. Following a whispered conversation during the soup course; there was a pause in the proceedings. Then Abdel Rahman appeared with the Sherif's snappers on a silver salver., so he could now manage the croutons!

We had to watch a grand football match yesterday evening, the Builders v the Officials. Mima, the Sherif's youngest daughter wearing a bright red satin dress sat on my knee. Orangeade and sweets were served at half time. The Builders won 1 - 0. Everyone was very full of beans.

Christmas Dairy

December 23rd.

Arrived El Obeid. Staying with Tony and Wendy Husband though we are actually sleeping in the rest house. Childrens' party in the Club, Father Christmas arrived in his sleigh drawn by a donkey. Tea afterwards with the McComas's. Drinks with the Mantons (Inspector of Agriculture). Supper, Tony and Wendy.

December 24th. Christmas Eve.

Shopping. Anne to elevenses with Isobel Lorimer (Governor's wife) while M went to see the Governor. Lunch with Tony and Wendy.

4pm. Catriona Lumsden's Christening in St. Peter's Church followed by a tea party with champagne and Christening cake, given by the Lumsdens in the McComas's house. Frank Lorimer, the Governor, make an excellent speech.

In the evening, carol singing round the houses with a good crowd including the Hunters, Lumsdens and Wrights. This was followed by Christmas Dinner at the Governor's.

From 10pm-1.30am the Upcher's (C.O.Camel Corps) had a dance for their eldest daughter who is 18 tomorrow. Caviar and asparagus.

December 25th. Christmas Day.

Opened stockings and presents. 7.15 H.C. with the Rev David Brown, one of the CMS Missionaries who came instead of George Martin who is not well. (David later became Bishop of Guildford, but sadly died quite young).

Breakfast with the Husbands.

10am Mattins, M thought David preached well but some of the others thought he should have been more Christmassy.

This was followed by a cocktail party at the Governors'. Cold lunch, then three hours sleep till 5pm, when we listened to the Queen who was very good and spoke beautifully.

    8pm. The Husbands' Christmas dinner party. Turkey, champagne, crackers and all the traditional fare

    10pm Club Dance, reeled until 2am. Anne wore white muslin dress with red spots.

December 26th. Boxing Day.

    M to D.C.'s meeting. This was ghastly, never heard such hot air. The Sudanese Education Inspector and Commandant of Police talked for ever. We now have a Sudanese Deputy Governor, Abdulahi, who is very nice, also Sudanese D.C.s so the proceedings were all in Arabic, a sign of the times.

    A had a good natter with Mary Hunter, who came round to see her.

    Lunch with the Gillespies (Vet), the Lumsdens were there too

    2.30 Tennis tournament. Agitation as lunch did not start until 2 and A was the Governor's partner who would wish her to be on time. Fortunately, when we arrived, he was the only person there.

    M with John Haggar reached the semi-finals.

    Tea with the Husbands, then cold buffet supper with the Wrights and their three daughters, the Lumsdens and McComas's also there.

    9.30 Cinema, Gilda with Rita Hayworth (awful).

    12 Midnight. Bed.

December 27th.

    AM. M to another D.C.'s meeting.

    A to Wrights to meet Mrs Adbulahi, Deputy Governor's wife.

    PM. Cricket Match and walk round the fulas.

    Then saw Ralph Daly's coloured slides of Soderi and he ours of the Messeria.

    Dinner at the Husbands with Lumsdens.

December 28th

A to coffee with Isobel Lorimer to discuss the Governor General's visit. Then shopping.

Left after lunch, night in Abu Zabad.

PS. M...
Why I had to see the Governor.

The Kordofan press has said that District Commissioner Tibbs has "mocked at the new Government" and the M.P. for El Obeid has demanded his dismissal. The MP has also said that on its action over this imperialist the Government will be judged, so the people will know its good intentions.

I was asked what I had been doing, needless to say I had not the slightest notion. It transpired it stemmed from an incident when we came in to say goodbye to the Hawkesworths on the 6th December. Near Abu Ku, we overtook a lorry which was overloaded and had passengers on top of the load, which was forbidden. I stopped the driver and told him that he was breaking the law, but that if he dropped the passengers off, he could go on. The driver was very truculent and said how stupid it was. I had told him I was not responsible for making the law, but only for carrying it out whoever made it, the last government or this one. When I got to Abu Zabad I put a policeman on the road to arrest him if he had disobeyed. I suppose he thought if he was to be run in, he would get in first. However, Frank did not seem to worry too much about it. As Jack Hunter said, if they complain about you, you must be doing your job fairly well.

21. THE GOVERNOR GENERAL'S VISIT

As local Councils were set up through the Sudan, experience showed that many of them needed revisions of their charters to increase representation or to expand their powers. In our case, the Ngok Dinka had now joined up and we had shown that we were operating successfully. So, a new charter was due. The Governor General, Sir Robert Howe, had not visited Kordofan for some time. There was a strong buzz that he might be coming during 1953, but the elections put paid to that. Eventually we were informed that His Excellency (H.E.) would be coming to the Province at the beginning of 1954.

On the day that we left El Obeid after the Christmas celebrations, Anne had coffee with Isabel Lorimer, the Governor's wife. She wanted to know the exact arrangements we were making for HE's visit and enquired what Anne was going to give him to eat! We spent the night in Abu Zabad and came on the next day. We tried out the 'new road' from Abu Ku' to Rigl el Fula, cutting out El Odaiya. This was the road said to be all ready for H.E. to sail down on the 13th January, shortening the journey from Abu Zabad by 1½ hours. However, after a very bumpy hour we had covered 16 miles and the road petered out completely. We continued through tall grass and undergrowth for the next three hours; our so-called guide, having no more idea where we were than we had. It now being 8pm, we thought we would camp for the night. Then we heard dogs barking in the distance, so went on in that direction and suddenly found ourselves in Fula. Wasn't it lucky we tried out the road first? H.E.'s saloon would not have got very far. We now had to rearrange his route via El Odaiya.

We all had a shock on New Year's Eve. Just before lunch, Beshir, our cook was found lying on the kitchen floor almost unconscious. We called the temurgi, (male nurse), at once, but in spite of all his efforts, Beshir died a few hours later in our lorry that was taking him to El Odaiya where there was a small hospital. He had been with us for a year and had been discussing arrangements for H.E. the day before. He was only 45 and never ill, always willing and cheerful and we were very fond of him. We could hardly believe it. He was buried the same evening amongst the tebelgi trees, everyone came. The next day we all went and drank tea at A.R's house, as was the custom. I sent a telegram to his family in Fasher via John Rowley, the Governor and asked him to give them LE 10 to go on with.

Now of course we were cookless and H.E. was to arrive in ten days. We asked Geoffrey McComas if he could find us a cook in El Obeid and in the meantime Anne began teaching Ahmed, the seconda, to cook. He was very keen to learn. The preparations had to go ahead and everything thought out well in advance. For instance, Anne had to ask Tigani the shop keeper if he could kill a bull next week so that she could have its tongue in good time to pickle for the buffet supper,.There were not usually enough people in Fula to justify killing a bull, in the heat the meat did not keep.

The last ten days were an enjoyable nightmare, a whirl of painters, builders, carpenters and prisoners all capable of doing exactly the opposite to what we wanted, unless we watched them very closely. Hence, we were up and down to the house at all hours from 6am onwards. Jaundiced yellow paint instead of pale cream in the sitting room and violent Reckitt's blue instead of pastel sea green in the bathroom. Shelves with scallops and swirls instead of plain; the fireplace with BLUE pointing instead of natural cement; taps in wrong places and so forth might well have been the result had we not been on the spot to say very tactfully how we would prefer it, although their idea was very nice too. The painters, builders and carpenters were simply marvellous and worked overtime from morning to night to get the house presentable, it was a very near thing indeed.

Up to two days before the great day, one could not believe it could be straight in time, paint, cement, and bricks in all directions. We moved some of our things up on the Friday with our lorry and the help of dozens of prisoners. China and glass were carried up on trays, all the clothes from the wardrobe (which had to be collapsed to get it out of the rest house door), were borne aloft upon our double bed carried by four prisoners. The processions to and from were a very funny sight. All the population of the village came out to either help or look on. The turkeys were driven up, so were the cows and sheep. The chickens were caught while asleep and carried up all except one hen who insisted on sitting tight on ten eggs. The kitchen stove got cracked on the way, but the paraffin fridge flourished with renewed energy after its trip

Amidst it all, Anne was practising Ahmed with all the meals we wanted to produce as we had given up all hope of finding a cook. However a radio message arrived to say one Abdullahi was on the way, found by the Governor's safragi. He arrived, smart with medal ribbons, to find the kitchen in transit, but luckily seemed quite unperturbed and happily settled down to a campfire for a day or two.

As rooms in the house were completed, so we were able to unpack and arrange our belongings. The red tiled floors were scrubbed and then polished until they gleamed. At last we moved in and slept the night. We got up at 6 the next morning just before shoals of people came sauntering into the bedroom 'just to look over the house'. It had been the favourite walk in Fula while building was going on and it never seemed to occur to anyone that now we were actually living there, it made any difference. AR got very angry and like Mrs Tittlemouse came in behind polishing off their footmarks. Not knowing how Abdullahi cooked, Anne made a French chocolate cake, water biscuits and various other dishes. Then the new Council flag did not turn up, so we had to take the crescent off an Egyptian flag and Anne painted a large elephant on it with white enamel, the more she put on, the more it soaked in. Then I had to paint 'Meglis Dar el Messeria' underneath in Arabic.

Meanwhile the arrangements to do with the opening of the Council chamber had to be completed. Grass houses were going up in all directions for the Council members and guests. Needless to say guests started arriving the day before they were invited. Nazirs and various sheikhs appeared as we were covered in paint while painting our garden furniture or some equally inconvenient time, to say how do you do and get in some important say before the others. A lorry load of stores and fresh fruit arrived from El Obeid, on the Council's bill. It having allocated £E 600 to make grass houses and help to feed the company during the visit. The Sherif and Anne sorted it all out and divided it into different heaps. Some thirty sheep had to be divided up and in the evening Anne had no less than fourteen cows lined up outside in the garden to be milked. She rushed round collecting milk in buckets and putting it through the cream separator. Half the cream went to the Sherif for his house party. Various contributions to help with all the guests rolled in from those arriving. These included the loan of cows by Nazir Sereir; a huge jar of toffees made with rich semin from Nazir Ali: a box of fruit and veg from Mekki Amin; tinfuls of biscuits and cakes from the Sherif's wife, (so sweet of her, all made by herself); buckets of eggs from various people and two sheep from another guest. Meanwhile our fridge bulged with three of our own turkeys and a special sheep for H.E, from which Anne had selected the choicest parts.

Ian Cunninson, the anthropologist arrived and presented us with the 'Ascent of Everest'. Ian had travelled up from Abyie with the Dinka who were going to dance; forty were invited, so eighty came, all equipped with sparkling new white pants and vests. On the journey they had removed the pants to keep them clean but as it was cold they had kept the vests on.

Wednesday 13th January.

Up at 6. for a rush of last minute preparations. We had decided that H.E. should stay in our house so that the rest house would be free for the Governor and his wife. So, we had to put out all the things we needed to be transferred to our tent in the garden. I also went off in the lorry, escorted by outriders for a dress rehearsal of the next day's ceremony while Anne was in the kitchen making asparagus rolls for tea.

At 11am, ten minutes after the scheduled time, we set off in the lorry with policemen Mekki Tia and Musa in the back and an extra box car in case we broke down. Anne held the chocolate cake out of the window to keep it cool in the breeze.

We had not gone far before we met advancing traffic, lorry loads of Councillors and guests coming towards Fula. We stopped to greet three lorry loads of sheikhs we knew and then came across a dreadful lorry with its bonnet off containing Peter Hogg. He fished my District Commissioner's stripes out of his suitcase, so I was properly dressed at last and Anne could suspend sewing activities on a homemade version. (Although I had been doing the job for seven months, my actual promotion was dated 1st January). On again and met Jake Seamer, a previous DC. Messeria: the Public Relations Dept Cinema van, the Camel Corps Band, the Commandant of Police, the Education Inspector, the Agricultural Officers and so on, some 20 - 30 lorries on the road all heading towards Fula. A plush saloon taxi then appeared carrying Nazir Babu, now a Member of the Senate, he had come back from Khartoum for the occasion. Each time we stopped, but we had allowed for this and we arrived at our meeting place on the road near Abu Ku, as scheduled.

A grass shelter had been made under which we lunched on the crusts from the asparagus rolls, watched by the usual cluster of small boys. At 4pm, we posted Musa down the road and after two false alarms he blew his whistle and two saloons hove into view. H.E. got out, tall and broad, white haired rather pink faced, wearing white shorts, bush jacket with thick gold stripes and two thinner ones, oak leaves on his collar and a white plume in his hat. We all had tea on the famous asparagus rolls and the chocolate cake, the kettle had been boiled by Hassan one of our messenger boys. We found H.E. quite charming with a sense of humour and easy to get on with. Anne said she took to him at once

During tea a collection of local ladies appeared and started dancing in the road in front of us. This caused much amusement especially when H.E's three baggage lorries appeared and could not get by. On the previous day we had sent out a lorry to collect all the sheikhs who might otherwise have been tried to give H.E. tea en route. Freed from their husbands' influence, the wives obviously laid on the entertainment on their own.

Tea over, M got into the saloon with H.E. and Governor Lorimer, while Anne joined Mike Foster the Secretary, Isobel Lorimer and tha Sudanese ADC in the second one. H.E seemed rather tired but he brightened up as we got near Fula and I showed him the landmarks like where we had abandoned our furniture in the rains and where Ian Cunninson's lorry overturned. The roads had been lined with whitewashed stones, so it all looked quite impressive in the dark.

We stopped at the house. A.R. was there to hold our stable-type front door open. We offered him a drink, the Lorimers started making better-have-a-bath noises but H.E. very firmly said a whisky would set him up, and it did. M then launched out into the dark with the unexpected Sudanese A.D.C. to where he knew there was an empty rakuba (grass hut), only to find it full of the Hunters' servants. However, he found a much better and nearer one, so all was well. Having taken the Lorimers to the rest house we had a lightening bath in our tent, where we found A.R. had moved and arranged all our things including our double angareeb (rope bed), so we could hardly move with that and the trek bath. Anne then dived into the kitchen to put finishing touches to the pudding. We were both ready waiting when H.E. appeared, much refreshed after his bath. Soon after, the Lorimers arrived, then the Private Secretary from his tent in the garden.

Dinner went off very well. Afterwards, the ladies, Isobel and Anne, retired to the bathroom and the gentlemen to the garden. Anne and Isobel were much amused to see H.E.'s servant had laid out all his night things including a small enamel object, not under the bed, but under the table beside it. A had left her ornaments on her kidney shaped dressing table, including a pair of glass candlesticks with blue candles which had been lit; the blue flowered Harrods chintz frill and curtains looked very pretty. Everyone was very taken with the house, even H.E. said how nice it was and how out of the ordinary.

We all retired at about 11pm, but we sat up in bed until the early hours while A sewed M's new stripes onto his office dress uniform, he had to be properly dressed for the morning.

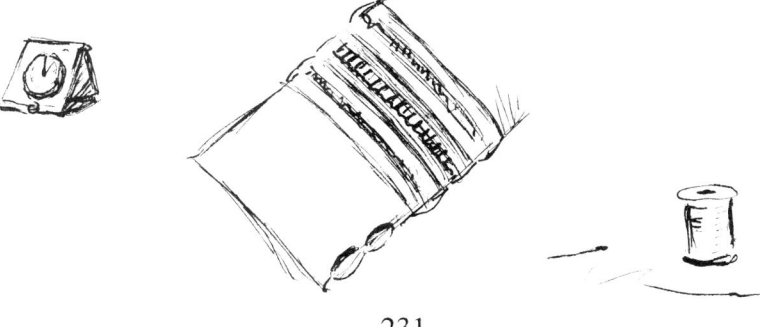

The Opening of the Council Headquarters

The Governor General Sir Robert Howe inspecting a police Guard of Honour with the band of the Camel Corps behind.

Nazir Babu   Sir Robert   Governor Lorimer

Cutting the tape with a Baggara spear

Thursday January 14th.

The day of the Opening of the Dar Messeria Council Headquarters.

At 9.30 M took Anne, Isobel and Mary Hunter down to the new building in Frank's car. Everybody was lined up round a square laid out with whitewashed stones. The Western Kordofan police provided the guard of honour with the Camel Corps band behind them, all looking extremely smart. Then there were the rows of Nazirs, sheikhs and notables, most of them in dazzling white against which the crimson Robes of Honour of the Nazirs made lovely splashes of colour.

At 9.40 the saloon came into sight escorted by four mounted police on their chargers, all doing a very controlled slow canter. H.E stood between the flags of the two Condominion Powers and took the salute. The band struck up and played while H.E. inspected the Guard. Various introductions were then made before Nazir Babu asked H.E. to open the iron gates (made at M's design like spears). He then cut a ribbon with a Baggara spear. M escorted him into his office and showed him maps and explained the work of the Council, this gave time for the guests to be shepherded into the Council chamber.

Once all were assembled, H.E, the Governor and D.C. took their seats on the platform. M called on the Governor General who made an excellent speech in English (written by M!). This was followed by a translation into Arabic by the Sub-Mamur, Mohamed Ibrahim Abdel Hafiz, Babu then replied. H.E. then handed the new Warrant over to Nazir Babu as Vice-Chairman. H.E. presented Sherif Ahmed Abu Gasim, as Executive Officer, with a watch and the Nazirs and Ahmed the Builder, with gold banded walking sticks to mark the occasion. Everything went very well with only two slight distractions. The microphones (supplied by the cinema van), supposed to be relaying the proceedings to the crowd outside, did not work. So, in the middle of the speeches a radio mechanic got under the table and started tinkering with the wires causing dreadful squawks and squeaks. M managed to kick the gentleman with his foot and told him to leave it alone, so he crawled out and retired into the background. Then there were off stage noises, violent popping and exploding of all the fizzing gazoozers having their lids taken off. All the British hoped it was champagne.

The proceedings over, the company adjourned to the courtyard where drinks and toffees were in good supply. M took H.E. and the Governor back into his office where the Nazirs and other notables were introduced in rotation and refreshed with pink and green fizzy, coffee and sweets. Omda Raheid from Abyad pleased H.E. most; he had been recommended and got a Robe of Honour in 1924 as the D.C. thought he would not live much longer. Now very old indeed he is still going strong and hunts elephant when he can. He attacked H.E. as the Game Warden would not give him a game licence, H.E. promised to look into it as soon as he got back to Khartoum.

Back to the house for drinks with the Mamur and Executive Officers. Slightly formalised as they kept standing and saluting and were about to sit down with their hats on. However M removed the hats which relaxed them a bit. We had organised a lunch party for H.E. while we went to the Lorimers.

The afternoon's entertainment was the dancing. This began at 3pm and by 4pm when H.E. arrived, it was really warmed up. Some of the best selections of dancing we have seen. We all wandered round informally watching the different groups. The Dinka were excelling themselves with leaps and bounds and also carried on a mock battle with skin shields and extraordinary looking helmets. We missed their lovely black oiled skins - A/Executive Officer Abu Gabr did not think they should dance to H.E. unclothed.

The Nuba from Kasha put on a wonderful display, conveniently most of the men were in Fula already - in prison, after their rock throwing harvest festival last year. They had made themselves very useful clearing and mending the road. While they were sweeping up the leaves in our garden they had asked M, who was painting our chairs, to lend them some paint. They must have somehow got hold of tins and tins of enamel as they were striped, spotted and patterned every colour of the rainbow all over and were a marvellous sight. Most of them wore skins round their behinds and we suppose for H.E.'S benefit, little pants underneath, most dainty but looking rather absurd with their tough muscular bodies. They were dancing and wrestling most actively and very entertaining to watch.

The next group was the Nuba from Tima, their speciality decoration was sun glasses, mostly without glass. The ladies of course all had their spikes of glass in their chins. We were much amused to see one gentleman with a large red handkerchief attached to a wart on his elbow. They were also very colourful and decorated up to the nines with combs, safety pins, feathers and match sticks in their noses. As a contrast the next group were the Dagu, not nearly so colourful but the great feature was their marvellous orchestra, they blew down long trumpets carved out of wood making a thrilling deep booming noise.

They and the trumpets originally came from West Africa. They have been in the Sudan for about 250 years but they have not lost their music.

The local contribution came from the Arabs in Mumu, which is quite close. A chorus of women, men and children stood in a circle clapping and singing. In the middle three girls behaved as though they were hypnotised. They swayed, twisted, then doubled over backwards with their heads and massive black plaits flopping on the ground. A thought they were very attractive but quite creepy!

All groups had their drums beating the time, while the constant background was the dull thumping of the nahas, the copper kettle drums, symbols of the Nazir Umum. It was all very festive. We retired to the Council courtyard for refreshment. M was surprised to see H.E. and Anne both dealing with very juicy and squirty oranges but with every appearance of relish. The tea made by our radio mechanic Mohamed Kafi was jet black and the hot water when it came, was even blacker, but no-one seemed to mind.

We dispersed at 6 to get ready for the next entertainment. Anne retired to the kitchen while M, Hassan and Segeir went to the mess tent (kindly provided by the Camel Corps), to rig up the projector. M found the board he had carefully painted as a screen had disappeared, but we found that Ahmed II had taken it as a roof for Mrs Ahmed's kitchen.

7.45 found us both changed, Anne in her long navy flowered organdie dress (Harvey Nichols), M in Red Sea rig. We both started in the pantry, A putting finishing touches to the salad, M mixing drinks. At 8 o'clock, everyone started to arrive, eleven British in Red Sea rig and eight Sudanese who were in suits except for Babu in his robes.. The party filled up the sitting room and overflowed into the garden. A ring on our ship's bell announced that the buffet supper was ready. This was laid out in the dining room, sliced turkey and tongue, a whole turkey on the side garnished with parsley, a variety of different salads in silver entrée dishes, glass bowls with fruit salad, silver sauce boats with cream, all lit by candle light and looking very pretty. After supper we all went over to the mess tent and saw our coloured slides - of the District for the benefit of the

Riqlel Fula Messeria Lodge

Our house is finished.

Looking through the archway to the dining room

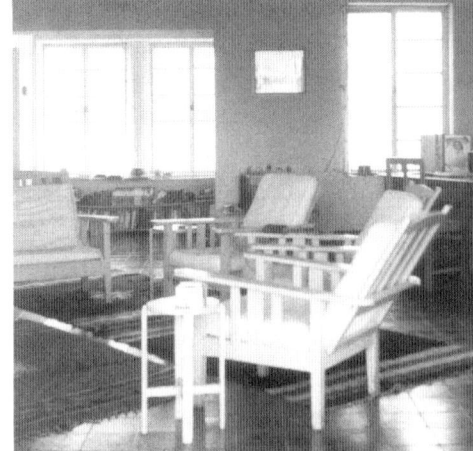

Front door beyond on right

Sitting outside the front door
Visitors, Mrs Hag Said & her son from Abu Zabad

Abdul Rahman brings tea into the garden

British and of England for the Sudanese; these included some of the Coronation which had just come and were excellent. H.E. was most amused by some of ourselves on trek. Bed by 11.

Friday 15th January.

We had breakfast with H.E. and Mike Foster having first taken them to see the horses. Willy had once belonged to H.E.'s nephew, Jack Hext. He got into the stables, inspected the tack and then the turkeys, ducks, sheep and cows. A thorough inspection which thrilled Abdel Rahman the scyce.

At 9 am the Lorimers arrived and it was time for them to go. H.E said some very nice things to us, wished he could stay longer in our hunting lodge, and said we must come and see him in Khartoum and let him know if we ever wanted a bed.

We had a relaxed morning with Peter Hogg and Jake Seamer who stayed for lunch. The relax of course did not last all day as we had a constant stream of visitors getting their points home before the Council meeting the next day.

Saturday 16th January.

We started bright and early with a Council Finance Committee. It was only then that M learnt that Deng Majok's rakuba had caught fire during the night. Fortunately no-one was hurt, but he had lost all his possessions including the walking stick H.E. had given him. So, our proceedings started with a whip round for Deng Majok. There was a rather embarrassed silence, while we all wondered how to start the bidding. Babu asked Mekki Amin to give us a lead. He came out with £E10, which we all followed.

The Council meetings continued through Saturday and Sunday. Deng Majok was a bit shaken and particularly sad about his stick but insisted on carrying on through the entire two days. Deng was taking advantage of the celebrations to go on to Khartoum, so we were able to give him a railway warrant and M gave him a letter to Mike Foster in the Palace. He came back beaming with new kit and a replacement walking stick.

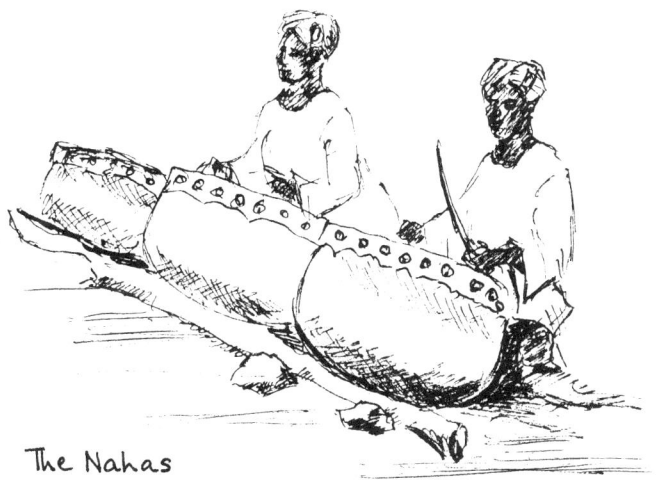

The Nahas

22.   A VISIT TO IAN CUNNINSON.

We have mentioned Ian Cunnison several times, but this may be the place to explain more about him and his work. The Messeria in Kordofan and the Rizegat in Darfur are the two large cattle owning nomadic tribes in the Sudan, but their way of life was beginning to change. The Zurug, that part of the Messeria tribe living in the east of the District around Lagawa, had already had their lives changed through the arrival of controlled cotton growing. It was felt that the Humr would not be able to retain their unique way of life much longer. So, in 1951, the Sudan Government offered to finance a full study. Ian Cunnison arrived in the District in August 1951. He made it clear that he wished to live as a member of the tribe and not as an official. So, it was arranged that he would be attached to the family of one of our Omdas, Horgas Merida. For the next two and a half years Ian lived with his adopted family, moving with them, eating what they eat and sleeping where they slept. His book, Baggara Arabs - Power and Lineage in a Sudanese Nomad Tribe was published by the Oxford University Press in 1966. Ian subsequently became Professor of Anthropology at Khartoum University and then at Hull.

Anne's account...

In February 1954, we had been to meetings at Toragi with the Jebels and Bentiu D.C.s. When this was over we drove to Abyad (15 miles) for breakfast. After a look round including a visit to the dispensary we went on to Azrug (31 miles) where we had lunch under some trees by a well and met Omda Reheid and a gaggle of other sheikhs. Reheid produced some rather nice fried pastries and some eggs for us. We left after about two hours, plus some elephant tusks, confiscated as the elephant had been killed nearby without a permit. The gentleman concerned was also on board on his way to start serving his sentence in Muglad. Ivory is of course valuable, the current price being between 75pt and £E1 per pound, so a heavy pair of tusks is worth up to at least £E100.

We pressed on to Keilak (50 miles), to find the lake was more full than we have ever seen it. The roof of the rest house had blown off recently, but had been repaired just in time for our arrival. Nur el Din came and filled us with a very refreshing native drink made from corn (not alcoholic). Our beds were put up outside as usual.

Wednesday 3rd February.

I decided to have a read in bed before getting up. However the rest house, having no hedge round it, was open to the public, so when all the little boys came past on their way to school, they found me quite an interesting spectacle and I thought it was time to rise. However carpenters had arrived and were swarming all over the rest house putting new mosquito wire round, so I had to call AR to shoo them away. We continued after breakfast to Muglad (130 miles), it was getting very hot so we stopped under a tree for two or three hours and had lunch. We got in at 8pm.

Thursday 4th February.

Muglad to Abyei, 126 miles. An uneventful journey stopping at Tebeldia for lunch and snooze. Arrived at Abyei rest house. We had taken the keeper to El Obeid at Christmas time to see about his eyes, In his absence the bats had taken possession in full force. Such a noise, squeaking and banging under the roof, and what a smell!

The next day someone poked them all out and they flew away in a great black crowd, but as soon as it was dark they all came back again. Mike says the roof must be taken off and replaced with seasoned wood which won't warp and let them in.

Friday 5th February.

As it was our rest day we decided to have a day in the country and try and find Ian Cunninson with his ferik. We were told, 'not far off' and were provided with a guide. So, after breakfast we set off with a picnic lunch, leaving all the servants behind except for Segeir our driver, Sagha his assistant and Ahmed Mattar, M's messenger boy. No-one could have more surprised than us when after an hour or so driving, the last twelve miles off the road bashing through the bush, we arrived at the ferik to find Ian sitting under a beautiful spreading tree with all the sheikhs. He perhaps was even more surprised to see us and delighted to have his post, which we had brought with us.

We had a blissful lazy time just sitting under the tree with Ian, Omda Horgas and the others, chatting away and watching the cattle wading and feeding in the nearby ragaba. (A river during the rains but now a luscious swamp). There was a lovely cool breeze and delicious smell from the blossom on the trees.

The lowing of the cattle, the buzz of bees and the occasional human voice from the ferik a few hundred yards away were the only sounds, except of course for the birds including the deep barks of the long legged water birds wading in the swamp. It was really lovely. Ian pointed out his four cows amongst the herd and his two horses amongst the others as they were led down to drink. Soon after we arrived, bowls of frothy warm robe (curdled milk) and a delicious mixture of honey and milk arrived in succession to refresh us. Ian and some others had gathered the honey yesterday. They find a tree with bees in it, smoke the bees out then scoop out the honey. Ian removed twenty-four stings from the face of one of his companions who did not mind a bit; he was an accomplished honey gatherer and was used to being stung.

When it got near lunchtime there were great whisperings and although we said we had brought our lunch, they insisted we must be their guests. They were not quite sure how it would be with Sa'ata Sit as normally all the men squat round the dish and the women are not allowed anywhere near. The Omda tactfully decided to tell everyone to move off and leave just the four of us to eat on our own. (Ian told us all this in English when we enquired what the whispering had been about)

In due course all the sheikhs, about fifteen of them, moved off to another tree; meanwhile two handsome shawls were laid out for us to sit on, which we did, cross legged; our hands were rinsed in turn with water from a water jug.

Then, various enamel bowls of different bright colours and patterns, all with lids on, arrived and three were put in the middle. The lids were removed disclosing a bowl with pieces of fried beef, another with slices of knob-nosed goose and the third with white faced duck all shot by Ian that morning. Using only right hands, we dipped into each bowl in turn and were able to throw the bones away over our shoulders where a dog or two finished them off. It was beautifully cooked and tender, with a lot of hot spicy sauce over it

Next came a huge bowl of boiled rice in milk with a pool of semen, (oily butter), floating on the top. One attendant gave it a stir while another flapped a rush lid to keep away the flies. Four rather antique spoons were produced for our benefit and we all tucked in to our corner of the bowl. After that we had a sort of dough surrounded by hot spicy gravy, one took a handful of the dough and dipped it into the gravy. Our hands were then washed again, this time with soap as well. Then we got up from the ground, sat on the angareebs (string beds) and drank tea.

Before we left, I was asked to go and see the women of the ferik. I went over to their matting houses where a great crowd of ladies surrounded me, with babies and children all dressed in their best clothes. I shook hands with each of them in turn as the usual greetings were rattled off; after which they just stood and goofed, except for the particular one I was talking to who answered politely. Meanwhile, much to my amusement the others were being prompted by Ian's guide as to what they ought to say. So when I had finished talking their shyness disappeared and they all started at once, saying how glad they were to see me, the first white Sit ever to have come there etc. We all shook hands again and said goodbye, and I went back to the others followed by warbles and cries from them all, especially when I turned and gave them a wave.

In spite of our protests, two sheep were loaded onto the lorry but the Omda insisted. He also wanted to give me a guinea as well, but Ian advised him not to. We drove back via the river and had tea on the bank as the sun was setting, perfectly beautiful and how we longed to plunge in.

Ian told us afterwards that in celebration of our visit to Omda Horgas and the ferik, the tree under which we had been entertained to lunch had been named 'The Queen's Tree'.

Saturday 6th February.

Abyie to Tebeldia (86 miles). On the way we saw some gazelle, a baboon, an ostrich, and a wart hog. When it was just dark a huge pair of wart hogs and several jackals got into the headlights. We slept at Tebeldia.

Sunday 7th February,

We went into Muglad so M could have a morning in the office. In the afternoon we went to Tibbun near the Darfur border with Nazir Ali, (75 miles there and back), to look at the new deep bore. An Italian driller was in charge of some huge machines and engines. He had got down to 260 feet and still had to go another 100 before reaching water, meanwhile the people have no water at all except from water melons or from Muglad 37 miles away. Segeir then told us that we had two broken springs. Fortunately we had the Council lorry with us so we returned in that as we had Anna Redman (Education Inspector) to dinner.

Monday 8th February.

Our lorry was found to be irreparable, so spares would have to be sent from Nahud. We hired a suq lorry to take us home; we had to wait in the suq (market) while the chap in charge of the petrol dump could be found. What time a haboob (sand storm) blew up and we had to cover our heads so they did not get blasted off. Eventually we started off. It took us seven hours to get home instead of the usual three. We had to stop fifteen times altogether when the Purple Roarer as we named her just stopped, ran out of petrol or boiled!

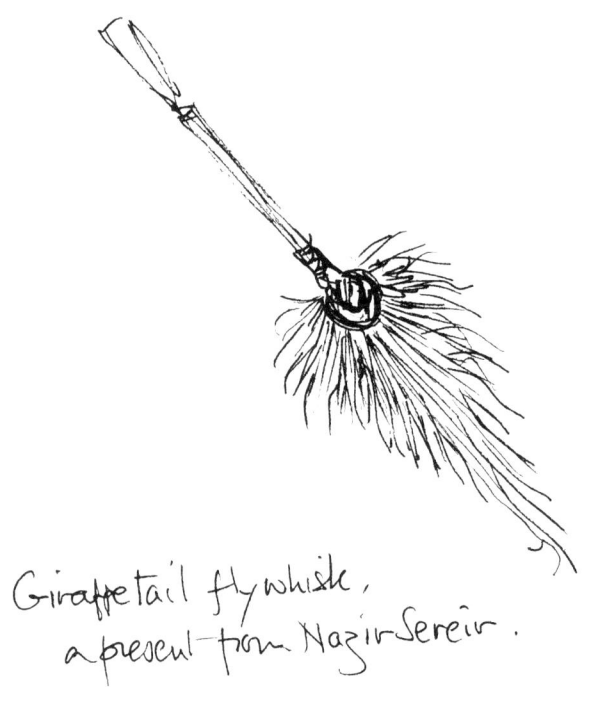

Giraffe tail flywhisk, a present from Nazir Sereir.

23. NEARING THE END.

We had been so busy in getting our house finished, preparing for the visit of the Governor General, carrying out all the office routines, going on trek including the quick whizz to El Obeid to say good-bye to the Hawkesworths and then again for Christmas, that we had not really had much time to consider what was going to happen to us. Living as we were out in the blue, perfectly happily with our friends all around us, the thought of having to leave it all seemed quite unreal.

We had begun to have one or two indicators that things were not going to be the same. Once during 1953 we arrived in Abu Zabad and started to move into the rest house only to be told very firmly that it was occupied by the DC from Nahud AND his wife. Normally this would present no problem but we decided we would tactfully move on to Kasha and stay there. At Lagawa we found the D.C.'s rest house full of a veterinary team, who really ought to have been in the council rest house along the road. We were told Nazir Babu already occupied that. At last very grudgingly, the Veterinary officer vacated one of the four huts for us, but his retainers continued to occupy all the others as well as the central dining room.

In February, Geoffrey McComas stayed two days and gave us the latest news, such as it was. The Prime Minister, Azhari had flown through El Obeid at the beginning of the month. Governor Frank Lorimer was there with a Guard of Honour, then went into the waiting room with the P.M. The Minister of Works, who was also in the party, stayed outside, got hold of the microphone of the loud speaker van and harangued the crowd. He ended by saying that they could all be reassured that the hated colonialists would be shot out as soon as possible and the corrupt administration with it. What time poor Frank was going livid with rage.

We have all been waiting to hear whether and when we are going to get our notice and about our gratuities. There is no news, but our Union (of senior civil servants) is taking it up in a big way. I had a firm contract, but no one knew if it would be honoured or not.

The new Parliament was opened by the Governor General at the beginning of January. This was so that the new Government could begin operating but there was to be a Formal State Opening on March 1st. Babu, now a Senator, came through during a recess, he seemed to be a bit fed up and was going straight off to the Jebels to try and convert their M.P.s who are all National Unity to the Umma party. He said that in Khartoum the M.P.s from the backward areas were all more or less locked up, they never went out unaccompanied by a 'galaba' (townie) so people like Babu of the Umma party can't talk to them! We have also heard that Sayed Zain el Din, the Pakistani Chairman of the Governor General's Commission went round El Obeid and then the Jebels. He stayed with the Jack Hunters, they took him for a drive as he had asked to see a local house. Jack showed him a tumble down Nuba house with a naked woman outside. When he explained this was the local M.P.'s house and this was Mrs M.P. the man nearly had a fit and said that the Sudan was at least a thousand years behind Pakistan.

Sir Lawrence Grafty Smith, the British member of the Commission was also supposed to have come round, but the Pakistani told him not to as it would be too tiring for Lady G S. Important observers, journalists and visitors seemed to have been wandering all over the place during the elections and the run up to the formal opening of parliament, but not to us, we were too far out. However, we had seen some visitors just the same.

At the end of February, we were spending a Friday clearing up our store when we saw a lorry coming up the drive. "Blast" we said "an Inglese". It turned out to be Frank Wherrall, from the PWD (Public Works Department) in El Obeid who had come to service the donkey (deep bore pump). He had brought all the family, wife Vivian and two delightful daughters of 7 and 3. They have all come to lunch and tea twice, sitting up and behaving beautifully. They have given dates to the horses, corn to the sheep and poultry, collected eggs, watched the cows being milked and stroked the lamb.

As soon as they had gone, we had a tea party for our Sub Mamur Mohamed Ibrahim Abdel Hafiz who was leaving. The party was in charge of Kaboze the accountant and Mohamed (gold teeth) Kafi the 'over' operator. They all ended up in our kitchen with Adullahi while Anne flitted in and out as Reckitt's blue got poured in to deepen the colour of the icing on the cakes. Anyway we had a good party outside the Council building. We are sorry to see him go, as he is very good. We then had John Hunter's relief, the new Sudanese Resident Magistrate, who arrived for lunch.

We were in Muglad on March 1st which was the great day for the State Opening of Parliament. We went down to the market to listen to the ceremony on the wireless, only to hear it had been cancelled owing to disturbances in Khartoum, so we went for a walk instead. We came back and had tea with Abu Gabr (Assistant Executive Officer) and heard from London on the BBC Overseas service what had happened. Supporters of the Umma party and Ansar, the religious counterparts, had flocked into Khartoum (later I found that many of our people had taken part). They had demonstrated outside the Palace and the Secretariat. The Ashigga, the government supporters, assembled in a counter demonstration. Violence followed and the British Commandant of police was amongst those killed. The State Opening had been cancelled.

Sometime later we heard the English weekly news summary on Omdurman Radio. Always interesting and full of tit bits, it was a highlight of our Friday evenings and was given by David Evans, now Director of Public Relations. Now it seemed that David had to restrict himself to news only. He had no more to say after 20 minutes so he said he would play two records of English music, the titles 'Ostracised' and 'Rolling Home'. We roared with laughter.

At Muglad we met Ken Lea-Wilson, the new Senior Agricultural Cotton Inspector from Kadugli and went down with him to Nyama, 80 miles south east of Muglad. We had quite a party as Abu Gabr and Nazir Ali came too. I was anxious to see how the cotton growing was catching on and if there were any problems, we could sort out on the spot. Much to our joy we saw a lion on the road. Anne as usual was looking out for anything and suddenly spied two eyes ahead gleaming out of the dark. As we drove round the next corner a female lion ran across the road, unfortunately she was in a hurry and did not stop and the trees were too thick to follow her. Just before that we had seen two civet cats playing in the road, they were so enchanted with each other they continued playing in the headlights for several seconds. They were such a pretty sight with their huge pointed ears and beautiful markings.

Although Nyama has a cotton market, there is nothing there except for a 'ragaba' (river bed), but there are an increasing number of people growing cotton as the soil is so fertile. The next day we went on another 18 miles to Subu, again a name rather than a place. We walked quite a long way round the plantations accompanied by a tame ostrich and Abu Gabr. It was very hot and Abu Gabr nearly blew up, he is rather over weight and we were quite worried about him, we revived him with a cup of tea with six lumps of sugar in it!. We went on and camped alongside a very pretty stretch of water with lots of duck. Abu Gabr and Ali camped with one of the feriks but came to tea.

We enjoyed being with Ken Lea-Wilson. Although John Manton and Ben Bradford of the Agricultural Department had been to see us in Rigl el Fula, it was refreshing to find an Agriculturist who was willing to come on trek with us. The Council members had asked for a cotton market at Subu, but I had to know whether the cotton was being grown correctly and the stalks burnt properly to avoid infection. Now that the D.C, an Inspector of Agriculture, the Assistant Executive Officer and the Nazir had been there together, we were all in the picture. On a domestic note we think we were helpful to Ken. He was wondering if he should propose to his intended and bring her out to Kadugli. We think we showed him that he could; anyway, later on he did.

The next morning we carried on to the 'Darfur dash'. This was a broad cutting the Agricultural Department had made between Abyad and the south of Darfur with the idea of opening up the area. It was not really a road and had been completely churned up by giraffe and elephant. There were enormous elephant footmarks. Anne longed to come back in the rains to see all the animals, but sadly it was not practicable.

Eventually we arrived at a place called Koiya, a little lake with water and a small ferik with an Omda who was delighted to see us. As he entertained us he exploded about the new set up. I could hardly get a word in to explain about democracy. He had not heard about the new Sudanese government and was quite incredulous when told we would soon be leaving. We had a relaxed day and went round and chatted to everyone. Just as we were having a drink in the evening the Omda came over and asked us to see his brother who was dying. We found a poor man, very ill indeed, lying on an angareeb (rope bed) with a matting screen round him. He really appeared to be at his last gasp, clutching his tummy and groaning away. His relatives were all round him wailing. There was really no way we could tell what was the matter with him, so Anne decided that whatever she did, even if he had acute appendicitis it could not make him worse, so she gave him a large dose of castor oil.

The next day while we were having breakfast, a very chirpy citizen appeared, full of life, gratitude and praise to God and Sa'ata Sit for saving him. She had done it again!

Sketch from Anne's Watercolour

We bumped on into Abyei which took most of the day. Anne, once again recorded the peaceful scene…

Rather than stay in the batty resthouse, I came down with Mike and settled under a shady tree by the water. M thinking it is much nicer than the office, has had his desk carried down here too. He is holding forth with everyone who wants to see him while I sit listening or not as I wish. Numerous little cups of coffee keep arriving from different people. I have been attempting to paint the scene, which is lovely. In the foreground is an enormous tree under which all the passers by stop to exchange gossip or sit down in the shade. Behind the tree is the water, blue and clear in which the people wade and fish while cows, horses, goats and sheep are feeding on the luscious green grass growing in and around it. All sorts of people are going by, mostly long legged tall Dinka with their spears or with baskets of dried fish on their heads. One little boy has speared a fish in the water and is very pleased with himself, he is now proceeding to chop it in half to share with his friend. A very colourful lady swathed in a richly coloured tobe has just stopped to stare for 15 minutes. She has a baby looking out on her back. Never a dull moment and the gleaming bodies wading in the water makes me long to join them, they look so cool and happy. There is one little boy swimming lustily, splashing as hard as he can.

We parted from Ken and went out that evening to Girinti (which means crocodile), to the west further up the Bahr el Arab. This was a favourite place of

Babu's and he had told us that we really must visit it if we had time. It came up to expectations, one could almost have been in a large water meadow by the Thames with the cows grazing peacefully on the banks of the river. On the other hand, it was in the Ngok territory, although the Arabs used to graze it in the spring, it was also on the borders of Darfur Province and while the Dinka tolerated the Messeria, neither of them wanted the Rezigat from Darfur there. It was therefore important for us to show the flag.

Rather reluctantly we started homeward. We arrived back in Rigl el Fula at about 8pm at night after travelling all day. We were astonished when the headlights picked up two policemen whom we did not recognise, then more and more, they were all over the place. We got in and before we had even time to sit down, AR announced a Police Officer from El Obeid. He came in and explained he had come on the orders of the Governor with a large contingent of the Reserve Police Company. He then produced a letter addressed personally to me. I opened it and there was another inside (rather like pass the parcel). This was again addressed Secret and Strictly Personal to G.M.G.Tibbs esq, District Commissioner, Messeria; Rigl el Fula. It was also sealed in three places with Frank Lorimer's own signet ring. I opened it with great trepidation and read it with unbelief.

The letter was from Frank in which he said that following the riots and unrest in Khartoum on 1st March it was feared that there might be a large scale rebellion against the new government by the Ansar, the followers of Sayd Abdel Rahman, whose Umma Party had been defeated in the general election. If this did happen it would start in the west. The Governor General had ordered that in such an event all British were to be withdrawn into Province Headquarters. The code word was "portmanteau". If this was broadcast on the wireless or received on the radiotelephone, we were to abandon everything and come into El Obeid immediately.

We digested this as we eat our supper. No one could have been more peaceful or friendly than those we had just visited on our trek. The next morning Mohamed Kafi started up the 'over' as usual, then put his head round my office door and said I was needed on the radio. I crossed the road into the little hut to find Geoffrey McComas on the blower. After a short greeting he became quite incomprehensible until it dawned on me that he was talking French. He said I was to come into El Obeid straight away without giving away that there was anything unusual about it "....avec Anne et ses malles ordinaires". Had I understood? I supposed I had and abandoned the office, went home and asked Anne to confirm that the message meant what I thought it meant.

We told the servants to let Segeir know that we had to go into El Obeid after lunch. and Anne started to sort out her things. As soon as Anne got out her dressing case, Abel Rahman asked "Why is Sata Sit going back to England?". Sadly we packed and before we went, took a photograph of us with all the staff and our faithful lorry. Abdel Rahman, Safragi; Abdullahi, Cook; Ahmed, Seconda; Abdel Rahman, Syce; Segeir, Police Driver; Sagha, driver's assistant; Ahmed Matta, Messenger; and the Kitchen, Garden and Stable prisoners.

Our lorry obviously did not approve of the new plan and behaved abominably, eventually giving up the ghost altogether about 100 miles somewhere between El Odaiya and Abu Zabad. As Sagha said profoundly "Arabya de, el jin gamat minha" - "This vehicle, the spirit has gone out of her". Eventually, after much blowing through of petrol pipes we limped into Abu Zabad at about 3 am. Not knowing what was happening in El Obeid, I went to the police station and after much furious winding of the handle of the telephone, managed to get through to Geoffrey McComas, his house being only one of three in El Obeid to be on the 'phone. He asked what on earth was the time. I explained and said I supposed we could try and continue the journey but would much sooner go to the rest house and get some sleep. He said we could, but must come on first thing in the morning

After an early start we got to the Muderia (Governor's Office)) at about noon. Governor Frank told me that things were very tense and that the Governor General had ordered that all British women and children were to be sent home out of harm's way. "If anything happens and we have to be tough, we will be much better without our women folk." Tough with what? one wondered.

We were told to go straight to the airport as a special flight was due. Much to Anne's delight we were late and the Dove took off as we arrived. John and Mary Hunter, now in our old Powder House were very kind, gave us lunch and somewhere to have a rest. (Mary as a doctor living in El Obeid was exempt from the evacuation order). However another special Dove came down in the evening and Anne had to leave. She went to stay with the Bells in Khartoum before going back in the Airwork Viking to England and Bunchfield.

Abdel Rahman was wonderful and told me it was much better, I was not to be too sad, he would look after me. When I got back to Rigl el Fula all our friends were amazed that Anne had gone and could not understand it. The sheikhs all told me that if I had been worried I should have sent her down to the river (Bar el Arab round Abyie) and they would have looked after her there.

24. SAD FAREWELL.

Water problems in Muglad

I spent about six weeks on my own before I was able to come on leave and rejoin Anne. Much of the time was spent in going through the old Messeria District files, which I had taken with me from Nahud, and getting them up to date. Ahmed Abu Gasim had very inconveniently elected to go on leave as soon as the Governor General's visit was over, so I had a lot of his work to do as well as my own. The night after Ahmed Abu Gasim had returned, I was fast asleep in the verandah on our large double angareeb, when Abdel Rahman woke me up and said that Bukr wanted to speak to me. Bukr was our Executive Officer in Lagawa, but had come over to help us in Rigl el Fula for a while. He said that the Omda from Muglad, Mekki Aly el Gulla had arrived with several of the merchants to say that the donkey (deep bore pump) had broken down. They had been very abusive to Ahmed Abu Gasim and told him the government obviously did not care if they and their children were going to be left to thirst to death by the departing British; the Council and particularly its officers were corrupt and inefficient etc. etc. Bukr said that he was driving straight into El Obeid, he would report to the Governor, ask the PWD to send someone to mend the pump and ask the Camel Corps for the loan of some tankers to bring water into Muglad from outside. I gave Bukr a letter to the Governor and said I would go down to Muglad as soon as possible in the morning and wished him luck.

Being wide-awake by this time, I decided to go down at once. So, Segeir, Sagha, Ahmed Matta and myself set off at 4am down the valley to Um Kedada, a lovely drive as the sun came up. We got to Muglad shortly after 7am to find quite a crowd of people waiting to fill their tins and water their animals. I stood on a box to talk to them, then wandered through the crowd assuring them that help was on the way, in the meantime they must be patient and God willing they would not have to wait long. At 8am the radios in some of the little shops were blaring out the news. The corrupt British administration had sabotaged the wells in Muglad, angry crowds were calling for vengeance and no one in authority was doing anything about it. Mekki and co had not, as we assumed, gone back to Muglad but on to Nahud from where they could telephone the press in El Obeid. The shopkeepers were very good in giving out drinks to those who were thirsty, but by the afternoon Bukr had come back from a 400 mile return trip with some SDF tankers and an engineer. I was able to get back to Rigl el Fula for a late tea.

I had always been rather sorry for Mekki Ali el Gulla, he was Babu's uncle and much in his shadow. None of my predecessors had thought very much of him and he was well known for intrigue but I reckoned he had been doing better lately and could do with some encouragement. So, I had been writing out a recommendation for a Robe of Honour (Class 3), which I now tore up.

Abyei again.

Now that the Council's remit ran in Abyei we all thought that we should have an Executive Officer of the Council there, rather than leave it all to Deng Majok and the Sergeant of Police. One of the most difficult decisions of the year was when to send grain down to Abyei before the rainy season. At each of the main centres, there was a Government shuna (grain store, a large concrete tank in the ground with a locked iron top). Like Joseph in Egypt, grain was bought in the time of plenty so that it could be issued out if the rains failed. The Dinkas' main preoccupation was with their cattle although they grew enough crops for a subsistence economy. Sometimes their harvest was ruined by too early flooding, and the police had authority to open the shuna if necessary. The other hazard was that if the locals knew the shuna was full, they would not bother to plant their crops in the first place. After all, it was much less of an effort to get grain from the government hand out. The trick, therefore was to send grain down the road at the crucial moment after the planting and before the road closed for six months. The timing of this was one of one's most important decisions during the year.

The Ngok used to complain that if they did have surplus grain, they could only sell it to local Arab merchants who would then sell it on at an exorbitant profit. So, I had got hold of the rules and regulations for registered co-operative societies, but if we set one up, it would need someone competent to run it; another job for a resident executive officer.

So, another visit to Abyei and lengthy meeting with Deng Majok and the other notables. We had discussed the question of 'who' before. Deng's eldest son Ahmed had been working in the new offices in Rigl el Fula. Deng was very insistent that Ahmed, or 'Mamid da' as he called him should do the job. I was not so sure and had thought he should get more experience first, such as a spell as an army officer; in the meantime we would find someone else for five years.

I had never been to Lau, about three hours drive out to the west of Abyei. It was a beautiful place, just a few trees and lusciously green, so I decided to stay a whole day there and write my annual report in peace and quiet.

On returning to Abyei, there was another unexpected problem. We had become friendly with two of Deng's other sons. They had turned up one day in Nahud and asked for a lift down to Abyei for their holidays. They were both at that time at Rumbek Intermediate School in Bar el Ghazal Province. They had their initial schooling with Lino Wor in Abyei and also been baptised as Roman Catholics as Zacharia, Dinka name Bol, and Francis, Dinka name Madeng. I found out that Zacharia Bol had been thrown off a lorry and had injured his leg so I went to see him. He was lying in a hut, obviously in pain and the leg had not been properly set and looked as if it might go gangrenous. He was being treated by a local medicine man but I said he should have proper treatment and I would take him to Nahud hospital. This caused a lot of discussion, the elders did not want him to go, but in the end Deng agreed. We made Zacharia as comfortable as we could on a bed in the back of the lorry and were able to get him up to Nahud where the leg was reset before he had another uncomfortable transfer to El Obeid hospital. I was very worried about him, but he recovered apart from a slight limp.

We had a Council meeting in Rigl el Fula at the beginning of April, after which I was able to rejoin Anne in Lynchmere.

Our last return.

In early June, we were sitting in my father's study in the Vicarage having elevenses when the telephone rang "It's for you". "I am ringing for the Sudan Agent. You have been recalled from leave, your passage with Airwork has been booked for Tuesday next week". "Can my wife come too?". The voice said it would have to find out, but, praise to God rang back with "Yes"

By the 21st June, we were back in Khartoum staying with Gawain Bell, now Civil Secretary though under the title of Permanent Secretary to the Ministry of the Interior. We had four days while waiting for the next train, during which I paid a number of courtesy visits. These included breakfast at Clergy House with George Martin; coffee at the Grand Hotel with Hammad Mohamed Dafaala, our MP for the Zurug and signing the Visitors' book in the Palace. I also tried to find out from Robin Young now ic. the 'Jug and bottle' (personnel department) in the Secretariat when we would get our final notice. While I was in the Secretariat someone came up and said, "You are dining at the Palace to-night". Not being aware of protocol, I naively replied that we could not as we were already going to Bill Monteith. "Don't worry," I was told, "that has already been taken care of."

Anne takes up the story....

Dinner at the Palace.

Jock Duncan, the Private Secretary asked us for a drink before hand, they live in the Palace grounds, so from there we were able to walk through the gardens and arrived punctually at 8 o'clock. H.E. was sitting out in the garden and we were ushered across the lawns by David Eales, the Aid-de-camp who looked immaculate in mess undress and miniatures. (M had to borrow Gawain's white dinner jacket as his own was in Rigl el Fula).

We sat and chatted over a drink for about half an hour until dinner was announced. H.E. did not attempt to move, so it was announced again 10 minutes later. It was really a beautiful setting. A lovely star lit night and across the lawns, the Palace was all floodlit, so that it was a silvery white against the dark velvet sky. In the formal gardens, a fountain played surrounded by beds of beautiful coloured flowers. Behind us was an enormous mango tree, laden, in fact weighed down, with golden mangoes looking like glowing lanterns. Night birds chattered loudly in the trees and the smell of dinner wafted acrosss the lawn from a small charcoal furnace roaring as the cook grilled the chops.

We moved over to the dinner table, I had the misfortune to put my foot through my petticoat so had to hobble, hoping that the rip of taffeta had not been too loud; I managed to disentangle my leg after being pushed up to the table on my chair by one of the safragis. There were three to wait on us . The cook in the background had a table with his pots and pans, and there was a serving table as well. We each had a menu in a silver holder in front of us - Onion soup, grilled chop, potato puree, carrots, brussel sprouts. Mango fool. Dessert and coffee. White wine, Liqueurs.

The sprouts and carrots H.E. announced were grown in the Palace garden and they were very good; the mango fool was almost thick cream and very rich. I nearly had an embarrassing time sucking a mango for dessert, as when it was offered we were very busy discussing the pros and cons of carting hay in a Hillman Husky. H.E.'s activity at his farm in Cornwall. Thank goodness, I diverted myself to some dates just in time.

Dinner over, the ADC conducted me to the ladies' powder room inside the Palace. There was a lovely red stair carpet going up the outside grand staircase and I was looking forward to sailing up it, but instead I was taken through the huge hall around which hang all sorts of trophies from game to spears. As I went through the sentries clicked to attention.

We met in the hall and the sentries presented arms this time. The huge red Rolls was drawn up in front of the Palace and we got in, H.E., M and myself in the back and David in front. We were escorted by police out-riders on motor bikes who scattered the traffic in front of us. We sailed sedately along the avenue of trees on the bank of the Blue Nile which twinkled with different coloured lights and reflections. After about a mile we stopped at the Blue Nile Cinema to be welcomed by the Manager and were ushered into the Royal box, very comfortable with arm chairs. There was a newsreel, cartoon and then the 'Broken Journey' a somewhat tense and morbid story of a load of people in a Dakota, which landed on the top of some icy mountains. At the end we sat until everyone else had gone and saw several of our friends somewhat surprised to see the Tibbs in the Royal box. Then escorted by the Manager we re-embarked in the red Rolls and drove back to the Palace where we got out, said good bye in the hall and were then sent home in an equally large red Humber. Sir Robert was very hospitable and easy to talk to and offered any help in finding M a job which was very nice of him.

Return to Rigl el Fula.

We arrived back in El Obeid on 25th June to find a sea of faces to meet us, the Governor, Deputy Governor, Geoffrey McComas, John Hunter, Nazir Babu, the Sherif Ahmed Abu Gasim and the staff. Abdel Rahman had met us in Khartoum; he very kindly brought us some mangoes from his garden which we ate in Gawain's bath. We stayed with Geoffrey, neither he nor John had brought their wives and families out. Geoffrey was busy painting his furniture bright green, and had even enamelled his fridge (white!). Abdullahi our cook wis very happy as his wife was expecting, we were very glad, as they had been married for seventeen years and its the first time since their little son died when he was six. Our lorry and Segeir had not turned up yet as it had broken down, but about four other lorries seemed to have arrived and Geoffrey said he had been interrupted all yesterday by people delivering our trek boxes and enquiring when we were coming.

It took us two days to get back to Rigl el Fula as we had to come via Nahud. The direct road was too wet. In Nahud we were asked to breakfast with the new doctor. We arrived at 8.30 but it was not until 10. when after much shuffling behind the scenes did breakfast appear, lentil soup, fried chops, boiled eggs, liver then bread and jam, melon and coffee. We got to El Odaiya in time for lunch with a Second Lieutenant in the Camel Corps which was now having a Company posted there. A barracks was already on the way up just outside the town, much to Babu's indignation. (A sign of the times, the government obviously wanted some troops on the spot to crush any sign of unrest, a far cry from us and our handful of police). A very nice young officer, one of three brothers all in the army following father, and grandfather's footsteps.

We were travelling for the first time in the 'bus' a new Council lorry that M had designed, it had two bench seats in the front to take ten. all the luggage and servants can go in the back. It was quite comfortable to drive in except that the second row of seats was not sprung. We arrived home at about 5pm. The scene from above must have resembled a juicy victim landing in an ants' nest as everyone appeared from all directions at once. We shook hands, once, twice and then three times with everyone who were all very pleased to see us both back again. The old gardener stood beside us chanting greetings for a quarter of an hour. The Sherif's wife had tea already waiting for us. Ahmed had cleaned the house, lit the fridge, seen to the bath water and everything was all ready. Then we visited the farmyard. Abdel Rahman the scyce led each horse out of the stables and trotted them up and down for us to see. They both did a little bucking bronco act to show us how well they felt. The cows, sheep, turkeys, chickens and of course Rachel were all fit and well.

Council Lorry (designed by G.M.G.T.)
10 seater   5 front row
Commer   5 second row (unsprung)

Aleak   Arnouk
Rachel and her turkey children

Turkey Top

In the morning we walked round on a tour of inspection. Grass only a few inches high as yet, is springing up everywhere.. A lovely change from El Obeid and Nahud where it is all dry and dusty still.

Our own house looks lovely now it is thatched and its stone walls are set off with bluey green shutters.

New buildings have shot up since I left. Everything looks so nice, we do not want to leave it all so soon, especially our own house and farmyard.

several new houses, dispensary, school, prison and merkas (government office).

The old Council gardener was thrilled with the little trowel we gave him, he kissed it, waved his arms and rushed off to try digging with it. He comes up to see me with his pockets full of tebeldis or black tomatoes. I was able to give him some mustard and cress I grew on a bath towel, it was ready to eat in four days.

Michael continues

We are of course still waiting to hear about our future, we were told that a compensation bill was agreed by all concerned and would be going to Parliament. When eventually it was announced on the wireless that it had been through both House of Representative and the Senate, there was a thunderstorm, which blotted out most of what we wanted to hear. One brave southerner voted against the bill as he thought we would stay if it did not get through. Nazir Sereir has now moved here and built thirteen grass houses for himself, his four wives his concubine and countless children. He thinks they have all got to subscribe to my compensation, so he is not going to so that we can stay.

Our staff all seem to know what they are going to do. AR wants to return to Shendi where Zeinab's father has some cultivation, to open a small shop, Ahmed wants to open a laundry in El Obeid, Abdullahi will work on his little farm and Abdel Rahman the scyce wants to work in the forestry department round Rigl el Fula. We are the only ones who have no idea of what we are going to do! We have been busy painting up our veranda furniture. We have made a businesslike book and priced a full list of everything, Sherif Ahmed Abu Gasim kindly went through it and lowered some prices and put up others, then he bought our dresser and both beds. Nazir Serier came to tea and asked about the wireless. We had already tuned it to Radio Omdurman and it blasted out so much he bought it at once, but disbought it the next day in favour of our tent.. The Sherif is adjudicating any double bids and also collecting the money for us, stopping it from the purchasers' pay if necessary, saving us a lot of trouble.

We had to go down to Muglad in the new lorry with the police sergeant, his wife and Omda Musa Shwein in the front row, the Sherif, Ian Cunnison who suddenly turned up, and ourselves in the back row. It rained the last 10 miles but we were very comfortable in the front and there is a tarpaulin over the back so the troops there were quite dry. With so much space in front we can talk as we go along. Even at this stage the sheikhs do not believe we are going. When Ian told his friends we were packing up they shouted him down and said he was a liar.

The Prime Minister made a speech to Parliament the other day saying he was grateful to the Governor General for consenting to the Compensation Bill. He ended by remarking that the British had not starved and massacred the

Segeir

Our loyal police driver who drove us many thousands of miles in our Commer lorry.

Marraslas
(Messengers)

Hassan

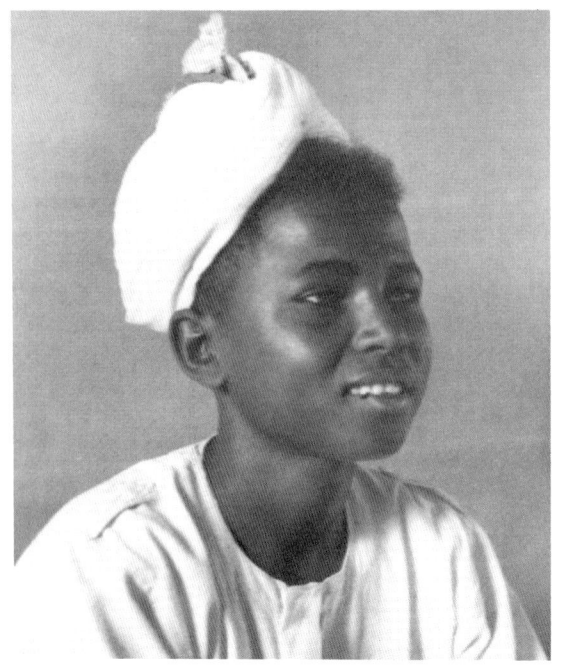

Gibril

Ahmed Mattah

Our faithful servants.

Abdel Rahman - safragi

Ahmed - seconda

Abdullahi - cook

Abdel Rahman - syce

Sudanese like they had the Indians, or colonised them like they had the Ugandans and Kenyans. The British here were of a superior type, unlike the Italians. They (the British) had come to serve in the Government only, and had all come from Oxford and Cambridge and had beautiful houses in England surrounded with tennis courts and playing fields.

There has been trouble in Muglad. A lot of West African nomads, the Um Borroro, have come in without permission. They are very destructive as they light fires and use our Arabs' grazing. The Council decided to take two years' tribute from them and try and push them out. It had been reported that Nazir Ali and friends rounded them up, taking all their sheep, selling them in Kadugli, paying some of the money to the Council but keeping the rest! We are trying to sort it out but needless to say no one has any receipts.

We were able to go duck shooting in the evening and got six but unfortunately a cat invaded the kitchen during the night so we only had one duck and apple sauce. In the morning there was a cattle auction, we sat under a grass shelter while 106 bulls and cows were sold, they had been taken as fines from parishioners who had not paid their taxes.

Goodbye to Lagawa.

At the end of July we went to say goodbye to Lagawa and our Nuba friends. We took two lorries, Segeir's full of prisoners to push. Our letters record a dreary catalogue of water on the road, boggings and squelch. It took two days to get to Lagawa where they were all taken by surprise, first that we ever got there and second that this was our last visit. We found a frightful row going on between Sultan Faragulla of Kamdang and Nazir Izz el Din. It all started in 1929 (!) when the Sultan lent some cows to someone and he now wants them back. The Nazir had found for the defendant. That took a lot of my time. I also saw two cases, one an unlicensed rifle (7 months) and one pickpocket (two years). Sheikh Mulah, our friend of the horse treks was there as his stepmother had died. One of the merchants had died having been bitten by a rabid dog, so it was a rather depressing visit. I had promised my shot gun to Nazir Izz el Din who borrowed the money from Mekki Amin who gave me some cash and letters to his brothers in Abu Zabad and El Obeid to pay me the rest. I left the gun with the Sol (police sergeant major) with orders to lock it up until Izz el Din's shot gun licence was sent from the Governor.

While I had been on leave the District had been under the charge of Taj, the new Sub Mamur. I had told him to settle a cultivation dispute by riding his horse from point A along a compass bearing to point B. I had worked out the bearing and everything was ready for him, but he had said there was too much

Outside the Council H.Q. Rigl el Fula
Backrow: Ismail, Abu Bukr, Mahmoud Horgas, Mohamed Ahmed
Middle row: Kabous, Sherif Ahmed Abu Gasim, Anne, Michael, Tag el Din
Front row: Ibrahim, Ahmed Mattah, Gibril

All poshed up for the Governor General

Messaria Lodge, Rigl el Fula

Finished - complete with a row of zinnias and the hand chopped rock path

dew and he might get rheumatism. The Arabs were saying, so much for the towney government.

A tedious journey back with an increased load. An accountant going to Abu Zabad with most of his furniture, two women with babies, six boys going back to school in El Obeid and the two extra prisoners I had collected in Lagawa. By the time we got to Tima it was pouring, some of our passengers sheltered under the lorry and we let some of them come into the other half of the rest house, no doors of course. All during this time we had no news of when we had to go or whether we had been successful in getting a passage in the Warwick Castle leaving Port Sudan at the end of September.

When we got to Abu Zabad I managed to get hold of Geoffrey McComas on the telephone. He said that he and John Hunter were leaving in a few days and we had better come in, so on we went to El Obeid. In Geoffrey's house we found him with John Hunter and Ralph Daly eating on the floor as they had sold everything. Fortunately we were able to stay in the rest house. We were able to get our affairs sorted out a little. Everything had gone haywire as we had not had any news from home for ages. (We eventually discovered that the postmaster at Nahud had put our letters under the counter and never sent them on).

Back to Abu Zabad, where we added Hag Said and his family to our load. Hag (Pilgrim) was a dear and very holy; he was our cashier and accountant in Abu Zabad and was going to help out in Rigl el Fula for a bit. The story goes that the Government Auditor arrived one day and sent a message to say he would come to check the books after lunch. Hag Zaid was way behind with his entries, although everything was written on little bits of paper and chits under the blotter of his desk. His friends urged him to get cracking and perhaps he would be able to fill in the proper columns in the cashbook before the auditor came back. Instead, the Hag went off to a quiet place to pray. He was back in the office at the appointed time and met the Auditor who apologised that he did not have time to look at the books after all or he would be late in getting to Lagawa! (Power of prayer?)

Then, a ghastly journey back to Rigl el Fula on our new direct road, which took two days. All the khors were flooded and everyone had to push and pull on ropes. We got bogged at lunchtime when both lorries stuck, the bus right down on one side. We toiled all day, then camped and lit a fire to dissuade the bugs which were in biting form finding us very juicey. As all the others were helping with the lorries we fried sausages, bacon and tomatoes on the fire and had banana for pudding. A hyena howled very close at intervals and Mohamed Kwal, one of the policemen went off to shoot it, but of course it ran away and howled happily all night.

 The next morning I got stung by a scorpion as I picked up a piece of wood. Anne cauterised it with our little scapula, sucked it and rubbed in permanganate of potash, but the real cure came from Hag Said. He rubbed it with one of his little amulets, which carried verses from the Koran. He then chanted verses and spat them onto my finger, it was very effective indeed.

We struggled on, at one place crossing a khor waist deep in water; we got through but then the carburettor was full of water. It took another two hours to clean it and the petrol pipes.

Eventually we had to leave the bus and got to Rigl el Fula in Segeir's lorry after an exhausting journey, everyone was very relieved to see us. A search party with another twenty prisoners had been sent out with extra rations but had also got bogged and failed to find us.

Anne recorded 26 boggings for the 'bus', 13 to Segeir's lorry, 39 in all with 14 hours of digging, heaving, pushing and pulling by an average of 17 people, often more. It was found that the bus's big end had gone, spares coming by horseback!

Goodbye to Muglad

We made a final visit to Muglad. The doctor from Nahud and a chum also came, staying with the Sherif on the way. We had warned them that they must stop in Gubba, twenty miles north of Muglad. This was the last resting place of a holy man who had accompanied the Mahdi's army at the battle of Omdurman. He fled back to Kordofan after the battle, but only got as far as Gubba. Just before he died he decreed that all travellers should stop to pay their respects or they would suffer for it. We always had a cup of coffee in the little grass cafe. While we were doing this, the two doctors rushed through blowing their horn and would not stop. We were not at all surprised to find them axle deep in a huge hole three miles on.

There was an enormous tea party in our honour on the space in front of the offices at Muglad. All the Nazirs, including Deng Majok who had ridden all the way up the 120 miles from Abyie, the Court Presidents, the Omdas, the merchants and the shiekhs were all there. Babu made a speech and one of the merchants who was on the Council also insisted on making an unofficial speech and then it was my turn. (See appendix). Afterwards we went slowly round and shook hands with everyone.

In the evening we gave a slide show projecting the slides on the white wall of the prison. We showed pictures of places in the District and then of England. Our homes, Lynchmere, shops like the Macfisheries in Haslemere, London and finally some of the Coronation. I tried to shout a commentary, but they all got far too excited to listen. Ian was on the outskirts of the crowd. As a picture of Buckingham Palace came up, one said to another "What on earth is that?" "Don't be silly, look at the flag on top, it's a river steamer".

Goodbye to Rigl el Fula

Back in Rigl el Fula we loaded lorries with 24 packing cases of various shapes and sizes, then got busy distributing our furniture to its new owners. It was odd seeing it somewhere else, especially our dresser in the Sherif's household, needless to say the carpenters had not assembled it properly. Although we have had lunch there twice it is still not right. They had been very kind, although we suggested we should have Sudanese food they have insisted on giving us roast chicken and stew off our own green spotted dinner service.

As well as dispersing our furniture, we had to find new homes for the horses and farmyard. Brown Willy is going to Bukr in Lagawa while Taj, the Sub-Mamur is having Turvey; this is a relief as both will still be on government certificates and be properly looked after. Ahmed Abu Gasim is having the turkeys, we have given Rachel our duck to Omer, his second son.. We are leaving the sheep Daisy, Buttercup and Dandelion with Abdel Rahman the Syce while the cows are being returned to their proper owners

We heard on Radio Omdurman that my relief is to be Mohamed Ibrahim Abdel Hafiz, our last Sub-Mamur who left us earlier in the year. I was lucky to become a substantive District Commissioner in five years, but he will jump through two ranks, Mamur and Assistant D.C in one go. The last official letter I had from the Governor's office was to say that the Province Board of Public Health had approved the plans of the District Commissioner's House!

We had a very happy tea party in front of the Council. The courtyard was gay with flowers, some of which had been picked for the top table which had four long sprigs. All the officials, police, warders, merchants and builders were there. Babu and Abu Gabr had come from Muglad and Bukr from Lagawa. The rest of the population was looking over the wall. We had cake (made in our kitchen during the two free days Anne gave our servants to do their own packing - they and our prisoners had been beating furiously), biscuits, fizz, tea and sweets. Then the Head Accountant said there would be three speeches. Three there were, one from Ahmed Abu Gasim who talked about our friendship with all the people in Rigl el Fula. Bukr said how sorry he was that they had not been able to give a party in Lagawa but they had been in mourning, then Ismail, the Head Clerk talked about the work we had done. There was just one more day, we went round giving the presents we had brought for people and they were most generous to us. Ahmed Abu Gasim and his wife gave Anne a gold ring especially made in Khartoum, the Sergeant of Police gave us an ebony cane, the cook's wife a pair of leopard skin slippers and so it went on.

At last came the sad day when we piled into the Council lorry. We left at 8.30am on the 6th September, 1954 and everyone turned out to say goodbye. Then they jumped into the other lorries and rushed ahead to say it again four miles out. We drove on another few miles and stopped, we had to take the dynamo to pieces which took an hour and a half!

POST SCRIPT

People were very kind to us both in El Obeid and Khartoum as we went through. In El Obeid we stayed in the resthouse but had meals with everyone, including the Sudanese Deputy Governor, Abdullahi. In Khartoum we stayed with Peter and Joanna Hogg. His Minister had congratulated Peter on his promotion to Director of Local Government. The next day he found his dismissal notice on his desk! We had a great send off from all our friends as we set off by train to Port Sudan, taking Abdel Rahman with us as far as Shendi. All his family were there to greet us; Zeinab still looking young and pretty with her father and mother and Salma; a chubby little baby with a lot of black hair. She was very pleased with the squeaky toy that we gave her. We were very sad to have to say good bye to our very great friends.

So, on to Port Sudan where we stayed at the Red Sea Hotel and were looked after by Joseph, a Syrian merchant and friend of Nubar Ebipane in Khartoum. Just before the Warwick Castle arrived, Anne was very ill with a very high temperature. A lady Polish doctor came to see her and helpfully announced that she could not possibly travel and must wait for the next ship! With Joseph's help, I was able to get all our packing cases on board, our passports stamped and find our cabin. Joseph then picked me up from the gangway in a small boat. In front of the hotel Anne got in, I rowed out to the ship and she was in bed in our cabin within ten minutes of leaving her bed in the hotel. Thank goodness she recovered very quickly.

On my way from El Obeid there were two things I had to sort out: -

I had discovered to my horror that a team had been through the west, surveying the route of the new railway. They had decided it should go through El Odaiya instead of Rigl el Fula. There had been no reference to us and we had no idea they were coming. One of Rigl el Fula's raisons d'etre had been to be the western terminus of the railway before a further extension was made down to Wau. I asked the Deputy Governor in El Obeid to take this up with the powers that be. I also went to see the Sudan Railway department in Khartoum. I do not suppose that this effort had anything to do with it, but the line was routed through Rigl el Fula on its way to Wau in the south and Nyala in the west.

My other parting task was to see the Province Education Inspector and the Headmaster of Khor Tuggart School, the secondary school near El Obeid. After long talks with Deng Majok, we had decided that if Francis and Zacharia (Bol) were to hold their own in the northern Sudan of the future, they should go to a northern school.. The Inspector and the Headmaster were very understanding and co-operative. Both boys were admitted to Khor Tuggart and wrote very kind letters to tell me how they were getting on. They have both had remarkable careers. They both went to the University of Khartoum, where Francis read law and Zacharia economics.

Zacharia concluded that economics was not for him and decided to do medicine. He got a scholarship to Leipzig, learning German as a start; then he mastered Italian and finished in Padua and Bologna. He then came to the United Kingdom for postgraduate medical training. Returning to the Sudan, he entered the Southern political scene. When General Nimeri approved the setting up of a parliament for the South, he became the Speaker. The parliament was suddenly abolished, so Zacharia practised in Khartoum, but later had to come back to this country as a political refugee. He is now a General Practitioner in Birmingham.

Francis graduated in law, then came to England for postgraduate studies. This was when we re-established contact with the brothers. Francis went on to the U.S.A. obtaining a doctorate at Yale. He then joined the Human Rights division of the United Nations in New York. Returning to the Sudan he entered the diplomatic service and was successively Ambassador to the Scandinavian countries, the U.S.A and Canada and Minister of State for Foreign Affairs. He resigned when President Nimeri imposed Islamic law on the country and abrogated the Addis Abba peace accord, triggering a return to the civil war in the South. Francis subsequently became an Associate or Fellow of the Woodrow Wilson International Centre, the Rockefeller Brothers Fund and the U.S.Institute of Peace. Since 1988 he has been Senior Fellow at the Broodings Institution where he is head of the Africa branch of the Foreign Studies Programme. Since 1992, he has also been Representative of the U.N. Secretary General on Internally Displaced Persons. Francis has written extensively in the fields of law, conflict resolution, human rights, anthropology, folklore, history, politics and two novels. His books include 'The Man Called Deng Majok', a biography of his father and 'Bonds of Silk', the Human Factor in the British Administration of the Sudan

Deng Majok died in 1969. Both Francis and Zacharia were able to get back to Khartoum, where he had been taken. They flew him to Cairo for treatment there, but his condition was hopeless and he died. Through superhuman efforts they fulfilled their last promise and managed to fly his body back to his beloved Abyei.

Nazir Babu, accompanied by Nazir Ali, came to England again in 1981 to see a heart specialist. It so happened that one of Babu's sons, Asim, had just become a Member of the Royal College of Physicians of which I was Secretary. They all stayed with us in Lynchmere; we had a wonderful time catching up with the news and reminiscing about old times. They also joined us in the Isle of Wight where we were staying. Babu died the next year. Who would have thought that the last time we would see him, he would be waving from the deck of the Yarmouth to Lymington ferry?

Our younger son, Christopher has been to the Sudan twice. First, in 1978, when he was reading zoology at Oxford. In 1983, through the kindness of Dr Halim Mohamed Abdel Halim FRCP, Christopher, then a medical student, was able to do his obstetrics and gynaecology in Khartoum. He has kindly written the Epilogue for this book.

A friend of ours visited Shendi three years ago. We asked him to call on Abdel Rahman and Zeinab, which he did. Sadly, Abdel Rahman had died the year before, but 'Praise be to God', they had both been able to go on the pilgrimage to Mecca together. Zeinab sent us her greetings and a photograph of our dear friend. . A few years ago, Abu Gabr's son wrote to tell us that his father had died. We have also learnt that our friend the Sherif Ahmed Abu Gasim has passed on.

We hated leaving the Sudan when we did. I had always hoped for another year or two in Rigl el Fula to see through the major projects we had started. Looking back now, all these years later, we realise how lucky we were to have lived such a life, which has now gone. The reports, such as they are, about the Sudan, and in particular about the Nuba and the Ngok Dinka are chilling. One can only pray that the light will dawn again.

Our administration may not have been perfect in all respects, but it was summed up by one of our Nuba who came to Rigl el Fula for the first time while we were on leave. He was most impressed by the buildings and said to Ahmed Abu Gasim

"I do not know why the British are leaving us. Before they came, our people were always full of fear. I have just been all the way to Khartoum and Port Sudan for the pilgrimage, then all the way back again without fear. I have never been afraid. We have peace".

EPILOGUE BY CHRISTOPHER

It is a witness to the compelling fascination of the Sudan, which was so much a part of my upbringing that I have always felt a little cheated that the premature demise of the Sudan Political Service meant that I was not raised there. The twenty-year contract would have ended when I was ten, but it was not until I was twenty that I first visited the country, which I always felt to be a part of me. A childhood in the Sudan was often imagined, so vivid were the images which I had, of lorries and swamps, deserts and bull trains of the Messeria, the Dinka, the Nuer and the Nuba.

On my first visit in 1978, I learnt little of the Sudan of my parents. I was involved in a research project on the coral which fringes the Sudan coast of the Red Sea. We spent most of the time living on platforms built out in the sea. The undersea life of the coral reefs below us, was as colourful and exciting as Port Sudan itself was hot, sandy, drab and uninteresting. Elegant ships of the Union Castle Line no longer graced the harbour. The Red Sea Club still existed and was run by a British manger but it cannot have seen a dinner jacket for 20 years. Our base house in the town rang to the amplified cries of the mullah and the night-time streets echoed to the drums and celebrations of nightlife during Ramadan. All the members of my expedition were stricken by dysentery. We departed after two months, thankful to be in one piece.

My second visit to the Sudan was in 1983, 28 years after the way of life portrayed in this book had ended. This time I was able to go back to the imagined place of my Sudanese childhood and meet many of the characters so lovingly recollected in this book.

First was the quest for Abdel Rahman. The trail led to Shendi, a town of mud brick houses on the palm-fringed banks of the Nile some 200 miles north of Khartoum. The train running on narrow gauged tracks originally laid by Kitchener, must have been the same set of rolling stock as bore my parents on their final trip to Port Sudan. Given the unpromising address of 'Ata el Seed Sid Ahmed, c/o Grain Market, Shendi', I was surprised to have made any contact with AR's family. However, within an hour of arrival, the network had established whom I sought. After a night with some of AR's relatives in Shendi, I was taken to a house in a village further up the Nile, where Zeinab, his wife, overcome, greeted me as a prodigal son. Hashim, one of his sons, at that time studying agriculture at Khartoum University, showed me round and the next day returned with me to Khartoum where we met Abdel Rahman.

AR and I were both overcome by this experience, although we could not communicate save through the interpretation of Hashim; the pressure to get over 28 years of mutual news was emotionally draining for both of us. At that time he was working as a cook and house servant at one of the womens' hostels of the University. He proudly led me out through the streets of Khartoum and had a handsome galabia made for me. I saw him a number of times while I was in the Sudan; our cheeks became weary with our mutual smiles as we both remembered how things had been and would never be again.

From Khartoum, I travelled to El Obeid where I had the great fortune to be the guest of the then Governor of Kordofan, El Fatir Bushara. He was the very model of servitude to the regime in power at that time. President Nemeiri was in his 18th year of dictatorship shortly before the declaration of Sharia law in September 1983 which put the final seal on the division of the country. Naïve as I was to the nature of power at that time, I was happy to be entertained in the Governor's garden in the evening, like my parents before me. I spent the days working in the hospital, until armed with two 40 gallon drums of petrol, a driver called Tadj and a Landrover, I set out with two of Babu's sons to the Messeria.

The desert had advanced over the intervening years; where there had been cattle grazers, there were now camel herds; where there had been water, there was now parched earth. The drive across the desert loosely followed the graded stream of tracks running parallel to the railway line, which now ran west from El Obeid. Near Abu Zabad, we met the only traffic, a small box car whose passenger turned out to be Bukr Ali, who had been the Assistant Executive Officer in Lagawa 28 years before. Then, about 20 miles short of Rigl el Fula we were flagged down by a venerable grizzled man in a spotless galabia, who just happened to be standing under the only tree for several miles. His eyes immediately lit up at the name Tibbs and to our mutual astonishment, we found a photograph of him in one of the collection of old prints I had taken with me.

In Rigl el Fula there was a reception committee led by the current DC, Nazir Sereir and Segeir (my father's Police driver). It also consisted of all those who could lay legitimate claim to have known Mr Tibbs. There were a good many, but it was a good excuse for a party, which was held in the garden of the house built by the first DC to live in Dar Messeria, 30 years before. Segeir was delighted to hear that Mr Tibbs had affectionately called his first car in his memory and later I met his entire and considerable family.

The DC's house, in which I slept, had been extended at both ends, but was instantly recognisable by the fireplace, the arch in the drawing room and the mosquito netted verandah. The old range was in the garden and the stable door and gravel paths had paid the price of time. The next day I saw

Mr Tibbs's office, his lorry (half-covered in sand), the Council Offices and Chamber, the Suq, the hospital (Russian built and doctorless). In the evening we went on to Muglad.

In Muglad, which was the tribal rather than the administrative centre, I spent two days greeting friends of Mr Tibbs, who travelled several miles on foot or donkey to see this reincarnation from the past, bearing gifts and endless reminiscences. We sat in the cool of a large thatched roof outside the house of Nazir Ali and talked and remembered and ate and dozed. The entire town went out for a picnic in the bush in my honour.

I returned to Rigl el Fula for another village picnic the next day. The persistent outpouring of hospitality, of genuine fondness for the previous generation of Tibbs's remains vividly with me to this day. As I drove away towards the Nuba mountains, I realised that although their respect may have been amplified by nostalgia and by the conflict, drought and corruption of the intervening years; they still held a lasting respect for that small band of dedicated men who had tried to serve them and nurture their land, the perceived decency of democracy and morality of mutual respect.

I was not allowed to go to Abyei; the Dinka were too unpopular with the Governor at that time, so I headed west to the parched Nuba hills. We saw few people there, save for weary lines of women trudging to wells dug in dried streambeds. They returned to their villages with a colourful; selection of plastic water containers. Without the escort of the Nimrs who had heralded my passage through Rigl el Fula and Muglad, there were no more recollections of Tibbs until I reached Kadugli. Here I was greeted by the District Governor with "You are wearing your father's bush jacket". This was Abu Gabr Hag Agbar who was Assistant Executive Officer in Muglad when GMGT had left 28 years before. He told me that he last saw me when he had stayed with us in Lynchmere and I was three!

In the last year, I have had a Sudanese Registrar working with me in London. We have often talked of her troubled homeland, its gentle people and eternal difficulties. It seem as though the days of the District Commissioners that we read about here, had given the Sudan an oasis of peace in the conflict of many centuries at the hub of Africa. She tells me that she could never be happy living anywhere else, because the Sudanese people who are in the country remain the same, unbowed, resilient and above all, cheerful, just as they were in the days of Tibbs.

(Christopher is now a Consultant Physician in a London Teaching Hospital).

APPENDIX 1.

Governor General's speech at the opening of the new Council building.
BULLETIN NO. 6.   PROJECT FEATURE NO 403
Date line – Khartoum 14.1.54.

HIS EXCELLENCY THE GOVERNOR GENERAL'S SPEECH
AT THE OPENING OF THE DAR MESSERIA COUNCIL

Chairman and Members of the Dar Messeria Council.

     I am very pleased to be again visiting Dar Messeria, to be able to congratulate you on your new warrant and to declare open these fine new buildings.
     Your building organisation, in completing not only these administrative buildings and eight houses for your officials, has, I understand also built three houses for central government and eight rest houses. These are fine achievements and I am confident that the Council will carry out the many other tasks both of daily routine and capital development in the same way.
     This Council in one way resembles the Sudan as a whole with its different races living alongside each other in the same area, Arabs, Dinka, Nuba and Dagu. Until recently each section has been pursuing its own path; you are now (differing as you are in origin, race, religion and tradition) combined in one council and your aims are only directed only towards working for the common good. Tolerance, patience and appreciation of the other point of view are going to be of paramount importance and I know I can rely on you o exercise these qualities. You all have a share in these fine new headquarters at Rig el Fula.
     You have two main responsibilities. The first to be in close touch with your constituents, so that not only can you keep them informed of the Council's activities and plans, but also give them a chance of passing on to you their ideas. Secondly, you are the policy makers. Without your direction and planning the Executive Officers of the Council can do nothing. In the same way as the District Commissioners carry out the orders the Central Government whatever that government may be, so to will the Executive Officers carry out your orders. So plan your policy well. Yours is a great responsibility and I am confident you will honour it.
     You owe a lot to Ahmedi Effendi Abu Gasim who has been responsible not only for the execution of these buildings but also for the setting up and growth of the Council five years ago.
     I have great pleasure in declaring this building open and in presenting you arrawith this new wnt.

PRO/140009. Public Relations Branch.
.Khartoum, 14.1.1954

Usual Dist. PRm.O/145100   Abdallah

APPENDIX 2

FAREWELL SPEECH IN MUGLAD (English Version)

Sayeds

British Inspectors have worked in the Sudan since 1899. Now, after 55 years the time has come when we hand over our duties to Sudanese District Commissioners from your own country. Today you have provided for me this party, but it is not just to me that you are saying goodbye, but to the last of your British District Commissioners, so I speak with this in view.

Let us turn first of all to the past. When the last government came to the Sudan there was hardly any administration the country, though you had your Nazirs. In 1911 Omdas were appointed to be responsible for their omdias, but it was not until 1937 that the first step to unite the people of Dar Messeria was made. In this year the Humr Felleita united with the Agaira. In 1942, the Zurug united with the Humr and the Messeria were united again after more than 100 years. It was the Government's policy to unite the people of the District because if everyone tried to go their own way, there is no stability. If there is no stability it is not possible to develop the resources in the area to their best advantages. The people in a ferig all have to work together for the good of all. Some cultivate, some look after cattle, some go ahead to find where the best grazing is. If everyone worked by himself, it would not be possible for him alone to find the best grazing, to cultivate and to look after his family and cattle. That is the reason why the Government has tried to unite the Sudan as a whole.

It became clear that the Sudan would soon be ready to look after its own affairs, but if you are to have a democratic government, one government in Khartoum is not enough. Everyone must have a voice in the affairs of his balad; so, in 1949 the Council was formed. In 1950 the Nuba and Dagu came into the Council and in 1952, the Dinka also. In 1953, the Dar Messeria District was split off from Western Kordofan. That brings us to the present.

At the present time the Council covers the entire District. Now what do you think is the must important function of the Council? The thing that affects you most is the tax that you pay. In the past you have had no say in how much your tribute was to be, but now you have. Now, if you want more wells or roads or vaccination for your cattle, you have the right to ask for them through your Council Member. If the Council agrees, then you have to raise the tribute. If you ever agree to surrender your Council, you would surrender your freedom to raise or lower your tribute. Don't think that if there was no Council there would be no tribute, there would be, but you would have no say in how much it was, or how it was spent.

That you have realised the usfulness of the Council is shown by the fact that when the Council was started in 1949, the Tribute was £E27, 000, it is now £E57, 000 and the services have increased accordingly. Now five years is NOT a long time. It has been necessary to establish the Council on firm foundations and build its headquarters at Rigl el Fula. The Nazirs agreed this during 1948. It is now there, near the old headquarters of Nazi Ali Messeria in the time of the Turkia.

Do not think that because the Council has not been able to build wells on your own doorstep that the Council has done nothing. Before you build a house, you must build the foundations then build the house, put on the roof and then you can paint it and bring the furniture inside. We all know that you want more furniture inside. You need more wells, donkey (waterbores), grazing, haffirs (reservoirs), schools and markets; but God willing, these will come and the house will be complete.

Now for the future. The partnership between us, the British and the Sudanese is at an end. This was bound to happen after the agreement made last year between the British and the Egyptian Governments. You cannot expect the Government not to implement the agreement, although Sudanisation is going faster than you would like.

Remember this. Many of you have said that when the British go, there will be a mulahkbut and fitnas (shambles and intrigues). If there are mulahkbuts and fitnas, they will not start from the District Commissioner nor from the Officers, they will start from you. They will hurt no one except yourselves and they will hold up your progress. If you hear that someone said something about you, do not wait until the fly has become a lion, go and ask him, and you will find that the fly is easier to kill.

Remember also that your Council Officers take their orders from the Council. If they do something you do not agree with, it is because that is the will of the Council. Your District Commissioner and Central Government officials take their orders from THIS Government. If you do not approve of their actions, before you start writing to the newspapers, you would be advised to find out what is this law that they are trying to carry out. I am not saying that you are not free to complain; that is your freedom; but if you are not sure what the truth is, go and ask the Merkaz (District Headquarters) or Council official responsible and ask him. This will save your time and theirs.

If you do not like the policy of the Government or Council, you, each one of you, have the power, through the elections; to change it.

I had very much hoped to be your District Commissioner, living amongst you here, for at least three years; but now I have to go after two. There are still things that I have begun, but must leave to you to finish.

My wife and I are very, very sorry to leave you, and we would like to thank you for all the kindness you have shown to us, in this time that we have been with you.

I know that all previous District Commissioners would like me to thank you for all your loyalty to them as well as to myself. I ask you all to show the same loyalty and respect to my successor, and help him as much as you have helped me.

May God bless you all, and your families, flocks and cultivation's in the future.

APPENDIX 3.

HANDING OVER NOTES FOR MY SUCCESSOR.

These are very short on purpose. The history of the District both before and after the split from Western Kordofan can be gleaned from the files and Personality sheets.

GENERAL.

This is the only District, which has four distinct races; Arabs, Dagu, Nuba and Dinka all tied up in the Rural Council. As far as I know the Council is the largest in the Sudan with 57 members. The composition, wards, etc. are all in the warrant.

See my letter of 18th April 1954, copy attached, to Governor, which is my progress report for 1953/54, also my note in the District Handbook.

COUNCIL

The D.C. is Chairman and I would oppose any move to have an elected Chairman. The Vice-Chairman is elected.

The Executive Officer, Ahmed Abu Gasim knows the Council backwards and you can rely on his experience and advice. He is now on a three year contract with the Council but may resign on giving three months notice. If he does resign as he might, the most suitable person to succeed him is Bukr eff Ali, now Assistant Executive Officer, Lagawa. I suggest that the seconded Head Clerk Ismail eff. Mohamed should be appointed to Lagawa as AEO in this case. This would be a disappointment to Abu Gabr eff Hag Agbar (AEO Muglad and brother of the Nazir of the Felleita, Sereir Hag Agbar) who has done an Executive Officer's course, but Bukr is more experienced in the Council, is senior, older and has succeeded in getting all his tribute in while Abu Gabr is still a long way behind.

Abu Gabr is hindered in his work by the personal animosity of Nazir Ali. He can't help this but in the showing of their work over the last two years, Bukr is more likely to succeed, also I think Bukr would have more support. I also think that Abu Gabr would be opposed by the Agaira and the Zurug. As regards Ismail, he has been four years with the Council and has considerable administrative ability. Neither the Humr or the Zurug have anyone who could take the Lagawa job at the moment, though I am sure that lots think they could.

COURTS.

You have only the Dinka Court to look after. Mr Owen said it was the worst court in the Sudan. It still may be, but it is difficult to keep a tight rein on it when you can only get there December to April. The worst part is in the execution of sentences. Until now they have only had one court clerk for the President and the two Vice-Presidents, but we have another in the budget for this year. Another problem is that the Chief (Nazir) and Wakil (Deputy) Nazirs are always getting into debt with the merchants - the latest list is in the tribal file.

The other courts and Court Presidents work under the direction of the Resident Magistrate in Nahud, though I usually look at the books of outlying courts if the RM has not been.

POLICE.
You theoretically have no control over the police, which is most unsatisfactory. They should be either under your orders and divorced from Nahud, or else there should be a Police Officer stationed in Rigl el Fula who can arrange transfers from here. It is infuriating having unsuitable policemen foisted on a place like Abyie and being unable to get rid of them again. Also, if the police get dissatisfied and complain to the DC and he cannot do anything about it because he has to ask the Police Officer in Nahud. I have written numerous letters to the Governor and the Commandant but nothing has happened.
Later...At last the Commandant has agreed and 9 more policemen have been asked for Rigl el Fula. The Commandant has at last agreed verbally to divorce Dar Messeria from Nahud, but you must get it in writing.

PRISONS.
Theoretically under the Prison Officer at Nahud, at present he pays a visit to Rigl el Fula about every two months, but has not been to Muglad or Lagawa for years and never to Abyie.
The prison camp in Rigl el Fula is under the Controller of Prisons, but in fact we run it here and as it is most useful, I should keep it so. They would not let us have control of its budget last year, but if it does not come this year I should ask for it. The Bash Shawish, Mohamed Nur is excellent and I have recommended him for Sol, if not Prison Officer. (Note. Bash Shawish is a Sergeant Major, Sol is a Warrant Officer).

STAFF.
Sub Mamur Taj eff el Din has done quite well since he came and manages the Merkaz administration. He needs more outside experience and dealing with people. Send him on a boundary trek with a hamla (animals carrying the baggage) if you can.
Abu Bukr eff. the Clerk is very good and runs the office very efficiently.
Mohamed eff. Ahmed the accountant has not settled and wants a transfer to El Obeid. Although the Merkaz (District HQ.) was formed in April 1953, no accountant was posted here until December 1953, during which time the Sub Mamur or I tried to do the accounts. After six weeks the accountant went to El Obeid to get his family and never came back. So Mohamed eff. never had a proper hand over and at the same time Mohamed Ibrahim the Sub Mamur left. I have asked the Inspector of Accounts, Yousif eff Eisa to come and sort the office out properly, but so far none of the Headquarters staff has come within miles. They don't seem to realise in El Obeid that we are completely in the khulla (bush). We asked for things like administrative regulations, Financial Regulations, Laws etc over a year ago, but so far none have come, so if we don't know the regulations we have to do the best we can.

GENERAL ORGANISATION.
I have written this up fully in the District Handbook (actually Mr Cunninson has this at the moment but please put my new chapter in it when he gives it back). This supersedes the chapter on Administration written by Mr Howell.
(D.C.Messeria in 1948)

MEETINGS
There are always three meetings a year with neighbouring Districts and Provinces to discuss border questions.
1.   End January.   Western Nuer.   Jebels
                         Messeria   Tegale
Next years' hosts are Tegale. Look up the hunting files about giraffe. The Game Warden has been asked to come to this meeting to increase the number allotted to the Messeria which is now 60 - they want 150. In any case get all the applications in for permits BEFORE the meeting. Also, a police patrol of 4 should go from Muglad to the meeting and then patrol the hunting country. See Map in D.C's office and also their orders for the last year in the file.
2.   First March. This year, you are host in Abyie.
Western Nuer   Gogrial
                   Aweil   Messeria
Last year this was cancelled owing to CSM (Cerebral Spinal Meningitis) in Bahr el Ghazal.
3.   End March. At Wali. Only between this District and the Jebels. This year, the Jebels are the hosts.

BOUNDARIES
All in the files, though the Hamr-Messeria boundary files are in Nahud and there are no copies here.
The boundary west of Abu KU' need shigging (demarkated by blazing the trees). Either you or the Sub Mamur ought to do it during this rains if possible. Abu Zabad belongs to the Hamr, but we have an office there and look after the Abu Zabad - Abu Ku' and the Abu Zabad - Kasha roads including the bridge across the turda (a swampy lake). Don't let the Nazirs confuse you as they all agreed to the boundary and it is in the files in Nahud. I will ask Nahud to send a copy of the agreement. There may be a fitna (intrigue) when the railway comes there.

BUILDINGS.
I am sorry I have not had time to close the accounts for the Merkaz buildings. The total estimated cost was £E13,413. We have now run out, but the Sub Mamur's house and the last Class III house are not quite finished so I have asked for another £E500. There was no point in stopping work so we have borrowed some materials from the Council and gone ahead. Taj el Din eff. has been charge of the buildings since I went on leave in April and knows all about it. There is also a difference of about £E300 in the Council's records owing from the Merkaz and the amount we have asked the Muderia (Province HQ) to pay the Council. I have asked the Muderia to let us have this latest statement up to date and when it comes Taj el Din should go through the lists and agree the right figure with the Council .

The Muderia kept on asking for 'vouchers' but stores for the Council, Merkaz, Elections and all the rest are on the same voucher, so they have agreed to accept the Council's tulab (account). At first the Council ordered the stores and we paid as we used them. We had to do this as there was no merkaz accountant who could keep a check on them. Now we always keep the stores separate.

I have asked for £E3, 450 for buildings in Rigl el Fula this year (see building proposals) also £E, 6000 for Police housing (see file 9.B.2). There is also 100 metres of stone in front of the Merkaz and another 450 in front of the last Merkaz house, so you should have enough stone to complete all your buildings except the extra (guest) room for the D.C's house without bringing in more stone. This will save you a lot of money and you can repay the Council if they still have any other ohad (demand).

In any case you can get stone much cheaper now the prison is here as they cut it for nothing but you have to bring it in from the jebel. Originally we had to buy all our stone for £E1,250 a metre which was very expensive and a big drain on the funds.

RIGL EL FULA PLANNING.

This has been held up when we were suddenly told that the railway extension may not come to Fula after all. See SCR.1.B, which gives the reasons for splitting Western Kordofan into two. The town has been planned on the assumption that it would be the size of Nahud in ten years and would be a railhead.

Twenty shops were auctioned in February 1953, but so far only 7 have been started. The rest were given notice to build, this expires at the end of August.

An auction for 40 1st Class, 40 2nd Class and another 20 shops I tried to hold last February was a flop as no one turned up.

Until it is known whether the railway will actually come here it is unlikely that there will be a demand for anything except NLA (Native Lodging Area) This is east of the water yard, though it should be plotted properly and the register started. I was going to do this last year but the elections took up all the time and the staff but it must be done this year as grass houses are springing up all over the place. The roads were cleared for NLA orienting from the aredeib tree in front of the donkey (water yard), as is shown on the plan.

Nazir Sereir has been given a plot east of the suq beyond the lorry park and has built a grass house on it while he is saving up for a brick house. Nazir Babu has a plot north of Sereir's but Babu won't build. He has no money to build a stone house, the Government won't give him a loan and he refuses to live in a grass one.

The Town surveyor was supposed to make a plan two years ago, but so far nothing has happened. The present plan I have drawn myself from the air photographs, but it is far too small and I have not had time to enlarge it.

(Copy to   Rigl el Fula Building file)
              Rigl el Fula Lands file).

APPENDIX 4.

LETTER TO GOVERNOR OF KORDOFAN
18th APRIL 1954

Number:-DMD/57.D.1

DISTRICT COMMISSIONER'S OFFICE
RIGL EL FULA
18th April 1954

Dear Governor,
    I have just been writing my annual report which I shall leave for the Sub-Mamur to bring up to date while I am on leave. I thought perhaps you might be interested in one or two points that do not appear in the report.

1. Council. a) The Council ticks over all right, but the understanding of the members is not very high, and the temper of the Executive Officers sometimes gets a bit strained. Our system of having a Central Executive Officer and two and next year three Assistant Executive Officers is I think proving successful. The A/Executive Officer Muglad's area is a bit large, but next year Abyie will not be in his area, Ahmed Eff Deng will be supervised from Rigl el Fula.

    b) Tribute was very slow starting, but it now appears to be coming in n except for the Dinka which is very behind. The slowness in starting was as far as I can make out due to the Council members. I proposed in the Council that February should be the last month for tribute collection, after which a Sheikh who had not produced his tribute would not be entitled to any remuneration. The Council defeated this, and made the date the last of April, after which the members were so pleased with themselves that they told all their friends not to pay their tribute until April.

    c) The Council's Budget for 1954/55 has an anticipated surplus of only LE.1,000, but by sitting on our present surplus I hope we shall scrape through. The surplus of LE. 1,000 includes a 20% triennial increase. Although only 20% appears in the budget the lists go up by 25%, we have therefore allowed for a 5% failure, and have not allowed for additions, which will be made.

    d) The Council's building headquarters programme will be finished by the end of the year. Next year we shall concentrate on provision of Courts, Abyie Council offices and houses, and I hope a double-headed school at Lagawa.

    I think it may be said that with the end of this year, the building up phase of the Council has ended. The Council has been re-warranted.

1. The Headquarters at Fula has been built and opened.
2. The Council officials are all very adequately housed (except for Abyie)
3. The Council is adequately staffed with four Executive Officers, though the accounting side still needs some boosting.
4. Transport should be adequate by the end of the year. The Council will have 7 vehicles. One each at Lagawa, Muglad, and Abyie. At Fula one lorry will be for transport of the Nasirs, the E.O.'s box a station water cart, and a works lorry.

    e) The main job now of the Council staff is to "sell" themselves to the Councillors and people. This has begun, but will take a long time yet.

2. Merkas a) The Merkas has been built, and staff will move in before the end of this month (April). This only leaves the District Commissioner with his office in the Council. The accounts office needs an inspection. No accountant was appointed till December, I spent many long hours opening grant books with the accountant, and getting accounts up to date. The accountant then went to El Obeid to fetch his family and with no warning or explanation your office kept him and sent a relief with not much experience and so I had to begin all over again. The present incumbent is now finding his feet, and I hope he will not be transferred. With all the building going on accurate accounting for stores etc. is essential.

    b) The office is still handicapped by lack of any copies of Laws, Regulations, Province orders etc of any sort. I started asking for these in April 1953, but inspite of reminders, supplications, and threats nothing has been sent. This makes work simpler in some ways, but your office still seems to think that our memories must be infallible.

3. Tribal. a) After all the election fitnas (intrigues) things are nearly back to normal. On the whole relations are good. Relations between the Council officials and Tribal Heads are better. The Nazir Umum and Nazir Agaira were very opposed to the idea that Executive officers are responsible for tribute collection as they saw their powers wilting away, however, the Nazir Umum has now disappeared to the Senate, and the Nazir Agaira appears to have ceased obstruction.

    b) I do not know what the proposed tribal Authorities Bill will do about the separation of administrative from the Judiciary. I would be strongly opposed to the creation of administrative Nazirs and Judicial Nazirs, as has happened in El Odaiya in the Hamr District just to the north of us. I understand that the main function of the administrative Nazir at El Odaiya is tax collection, but here we have already taken this away from the Nazirs, and made the Omdas directly responsible to the Executive Officers. The Nazirs of course are supposed to help the Executive Officers if necessary and uncooperative Sheikhs are prosecuted before the Nazirs by the Executive Officers.

Internal tribal disputes and dia (compensation – blood money), are best dealt with by a Nazir with court powers, and in any case are surely part of his judicial functions.

4.Police. a) The Commandant at last agrees with me that the District is grossly under policed. He has also discovered that an increase of four approved last year to provide a patrol for Abyad, has been kept in Nahud. I had not realised it had even been approved.

b) I find that the unification of the W.K. police force is most unsatisfactory. The Police S/Mamur has paid three visits during the year. Once to investigate the Sayed El Fadil Mahmoud's case. Once for police shooting, and once with the Commandant. The Muawin has done one routine inspection. It is most annoying not having any control over police postings, or over the police officer, who naturally inclines to the District Commissioner in whose Merkas he is stationed. If the increase in Dar Messeria Police is approved and a Muawin appointed, this difficulty will be solved, but at least one additional lorry is essential for police work.

(Merkas fleet is now only two)

5.Prisons.a) The Fula prison camp has been started, the warders' houses have been almost finished, and the wards should be finished before the rains.

b) Division of a Prison Officer between the Districts iseven more of a failure than the division of a police Officer. For a start the Prison Officer hardly ever has any transport, which he has to get from Nahud. I was assured by the Controller of Prisons that the main job of the Prison Officer in March and April, would be to build Fula Prison Camp. He visited Fula at the beginning of March for a day, and for another in the middle of April, the building has been organised entirely by the B/Shawish who has done very well. The Prison Officer has not been able to obey his Controller's instructions because D.C.Hamar also ordered him to repair Nahud Merkaz Buildings in Abu Zebad and El Odaiya.

c) Muglad, Lagawa, and Abyie prisons have not been visited by a Prison Officer this year (as far as I know Abyie never has been)

6. Departmental and Development.

a). Relations between District, Council, and Departments have been good on the whole. Though both the council and myself are not very happy abou the way in which Departments having apparently exhausted their resources try and cover this up by demands on the Council or Merkas.

b). The following are among the requests made to the Council during the year.

1). Upkeep of Haffirs
2). Training and maintenance of midwives.
3). Appointment and pay of two public health overseers, for Muglad and Lagawa, with additional bucketman and water privies.
4). Appointment, housing and pay of a literacy officer, hire of a shop, purchase of books, brushes, lamps, slates, pencils and adult students for literacy campaigns.
5). Enforcement of rules and regulations, and provision of council police for policing of cattle routes.
6). Maintenance, medicines and pay of Temergi's for dressing stations.
7). Provision of double headed schools, and even Elementary schools.
8). Digging of rubber-lined haffirs in sands area.
9). Purchase of tractor to dig small haffirs in cotton area.

While we all appreciate the advice of the technicians the resources of the Council have now caught up with its commitments and little capital expenditure can be considered till the end of 1954/55. In fact the Council is taking over its haffirs from July 1954, and will try and provide a double headed school at Lagawa in 1954/55.

c). I am now trying to find out what are the development proposals of the Departments for the next five years, andwhat commitments the Council will be expected to undertake.

My own impression, which is strongly confirmed by Cunnison (the anthropologist), is that the Messeria (both Murug and Humr) will continue to be a nomad cattle tribe. They will not settle, though there may be more marked variation is their way of life to include cotton cultivation, and possibly increased grain production.

Any development plans therefore should assume that nomadism will continue, and not that there will be any great desire for settled agriculture.

I have just received Manton's Sands/20. B. 2 A/2 of 31/3/54 in which he is pressing for water supplies in the

Fula-Maglad-Muma Area, and Daggag. He is coming here tomorrow, and I will discuss his proposals with him, and the Council. It will be difficult to prevent settlement when the railway comes, and I strongly support his proposals to have a plan ready. But I do not think that the tribal leaders will be frightfully keen to have 72,000 foreigners squatting on their rains grazing.

I may be wrong, but it seems to me that there is too much segregation in the minds of the Agriculturists between Sands and Clays. Theoretically they are twin, but practically they must be considered together.

We now have the situation where one ferig is split into three, one party undertakes grain cultivation in the Muglad- or Daggag. One party looks after the cotton cultivation anywhere between Abyie and Lagawa and the third and most important party, which is the Headquarters of the family or Khashm Beit (family group), travels with the cattle. The Khashm Beits may now therefore spread over about 250 miles.

Increased agricultural production ought to be complementary but secondary to the grazing, I do not think it is practicable to try and settle ful (groundnut and grain producers on the sands, and cotton producers on the clays, and allow the cattle to have what is left.

Might I also point out that the District Commissioner and Council have to deal on agricultural matters with the General Manager N.M.C.I. at Kadugli, The Senior Inspector of Agriculture at Kadugli, the Inspector of Sands at El Obeid, the Inspector of Agriculture at Dilling, and the Senior Cotton Officer at Lagawa. All these are liable to give a different answer on the same subjects.

The first essential for coordinated agricultural development should be the appointment of an Agricultural Inspector for the District, with whom we can deal with direct, how many supervisors he has to satisfy, is up to his department. I would be most grateful if you could support this proposal I suggest he should be stationed at Fula. I can build him a house whenever I am given a chargable heading.

The Inspector of Agriculture Dar Messoria would be responsible for the planning and execution of agricultural development throughout the District, and should have his office in the Merkas and use Merkas files. This would not affect the cotton marketing organisation who are at the moment better situated in Lagawa. An Inspector of Agriculture stationed at Fula would also tie in with the S.V.S.'s intention to post a V.I. in Fula (whose houses and office have now been waiting empty for 18 months)

This brings me to:-

7. **The position of the District Commissioner.**
a. The District Commissioner is not responsible for the Administration which is done by the Council (although he is still Chairman), the Native Courts, (Resident Magistrate), the Police (Police Officer), Prison (Prison Officer), or Education (Province Education Officer) which in theory leaves him with only the Dinka Chiefs Court. In practice however he finds plenty to do, but as far as I can see his main duty now is to act as a catalyst and co-ordinator between the Departments, Governor and Council in his District.
b. I find that some of the Departments' idea of administration is to fly round ones' District, write a report, send it to District Commissioner or Executive Officer Rigl El Fula for action, and feel that duty is done till next year. I suppose this is inevitable, and so I have no real objection to it, but I do object to departmental officials who give one no opportunity of meeting them. The days have gone when it was polite to call on the District Commissioner, but it would be a great help if the technicians could let me know where they are going, and after they have gone, what they have done.

For instance the grazing haffir programme is the most important project in hand at the moment. Symons came here in October last by invitation, and broke it to the Council that the programme had been delayed a year, this was the first we had heard of it. I am told that he and Jefferson went right through the South of the District in February, but I only know they did, because one of their cars overturned, and it was reported to the Muglad Police.

Foster the Pasture Research Officer says he wrote a report last year on grazing haffir sites, and he is now going off to show them to Symons. The Council has made several suggestions for haffirs, but now apparently the sites have been chosen on the strength of Foster's report which neither the Council nor I have seen.

I am told by Lea Wilson that it has been decided the proportion of grazing haffirs to cultivation haffirs shall be 20: 5 I agree this is the right answer, but who decided it, on what grounds we do not know- although the Council will have to maintain the haffirs that are dug.
c. I have already written to you about the railway, and so will not bring it up again now except to say that I hope there is still some chance for Rig el Fula.

8. The Future. I hope when I go that the Council at any rate will have some sort of development plan to work on. I find that it has taken me over a year to get to know the District well enough to get my own ideas straight, another year to start putting them into practice, and next year should have some results, if all District Commissioners are the same this only gives one effective year in three. If however the Council has a programme always looking three years ahead, we may be able to diminish the even bigger hiatus when I go next year. It does not matter if the programme is altered, but we must look further than from one Council meeting to the next.

9. Finally. I should emphasise that our personal relations with departments are very good. Hassan Bahari the Cotton Officer at Lagawa has been most co-operative, the week's trek I had with Lea Wilson was most useful. Manton is most meticulous in letting us know what he is doing, although I may not always agree with him.

The cattle vaccination campaign was delayed owing to smallpox at Muglad, and has not quite re-covered but this is due to lack of co-operation from the Arabs who were all dispersed when the Teams came round.

The Sudan Medical Service has been very good in combating the smallpox promptly, and sending vaccination teams quickly.

I got a bit confused by many and contrary reports from various Inspectors of Education, but have now sorted this out with Mohamed Eff Hassan, and hope he will agree with my suggestion for the future, though progress will be much slower than he would like.

I should like to draw your attention to the way in which the Council and District staff have co-operated this year. Facilities in Rigl el Fula are, as you know almost non-existent, but there have been no complaints. I was particularly pleased last month when I was out for 26 days, and the Executive Officer was on leave and Mamur was transferred elsewhere, that the Merkas Clerk and Council Accountant supervised the buildings and transport, and the Council Clerk without any instructions from me supervised the transfer of Shuna grain from Muglad to Abyie.

Yours Sincerely

Michael

GMGT/AM.

(G.M.G.TIBBS)
DISTRICT COMMISSIONER,
DAR MESSERIA DISTRICT

APPENDIX 5.

ADMINISTRATION IN DAR MESSERIA DISTRICT AND COUNCIL, 18th AUGURST 1954

Number:- DMD/57. D. 1   **DISTRICT   COMMISSIONER'S   OFFICE**

                                                           RIGL EL FULA

25th AUGUST 1954

**Governor,
Kordofan Province**

    I attach a copy of a note on administration in this District and the Dar Messeria Rural Council as it is at the moment, for insertion into Vol II of your copy of the old Western Kordofan Handbook, which should now be called the Dar Messeria Handbook.

GMGT/AM

                      G.M.G.TIBBS
                DISTRICT COMMISSIONER
                DAR MESSERIA DISTRICT

Copy to:-
    Director, Ministry of Local Governemnt for information
    District Handbook
    Handing over notes
    Executive Offcier, Dar Messeria Council
    Mr G.M.G.Tibbs

ADMINISTRATION IN DAR MESSERIA DISTRICT
AND THE DAR MESSERIA RURAL COUNCIL
1954

The following note is intended to bring up-to-date the Political Development Chapter in the District Handbook. This was written by D.D. Howell Esq in 1948.

Headquarters:

The question of a headquarters for the Messeria rose as early as 1935, when Mr Robertson was District commissioner Western Kordofan, he proposed Kodruke.

Mr. Howell in 1948 suggested Fula or Kigeira, but decided Ful was more Central.

The advantages of Fula are:-
a) Reasonably central
b) Has good communications to El Obe-id.
c) Has an adequate and guaranteed water supply.
d) Has stone, wood, sand and good brick making material.
e) Is one of the few permanent centres in the Dar. There are nine permanent settlements near Fula.
f) The Humr would not agree to Lagawa being the centre, not would the Zurug agree to Muglad.
g) Neither Lagawa or Muglad have an adequate water supply for a large settlement. Neither are easily accessible. Muglad has no building material.
h) Rigl el Fula has a historical association in that it was the Headquarters of the tribe in the Turkia 1820-1870 when Ali Messar was Nazir.

A meeting at which the Nazir Umum, Nazira, Zurug, Felleita, and Agaira attended, was held at Abu Zabad in June 1950. It was then finally decided that the Council Headquarters should be built at or near Rigl El fula, the actual site to depend on the location of the P.W.D. water yard.

The water yard was built in 1950 in a site between Adoma and Rigl El fula. In 1951 the Council received a grant of LE. 8,000 from the Grants and Loans Board, and work was started at Fula the same year.

Apart from the headquarters it was necessary first of all to build a store for the building materials, and houses for the Executive Officer, Clerk and Accountant, a rest house, and also houses for the builders. The Council also decided to build staff houses at Lagawa and Abu Zabad. Three for Assistant Executive Officers, accountant and Sarraf at Lagawa and for the Accountant/Sarrag at Abu Zabad.

By January 1953 these works were nearly completed, and in February the Council Headquarters staff moved from Muglad to Rigl el Fula. A Second rest house was built at Fula during Janaury which was used as temporary office accommodation.

The Accounts of the project had by this time become complicated by the arrival of a series of accounts from the P.W.D. which were nearly 18 months old, and had been overlooked in the grants book. A meeting was held at Fula to reassess the buildings costs on 13th February 1953, this was attended by the director local Government (Mr. Buchanan). District Commissioner Western Kordofen (Mr. Hogg), Inspector Local Government (Mr. McComas), A/District Commissioner, Messeria (Mr. Tibbs), and Agmed Eff. Abu El Gasim Executive Officer. As a result of this meeting it was found that a further LE. 20,336 was needed to complete a further two houses at Fula for the Sarraf and Assistant Clerk, the second rest house and the Council Headquarters. Eventually a loan was granted for LE. 11,000, a grant made of LE. 4,450, and 5,064 fround from the Council's reserve and sale of surplus materials, making the total cost of the project LE. 28,336 distributed as follows:-

Council Buildings LE.	5,060
Furniture	500
Executive Officer;s house Fula	2,687
Four junior quarters Fula @ LE. 1,653	6,612
No. 1 Rest House	2,047
No. 2 Rest House	1,184
Store	1,250
Ostas houses	1,350
A/Executive Officer's house - Lagawa	2,687
Two junior quarters - Lagawa @ 1,653	3,306
One junior quarter Abu Zabad	1,653
LE	28,336

Offices had been already built in Muglad (1948) and Lagawa (1950), an office and two houses are now needed at Abyie.

The Council at a meeting at Muglad in September 1952 inspected various designs for Council Buildings, and finally decided on the Kabbabish plan which had been built at Soderi, though several modificaitons were made.

The Building forms three sides of a square, the square being completed by a wall, and iron gates, with upright bars in the form of spears. The square opens towards the East, on the south are offices for the District Commissioner, Executive Officer, and Clerk, and on the North for the Sarraf, accountant, and then a "Members" room. The Council chamber is 18x6 metres, with a spectators gallery at one end. There is a well in the middle of the floor leaving a strip of 1 metre down either side. The Members sit in two rows facing inwards. The Chairman is on the same level as the back row members, and is able to see all their faces clearly. There is a verandah all round the courtyard, and flower beds in the middle (an attempt to make a gold fish pond failed through the impermability of gold fish)

The Council offices were formally opened by H.E. the Governor General on 14th Janaury 1954, when he paid a two days visit. He also presented the new warrant under the Local Government Ordinance 1951, to the Council.

All the buildings are built of brown iron stone from the Jebel two miles to the west. The result is harmonious and quite attractive.

All the Council buildings have been executed by the Council's own buildings staff, and supervised by the Executive Officer and District Commissioner.

In January 1953 an announcement was made splitting off Dar Messeria from Western Kordofan. The Dar Messeria District was actually formed and split from western Kordofan on 1st April 1953, and moved to Fula in August 1953. Quarters for officials were somewhat cramped but by January 1954 houses for the District Commissioner, Merkaz Clerk, Accountant and six police houses were completed, and by the middle of the year the Merkaz (three offices), Mamur's house, lock-up and an Assistnat Clerk's house were up. All these Merkaz buildings were completed by the Council's building organization.

To complete the Rigl el Fula picture briefly, a dispensary and Elementary school were built by contract under Council and Merkaz supervision. A veterinary dispensary and two houses were completed by the D.V.D. in 1953. A prison camp was set up in January 1954 with six warders and seventy prisoners, this is primarily a quarry camp, but having built their own camp in stone, they are able to give assistance to Merkaz and Council buildings. Twenty shop sites were auctioned in 1953, but so far only seven shops have been completed in stone.

The District Commissioner's terms of reference when the Merkaz was formed, included the planning of Fula to be the same size as Nahud in 1963, in anticipation that Rigl el Fula would be the terminus of the railway. The route of the railway is still not decided finally, but the original plan has to stand until the route is finally decided.

NAMES

The new Town actually lies in the "parish" of Adoma, in the Omodia of Mumu. The Council preferred the name Rigl El Fula to Adoma, but then decided on a new name umm Haggar, which was their old home in French Equatorial Africa. This was vetoed by the Director of Surveys, as there were too many "Um Haggar" in the Sudan already. The Council then decided that Rigl El Fula was too long a name, and to call it El Fula. In prctice Rigl El Fula is used as a postal address, as letters addressed to "El Fula" sometimes go to another El Fula near Sederi.

The Council is called Dar Messeria Rural Council, as embracing all the people living in the area of the Messeria tribe whether members of the tribe or not. The Messeria do not have Dar rights in the same way as the Kabbabish have. This was the most satisfactory name rather than South Western Kordofan Rural Council or something of the sort.

DEVELOPMENT

In 1951 the Nuba and Dagu courts were reorganised, and their appeals taken from the District Commissioner to Nazir Zurug, and these to Nazir Umum. At the same time after a meeting held in Lagawa it was decided that the Nuba and Dagu should enter the Council, and come under the Council budget.

The future of the Ngok Dinka was decided at a meeting at Abyie in March 1951, when the Ngok finally decided that they would prefer to stay North, and join the Messeria Council. The Council formally approved this at Lagawa in January 1952. The Ngok are therefore full participators in the Council; but, are not members of the Messeria tribe, do not come under the Nazirate Umum, and have their own court with appeals lying to the District Commissioner and not the Resident Magistrate.

The whole of the District is new therefore, covered by the Council, and all races Arab Dagu, Dinka and Nuba are represented in it. The fifth race, British, disappears with the present Chairman.

COMPOSITION

The Council was rewarrented under the Local Government Ordinance 1951 during 1953, and the first meeting of the re-warranted council took place in October 1953. The warrant itself was presented to the Council by His Excellency the Governor General in Rigl El Fula on 14th January 1954.

Apart from the town of Muglad and Lagawa which are territorial wards having direct elections, the rest of the wards are Omodias, with one split Omodia (Awald Kamil). The

Nuba and Dagu also have grouped Omodias. All three wards have indirect elections.

There are nineteen appointed memebers in addition to those elected making a total of 57 members in all, as far as I know this makes the council the largest Rural Council in the Sudan.

The Chairman is nominated by the Governor, and is in fact the District Commissioner. I would deprecate any change in this for the time being. Apart from the Nazir Umum who is seldom here, as he is now a Senator, there is no one with the necessary personality to be Chairman. Further, the various segments in the council are always suspicious, unfortunately usually with some reason! The District Commissioner is respected as being neutral, and able to sum up any proposals fairly and on its merits.

The V/Chairman is elected annually, but cannot hold office for more than three years in succession.

Appointed members are the District Commissioner as Chairman, five Nazirs, seven Court Presidents, two Omdas. Two officials, one merchant, and one Tulleshi Sheikh. North Nuba have at the moment only one elected member (for Kasha, Shifr, Tabag, Abu Jenouk together), so the Court Presidents ought always to be appointed members. Tima and Tulleshi together are one ward, but in practice the elected member comes from Tima, and a member should be nominated from Tulleshi.

Government officials, Nazirs, Omdas, and Court Prpesidents may not stand for elections but may be nominated. An exception to this has been made in the warrant in the case of Dinka Omdas, who may stand for elections; the reason for this exception is the language difficulty.

The Nuba and Dagu representatives should be increased when the number of their tax payers increases.

ORGANIZATION

An Executive Officer was appointed to Muglad when the Council was started in 1949. In 1951 an Assistant Executive Officer was appointed to Lagawa, in 1952 another A/E.O. was appointed to Muglad, and in 1954 a third A/E.O. was appointed to Abyie. There is an office at Abu Zabad run by an accountant/Sarraf, but his work includes responsibility for roads, Nuba, stores etc, and he acts in fact as a general Wakil. The Final picture with staff is set out in the accompnying diagram.

The Assistant Executve Officers should always be referred to by their stations i.e. Lagawa, and not their area i.e. Zurug, as they should be interchangeable. If the idea gets around that A/E.O. Abyie is only for the Dinka, then complications will undoubtedly arise.

It will be seen that Nazirs and Court Presidents do not appear in the Council hierarchy. This is the beginning of the separation from the Administration from the Judiciary. As far as the Council is concerned Nazirs and Court Presidents are members of the Council, and therefore should assist the administration as much as possible, but in that 75% of their pay comes from the Central Government they are Central Government servants. Omdas on the other hand draw 2/3 of their pay from the Council, and are reckoned as being council servants.

The Executive Officers are responsible for tribute, and the Omdas are responsible to the Executive Officers and not the Nazirs. If an Omda or Sheikh eats or defaults with tribute he should be prosecuted before the Nazir or Court President by the Executive Officer. If he is late with his tribute administrative action should be taken by stopping his pay or gratuity. At the moment if a sheikh has not produced all his tribute by the end of April he forfiets his gratuity (resolution in October 1953 after some difficulty).

The position of Nazirs and Court Presidents vis a vis the council needs defining, but all has been held up pending the traditional Authorities Bill. At the moment the position of a Nazir is that he is the head of his tribe, and responsible for tribal custom. He is a Court President. He may, but need not be, a nominated member of the Council, and as such hold office in it. As a Court President he is responsible to the Resident Magistrate and not the District Commissioner.

A Court President (not a Nazir) is responsible to the Resident Magistrate and theoretically at any rate the District commissioner has no hold over him, though the District Commissioner is responsible for deciding his pay.

The appointment of A/Executive Officers has avoided necessity of having Court Nazirs, and Adminsitrative Nazirs, as has happened in the Hamar.

FINANCE

I do not intend to go closely into the budget structures as this can be best seen from the various budgets themselves. But it is interesting to note that revenue has more than doubled since the forming of the Council in 1948. Tribute in 1948 was LE. 20,000, in 1949 22,900, and in the current budget 1954/55 is LE. 64,864. The total revenue in 1938 was LE. 9,3000, in 1949 was LE. 25,731 and is now LE. 66,996.

Comparative Figures

Rabt	No. 1948/9	Rate %	No. 1954/5	Rate %
Camels	22	2501	21	250
Horses	594	220	516	230
Cattle	142,603	100	161,870	260
Sheep	43,437	030	40,710	040
Donkeys	1,991	040	2,012	085
Goats	11,613	020	12,458	030
Poll tax. Messeria	27,425	100	21,894	300
Dinka		250	6,300	800

(Note the Dinka pay only poll tax, and no herd tax)

Revenue	1948	1949	1954/55
Tribute	20,000	22,900	64,854
Courts fines	650	650	2,000
Animal Markets	45	55	800
Ponds	20	20	65
Licences Traders	315	337	1550
Other	30	40	388
Rates	72	80	229
Contribution for Collection of taxes for Central Government	11	18	63

The figures show that the number of animals listed has not greatly increased, but that the increased revenue has been raised from increased taxation rates. This indicates that an increase in services demands an increase of revenue, i.e. they must be paid for, and they are prepared to pay for them.

C O U R T S

Supervision of the work of Courts is now the responsibility of the Resident Magistrate. The Council is responsible for administrtion of the courts, transport of the Court Presidents as necessry, provision of court books and checking of court fines which go the the Council's revenue.

Present organisation is shown in the attached diagram.

T R I B A L

The position is still not clear until the Traditional Authorities Bill is published, and Government polcy is known.

The present organization shown in the attached diagram.

GMGT/ AM
Rigl el Fula. 21.8.1954

G.M.G.TIBBS
DISTRICT COMMISSIONER.
DAR MESSERIA DISTRICT

THE TRIBAL STRUCTURE

NAZIR UMUM, MESSERIA
Babu Osman Nimr Ali
    El Gullah

NAZIR, HUMR AGAIRA	Omda Naim Omer	Fadliya
Ali Nimr Ali El Gullah	Omda Horgas Merida	Mezaghna
	Omda Abu Gasim Musa	Fayyarin
	Omda Hammad Galo	A/Omran-Adal
	Omda Horgas Hamdin	A/Omran-Menama
	Omda Hammad Abdel	Galil A/Kamil
	Omda Mekki Alli el Gulla	Muglad Aghrab
NAZIR, HUMR FELLEITA	Omda Abdel Hamid Ismail	Mumu
Sereir el Hag Agbar	Omda Abu Gasim Tori	Salamat
	Omda Subeir el Hag	Jubarat
	Omda Adam Yousif	Ziyid
	Omda Musa el Shwein	Metanin
	Omda Gibreil Honowa	A/Serur
NAZIR, ZURUG	Omda Hammad Md.Dafaala	Duggag
Izz el Din Humeida	Omda Fudl Rabeita	Agrab Lagawa
	Omda Gadalla Abdullah	A/Abu Noaman
	Omda Bushara el Safi	A/Heiban
	Omda Ibrahim Ibeita	Eneinat
	Omda Balil Suleiman	Dira
	Omda Basha Hamadi	Zurug
	Omda Mohamed Alawi	A/Um Salim
	Omda Koko Gadou	El Ghazala
DAGU	Sultan Abdel Rahim Sobahi	Dar el Kebir
	Sultan Hussein Suleiman	Warina
	Sultan Nur Katafur	Selechi
NUBA	Sultan Faragalla Tobago	Kamdang
	Sultan Basha Kereisha	Tulleshi
	Sultan Khamis Gellab	Tima
	Sultan Ismain Adey	Abu Genouk
	Sultan Dangali Aly	Shifr
	Sultan Hami Suleiman	Kasha
NAZIR (CHIEF) NGOK	Omda Kon Tinglot	Dil
Deng Majok Kwal Arop	Omda Pur Col	Aoak
	Omda Lual Deng	Mareng
	Omda Abiem Bakat	Manyer
	Omda Akuei Deng	Aley
	Omda Madut Arob	Anyel
	Omda Fagwat Deng	Bongo
	Omda Achuil Bulabek	Aweng/Akyor

THE COURSE OF JUSTICE

THE MESSERIA, NUBA AND DAGU.

```
                        Appeals Court
                             ∧
                          Appeals
                             ∧
                       Province Judge
                             ∧
                          Appeals
                             ∧
                      Resident Magistrate
                             ∧
                          Appeals
                             ∧
                        Nazir Umum
                       Kordofan no. 6
                             ∧
                          Appeals
                             ∧
      Nazir Zurug          Nazir Agaira         Nazir Felieta
         6/1                   6/2                  6/3
          ∧                     ∧                    ∧
        Appeals              Appeals              Appeals

 Laqawa Daggage Ras el    Um  Muglad  Subu  Grinti  Keilak  Abyad
                Fil Kereisha
               (South  (North
                Nuba)   Nuba)
  6/5    6/4   6/9   6/10   6/6   6/11   6/12   6/7   6/8
```

Presidents and Vice Presidents (VP)

6/5	Fudlulla Mohamed Dafaal	6/6	Mekki Ali el Gullah
6/4	Mulah Mohamed el Faqir	6/11	Mahmoud Hamdin
6/9	Faragalla Tobago Khamis Gellab (VP)	6/12	not yet approved
		6/7	Nur el Din Serier
6/10	Rezigalla eff. Zaki MBE	6/8	Rehaid Dirhan

THE NGOK DINKA

```
                    Province Governor
                           ∧
                        Appeals
                           ∧
                  District Commissioner
              (Who may consult Twig Chiefs' Court)
                           ∧
                        Appeals
                           ∧
                     Nazir Ngok Dinka
                      Kordofan No 12
                        Appeals
                      ∧           ∧
               Vice President    Vice President
                 Col Gafur        Deng Abot Kwal
```

DAR MESSERIA RURAL COUNCIL, ORGANISATION

```
RIGL EL FULA   Executive Officer
                  Head Accountant
                  Head Clerk
                  Accountant (vacant)
                  Sarraf (Cashier)
                  Assistant Clerk

LAGAWA         Assistant Executive Officer
                  Accountant
                  Sarraf
                                    Omdas/Sultans
                                                    Sheikhs
         At Abu Zabad    Accountant/Sarraf
                                    Omdas/Sultans
                                                    Sheikhs

MUGLAD         Assistant Executive Officer
                  Accountant
                  Sarraf
                                    Omdas
                                                    Sheikhs

ABYIE          Assistant Executive Officer (Proposed)
                  Accountant/Sarraf
                                    Omdas
                                                    Sheikhs
```

DAR MESSERIA RURAL COUNCIL HEADQUARTERS RIGL EL FULA.

FORMALLY OPENED BY H.E. THE GOVERNOR GENERAL
14th JANUARY 1954.

Built by the Council's own staff and boys of its Builders and Carpenters Apprentice School.

Materials, local brown stone, mud mortar with cement pointing. Roof trusses and woodwork are mohogany, bought in Wau by the Executive Officer. Steel shuttered windows.

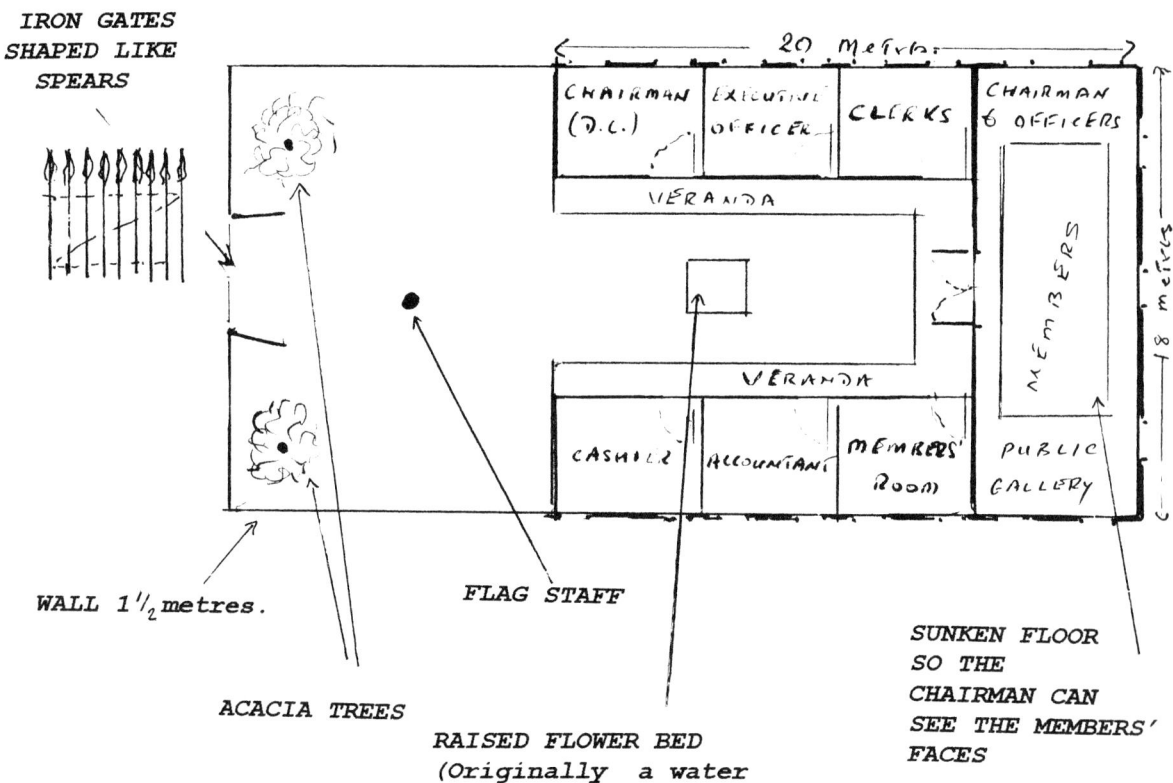

IRON GATES SHAPED LIKE SPEARS

WALL 1½ metres.

ACACIA TREES

FLAG STAFF

RAISED FLOWER BED
(Originally a water tank for mixing mortar. We tried to make it into a goldfish pond but the only goldfish we could find were in the Palace garden in Khartoum. So Anne collected poison trees which looked very pretty)

SUNKEN FLOOR SO THE CHAIRMAN CAN SEE THE MEMBERS' FACES

APPENDIX 6.

**Letter sent to District Commissioners
after the Election
by the Governor General.**

THE PALACE,

KHARTOUM.

4th November 1953.

My dear Tibbs,

    Since the passing of the Self-Government Statute and the formation of the Electoral Commission, the preparations for the elections which are due to be held this month have placed a heavy burden of responsibility on all administrative officials, a burden which they have shouldered in accordance with the best traditions of the service.

    An electioneering period is always one of tension and high feeling and I have noticed, with the greatest satisfaction, that no member of the Political Service has been deterred from doing his duty by the various attacks which have been made both on the service as a whole and on individuals.

    Neutral observers have commented with admiration on the way in which Governors and District Commissioners throughout the country are carrying on their task, undismayed and calm, at this most difficult time. The reputation, the good name and the honour of the Political Service have never, in its distinguished history, stood higher.

    I am confident that all members of the service will continue to carry on the difficult task with loyalty and devotion, and I wish to offer you my congratulations on all that you have so far achieved.

Yours Sincerely

R. Howe

GOVERNOR-GENERAL.

G.M.G. Tibbs Esq.,
Assistant District Commissioner,
Messeria (Fula), Western Kordofan.

Letter sent to District Commissioners by the Acting Civil Secretary.

PERSONAL

CIVIL SECRETARY'S OFFICE.
KHARTOUM.

12th December, 1953.

Dear Tibbs.

The Elections are now over, and I am writing to thank you personally for the part you played in seeing that they were carried through in freedom and fairness. And, not only that. The whole election period placed a great strain on every aspect of our administration, and it is much to our credit that things went as they did, and that incidents were so few. I know full well the difficulties you had to face, and I congratulate you on the way in which you fulfilled your exacting task.

(A. C. BEATON)
Acting Civil Secretary.

GMG Tibbs Esq,

Farewell Letters

From   The Governor General.

THE PALACE
KHARTOUM

12th September 1954.

Dear Tibbs,

Now that you are leaving the Sudan finally under the terms of the Anglo-Egyptian Agreement, I should like to thank you both personally and as a member of the Political Service for your services to the Sudan, particularly in the last critical years.

Transfer of power can never be an easy task, and the difficulties have been accentuated in the Sudan by external influences, which placed heavy extra burdens on the Political Service. It was the knowledge that I would always have the loyal support of all members of the Political Service, despite all difficulties, which made it possible for me to carry out the policy agreed on by the Condominium Governments in the Anglo-Egyptian Treaty.

It must naturally be with regret that one sees the end of the Political Service, but it has fulfilled its task in preparing the Sudanese for self-government, and in leaving sound foundations on which the new State can build. It has also left a tradition of service which I am confident will bear fruit in the new Sudan, and will be gratefully remembered by future generations.

The early termination of your service in the Sudan may have caused you worry and anxiety in looking for new work. While thanking you for your services here, it is also my sincere hope that you will soon find alternative employment in which I wish you all prosperity and good fortune.

Yours sincerely,

R.G. HOWE.
GOVERNOR-GENERAL.

G.M.G. Tibbs, Esq.,

Sir Tibbs

Dear sir

Congratulation to you, I am not cheerful for you have left us in darkness because there is no little Education in our area.

Hence we those of Dinka who are not well Educated we are not happy for your leaving and leave us primitive as we were in the long time ago.

We were not expecting that that British are going to leave within few years as you are going to fly away. We shall thank God for the british manner in the Sudan for they had been friendly to us.

God bless you forever

Yours, Omda
Achuil Bulakbek

Achuil Bulakbek, Omda Aweng/Akyor, Ngok Dinka

Sir mr tibbs

I am writing you this letter of mine just only for greeting because you are leaving to your home and you left us as orphans.

Hence I am not please for your leaving and leave us here and we are not well educated

God may give you good bless.

Yours

Malet-Ayoun
from Abyei

Malet Ayoun, a Ngok Dinka

WHO WAS WHO.

Here are the names of some of the characters mentioned in the book. Europeans are listed under their surnames. Sudanese who do not have family names are listed under their first names. We have briefly described who people were at the time we knew them. Only the names of those who appear in the book are included, there is a list of the names of tribal notables in Appendix 6 .(Note. 'Abdel' – means 'slave of' eg Abdel Rahman 'Slave of the Merciful'. In the same way Abu means 'father'). Apologies to those whose Christian or second names we cannot remember.

Abdel Garder	Schoolmaster, El Obeid
Abdel Rahman	Babikr. (AR) Our Safragi. Married to Zeinab. Daughter, Selma.
Abdel Rahman	Our Scyce (groom).
Abdel Rahman	el Mahdi. Religious head of the Ansar. Son of the Mahdi.
Abdel Rahim	Sobahi. Sultan of Dar el Kebir (Dagu).
Abdel Latif	The Hoggs' Safragi
Abdullahi	Deputy Governor, Kordofan, 1954.
Abdullahi	Our third cook
Abu Bakr	Clerk, Messria Council. Rigl el Fula.
Abu Gabr	Hag Agbar. Assistant Executive Officer, Muglad.
Abu Sita	A Kashi (Jebel Kasha), with six toes.(Nuba)
Achwel	Bulabek. Omda of Aweng/Akyor (Dinka)
Adam	Yousif, Omda Ziyud
Ahmed	Abu Gasim. Executive Officer, Messeria Rural Council. Married., Sons, Mohamed, Omer, Sadik. Daughters Fatna, Omeima. As a descendent of the Prophet, also known as the Sherif (Honourable).
Ahmed	The Builder in Rigl el Fula.
Ahmed	Hag Agbar. Policeman, Mugald. Brother of Nazir Sereir.
Ahmed	Khalil Mohamed. M's first Safragi
Ahmed	The Hunters' Safragi.
Ahmed	Our Seconda
Ahmed	Segeir, our driver.
Ahmed	Matta, one of my marasalas (messengers)
Ali	Nimr Ali el Gullah. Nazir the Agaira (Humr). Brother of Babu.
Arnold.	Canon. CMS Missionary, Sallara.
Asim.	Babu Nimr (son of Babu). MRCP.
Awad	One of my marasalas (messenger).
Azhari	Ismail. The Prime Minister.
Azzozo.	Ghaffir, (Caretaker). Tebeldia rest house.
Babu	Osman Nimr Ali el Gullah. Nazir Umum. Messeria. Senator.
Basha	Kereisha. Sultan of Tulleshi. (Nuba)
Beaton	Anthony.C.C. Deputy Civil Secretary. 1952-53

Bell	Gawain.W. DC Western Kordofan 1948-49, Deputy Civil Secretary 1953-55. Permanent Under Secretary. Min. of Interior 1954-55. Married to Silvia, Daughters, Peta, Amanda, Cressida
Bertoni	White Father from Verona and builder.
Beshir.	Our second cook who died suddenly in Rigl el Fula. 1954.
Blackley	T.R. ADC Western Kordofan 1927-28.
Bowcock.	Philip.P. MECAS 1950, ADC Bentiu 1952-55. Married to Brenda.
Boyle	Ranald.H.M. ADC Gogrial, Bahr el Ghazal, 1948-53
Bradford	Ben. Inspector of Agriculture. Dilling.
Brown	Rev. David. CMS Missionary.
Buchanan	Laurence.M. Director of Local Government 1952-54. Married to Doreen.
Bukr	Ali. Assistant Executive Officer, Lagawa.
Crole	Robin.L. ADC Nuba Mountains. 1951-54.
Cox	Department of Education. Wau, Bahr el Ghazal
Cumming	Duncan.C.C. Governor Kordofan 1949-50. Deputy Civil Secretary '50. Married to Nancy. Daughter, Ann.
Cunninson.	Ian. Our anthropologist living with Omda Horgas's ferik.
Daly.	Ralph.H. MECAS 1950. Executive Officer, Kabbabish RDC Northern Kordofan 1951-54.
Dee.	Brian.D. Civil Secretary's Office (Personnel)
Deng	Abot Kwal Arop. Half brother of Deng Majok.(Dinka).
Deng	Ahmed Deg Majok, son of Deng Majok
Deng.	Majok Kwal Arop. Chief/Nazir, the Ngok Dinka
Deng	Francis Madeng, Son of Deng Majok.
Deng.	Zacharia Bol, Son of Deng Majok.
Dew.	Heather. The Hoggs' nanny.
Donnelly	Rev James. CMS Missionary. Katcha and Sallara
Duncan	Jock.S.R. Private Secretary to the Governor General, 1954-55.
Epibane	Nubar. Armenian Merchant, Khartoum.
El Nur	Hag el Nur Ahmed. Commandant, Province Prisons.
Evans	David.M.H. DC El Obeid 1947-50 Public Relations Officer 1951-54. Married to Ruth
Fadal	Mahmoud Abdel Karim. Father in Law to Babu. MP for Muglad constituency
Fadl	Court Clerk. Abyei. (Dinka)
Faragalla	Tobago. Sultan of Kamdang. (Nuba).
Farouk	King of Egypt.
Forster	F. Michael.M. Private Secrtetary to the Governor General, 1951-54
Foster	Pastural Reserch Officer. Agricultural Department
Fretwell	Province Education Inspector, Girls Schools. El Obeid.
Garland	Patrick.S. DC Bentiu, Upper Nile
Gelsthorpe	The Right Reverend Maurice. Bishop in the Sudan.
Gibril	Ahmed Abu Gasim's marasala (messenger).
Gillespie	Ian. Senior Veterinary Inspector, Kordofan.

Grafty-Smith	Sir Lawrence, Member, Governor General's Commission
Hag	Agbar. Ex Nazir of the felleita. Father of Nazir Sereir.
Hagger	N John W ADC Province HQ El Obeid 1950.MECAS 1951 Nuba Mountains 1951-55. DC Tegali 1954-55.
Hammad	Mohamed Dafaala. Omda Daggag. MP for Lagawa.
Harper	Canon B J , 'Uncle'
Harrison	Rex. HRP. DC Nuba Mountains 1945-50. Married to Barbara.
Hassan	Mamur, Nahud.
Hassan	One of my marasalas (messengers)
Hassan	Zaki el Din. Ex Nazir, Bederia, El Obeid
Hawkesworth	Desmond. (Geoffrey's twin brother) Asst Civil Secretary (Political)
Hawkesworth	Geoffrey. Deputy Governor Kordofan 1945-50.Governor 1950-54. Married Mary Pullen. Son Mark
Hayes	Kevin, Province Judge of the High Court, 1951-54.. Married to Jan
Hext	Jack. Inspector of Agriculture (Sands) El Obeid 194.Married to Priscilla.
Hickson	Gordon.P.A. ADC Province HQ El; Obeid.1952-53.Married to Daphne.
Hogg	Peter. DC Western Kordofan 1949-53. Assistant Director. Local Government.1953. Director Local Government 1954-5. Married to Joanna. Son, William.Daughter,Margaret.
Hook	Hilary. Bimbashi, Camel Corps. 1951. Married to Jane.
Horgas	Merida. Omda, Awlad Omran-Menama.
Howe	Sir Robert, Governor General.
Howell	Paul.P.DC Messeria, Western Klordofan 1946-48.
Huddleston	General Sir Hubert, former Governor General.
Hunter	John.C.Finance Dept 1946-49.ADC Hamr, Western Kordofan 1949- 52..Resident Magistrate, Western Kordofan. 1952-54. Married to Mary.
Hunter	Jack.M. DC Eastern Kordofan 1948-50.DC Nuba Mountains 1950-55..Married to another Mary.
Husband	Tony, Doctor, El Obeid. Married Wendy Morris-Higgs.
Ismail	Head Clerk, Dar Messeria Council.. Rigl el Fula.
Ismain	Adey. Sultan of Abu Genouk (Nuba).
Izz el Din	Humeida. Nazir, Messeria Zurug
Kabous	Head Accountant. Dar Messeria Council. Rigl el Fula.
Karkanis	George. Government Geologist.
Khamis	Gellab. Sultan of Tima (Nuba).
Kia	Ora. Kujur of Tulleshi (d'cd)
Lappas	Cypriot Grocer, Abu Nigma,El Obeid.
Lino	Wau. Headmaster, Abyei Primary School. (Dinka).
Lea-Wilson	Ken. Inspector of Agriculture (Cotton). Kadugli
Longe	John. DC Um Ruaba 1934-39.Governor Upper Nile !950-53. Married to Mary. Daughter, Jane. Cousin, Vera.
Lorimer	Frank.C.S. Deputy Governor Kordofan 1952-54. Governor Kordofan. 1954-55. Married to Isobel. Son, Gordon.

Lumsden	Peter, G.R.C.DC Messeria, Western Kordofan 1948-50. DC Northern Kordofan 1950-55. Married to Nancy. Daughters. Susan and Catriona
Mahmoud	One of our Secondas.
Mahmoud	Horgas Merida. Cashier, Dar Messeria Council. Rigl el Fula. Son of Omda Horgas.
Manton	John. Inspector of Agriculture (Sands).El Obeid.
Martin	The Very Reverend George, Provost and Archdeacon of Khartoum. Married to Lena, Sons Michael and John, dauhter Ann.
McComas	Geoffrey, Inspector of Local Government, Kordofan, 1952-54. Married to Pam, son Alex, daughter Jean.
Mekki	Ali el Gullah, Omda Muglad Aghrab
Mekki	Amin, merchant, Lagawa
Mekki	Tia Kafi (son) Nuba Policeman
Moffat	Abbott, with wife and two daughters from New York. Stayed with the Cummings, Christmas 1949.
Mohamed	Hassenein Mohamed Hassan, Our first cook.
Mohamed	Ibrahim Abdel Hafiz. Sub-Mamur, then my relief as DC.
Mohamed	Kafi. Operator of the 'Over' (Nuba).
Monteith	Bill,W.N. DC Tegale 1949-53.
Molloy	Rev Robert. Presbyterian American Missionary, El Obeid.
Morris-Higgs	Wendy. Nursing Sister, El Obeid. Married Tony Husband.
Morrison	J.K.K. DC.Western Kordofan 1939-43
Mulah	Mohamed el Fagir. Court President Daggage.
Musa	el Shwein. Omda of the Metanin
Musa	Policeman. Nahud.
Negus	Sir Victor, Consultant Surgeon. Married to Eve.
Neguib	General, President of Egypt.
Nur el Din	Hag Agbar. Court President, Keilak. Son of Nazir Sereir.
Omer	el Tinai. Merchant, El Obeid.
Owen	Richard.H. DC Western Kordofan 1939-45. Governor, Bahr el Ghazal 1948-53.
Phillips	John.F.S.ADC Nuba Moutains1945-49.DC Wad Medani 1945-55.
Potter	Ivy. Nursing Sister, El Obeid. married Elliot Balfour.
Pullen	Mary. Nursing Sister, El Obeid. Married Geoffrey Hawkesworth.
Rae	Donald. ADC Messeria, Western Kordofan 1950-52.
Redman	Anna. Nursing Sister. El Obeid.
Rehaid	Dirhan. Court President, Abyad.
Rezilgalla	Zaki MBE. Court President, Um Kereisha (Nuba). Retired SDF Officer.
Richardson	Sammy.S. ADC Northern Kordofan, 1947-50.
Rix	Freddie. Public Works Dept. El Obeid.
Robertson	Sir James. Civil Secretary. Married to Nancy. His son, another James
Rowley	John.V.d'A.DC Northern Kordofan 1946-50. Deputy Governor Kordofan 1952-53.Asst. Financial Secretary 1952-53. Governor Darfur 1953-55. Married to Vicky.

Sadik	Headmaster, Lagawa Boys School.
Sagha	Driver's assistant
Said	el Hag. Dar Messeria Coiuncil. Saraf (Cashier) Abu Zabad.
Seamer	Jake.W.DC Messeria, Western Kordofan 1943-46 Commissioner and Registrar of Co-operative Societies 1953-55.
Segeir	Our driver, Segeir (Little Hawk) was really a nickname
Sen	Sukamar. Chairman of the Electoral Commission. (Indian).
Sereir	Hag Agbar. Nazir Fellieta (Humr).
Shaigi	One of my maraslas (messengers)
Sherif	The Honourable, Ahmed Abu Gasim.
Smart	John. Inspector of Agriculture (Sands) El Obeid..
Stern	Peter.L.Irrigation Dept. Blue Nile. 1949-51. (from Lynchmere).
Sulieman	Onbashi (Corporal). Driver to Peter Hogg, then John Hunter.
Symons	Conservation Engineer. Dept of Agriculture.
Taj el Din	Sub Mamur, Dar Messeria District, Rigl el Fula.
Tibbs	Michael and Anne – that's us! ADC Province HQ El Obeid 1949. MECAS 1950. ADC Province HQ El Obeid 1951-52. ADC Messeria, Western Kordofan 1952-53. DC Dar Messeria 1953-55.
Tibbs	Christopher.J.FRCP. Our younger son who has visited the Sudan twice. In 1978 as a member of the Cambridge Coral Starfish Research Group Expedition to the Red Sea. In 1983; Medical Student Elective for Obstetrics and Gynaecology, when he was able to visit Kordofan.
Tiernay	James.F. Governor Kordofan 1947-49, Governor Equatoria 1949-52
Tigani	Merchant, El Odaiya and Rigl el Fula.
Tilib	Driver's assistant.
Tom	Family name of the Nazirs of the Kabbabish, Northern Kordofan.(pronounced Tome).
Walters	Brian.R. MECAS 1950,
Watson	James.R.S. Province Judge, Kordofan, 1949
Wherral	Frank. Public Works Dept. El Obeid. Married to Vivian. Two daughters.
Wright	William (Bill). ADC Province HQ Kordofan (Lands) Married to Ethel
Young	Robin.G.C. ADC Nuba Mountains 1949-53. Civil Secretary's Office (Personnel) 1953-55.
Zain el Din	Chairman, Governor General's Commission. (Pakistani)
Zeinab	Wife of Abdel Rahman, our Safragi.

GLOSSARY

ADC	Assistant District Commissioner
Agaira	A sub-section of the Humr of the Messeria tribe
Aly wati	Up and down (the road el Obeid – Nahud)
Angareeb	Rope bed
Asharif	Sweet corn
Ashigga	Unity (with Egypt) party
Baggara	Cattle owning nomad Arab tribes
Bimbashi	Major or Company Commander in the SDF
CMS	Church Missionary Society
CSM	Cerebrospinal Meningitis
Cantonment	Lodging area for expatriates or troops
Chubak	Dinka greeting
DC	District Commissioner
Dagu	Hill tribe originally from West Africa
Dinka	Nilotic race living in the southern Sudan
Donkey	Water bore – from the donkey engine (Plural dwank).
Dove	Small aircraft of the Sudan Airways
Dura	Millet
Effendi	Title of the educated classes eg. Ahmed effendi
Eid	A religious holiday /from Medina to Mecca
Eid el Kebir	Major Moslem holiday – the flight of Mohamed
Emma	Turban like headdress worn by traditional Sudanese
Ferik	Family based baggara (nomadic) group.
Fula	Lake or reservoir
Gaiyl	Rest period in the middle of the day
Galabia	Long white gown worn in the more sophisticated areas.
Galaba	Baggara term for townspeople who wear galabias
Gezira	Cotton growing area, Blue Nile Province. (Lit. an island)
Ghaffir	Caretaker
HE	His Excellency (the Governor General)
Hakuma	Government (particularly the Sudan Government)
Khor	River bed, usually dry
Humr	One of the two parts of the Messeria tribe (Lt. Red)
Jebel	A hill or mountain (Nuba Mountains District)
Kabbabish	Camel owning tribe in the Northern District of Kordofan
LE (or £E)	An Egyptian Pound (equivalent to £1.1.0 now £1.10p)
Luak	Dinka round double storied dwelling for families and livestock
MECAS	Middle East Centre of Arab Studies in Shemlan, Lebanon
Mahdia	Time of the Mahdi
Meidan	Field or open space.
Mek	Nuba Chief (Nuba Mountains)
Merkaz (Merkas)	District Headquarters
Messeria	Cattle owning (baggara) nomad Arab tribe
Mudir	Governor
Muderia	Province Headquarters

Mufettish	District Commissioner – literally Inspector
Mustaba	Patio
Marmur	Administrative rank below ADC
Naggara	Messeria dancing to drums
Nahas	Copper kettle drums, the insignia of a Nazir
Namlea	Part of a veranda wired against mosquitoes
Nazir Umum	Paramount Chief
Nazir	Chief or Head of a tribe
Neem	Species of shady tree
Nuba	African race living in or near the Nuba Mountains
Omda	Head of a section of a tribe.
P&T	Posts and Telegraphs
PWD	Public Works Department
Piastre	100th of an Egytian Pound (like 1p Sterling)
Ragaba	Creek
Rakuba	Temporary shelter made with grass
Ramadam	Month of fasting for Moslems
Red Sea Rig	White shirt and cummerbund, white or black trousers
Rezigat	Baggara tribe in Darfur
SDF	Sudan Defence Force (i.e. army)
SMS	Sudan Medical Service
SUM	Sudan United Mission
SMS	Sudan Medical Service
SVS	Sudan Veterinary Service
Sa'ata Sit	Title given to a British lady "Her Excellency the Lady"
Safragi	Butler, who ran the household
Seconda	No 2. To the Safragi
Sheikh	Head of a family or village
Shehada	Testimonial
Shig	Blaze or mark trees for a trail or boundary
Shuna	Grain store
Sibr	Celebration (Nuba)
Sub Marmur	Lowest administrative rank
Sufga	Dancing to clapping
Sultan	Nuba or Dagu Chief (in Dar Messeria)
Syce	Groom
Tariga	The sections of Islam, literally a track or road
Tebelgi (or teleldi)	enormous spreading tree which could be hollowed out for water storage. Elsewhere known as boabab.
Tukl	Round grass or stone hut with thatched roof
Turk	Whiteman - according to the Dinka, who believed thy were all the same.
Turkia	C19, when the Sudan was ruled by the Khedive of Egypt
Um Borroro	Migrant West African tribe
Wadi	Valley
Yoke	Iron circle on which a well is built
Zurug	One the two parts of the Messeria tribe (Lt. Blue)